ExtGWT Rich Internet Application Cookbook

80 recipes to build rich Java web apps on the robust GWT platform, with Sencha ExtGWT

Odili Charles Opute

Oded Nissan

BIRMINGHAM - MUMBAI

ExtGWT Rich Internet Application Cookbook

Copyright © 2012 Packt Publishing

All rights reserved. No part of this book may be reproduced, stored in a retrieval system, or transmitted in any form or by any means, without the prior written permission of the publisher, except in the case of brief quotations embedded in critical articles or reviews.

Every effort has been made in the preparation of this book to ensure the accuracy of the information presented. However, the information contained in this book is sold without warranty, either express or implied. Neither the authors, nor Packt Publishing, and its dealers and distributors will be held liable for any damages caused or alleged to be caused directly or indirectly by this book.

Packt Publishing has endeavored to provide trademark information about all of the companies and products mentioned in this book by the appropriate use of capitals. However, Packt Publishing cannot guarantee the accuracy of this information.

First published: September 2012

Production Reference: 1030912

Published by Packt Publishing Ltd.
Livery Place
35 Livery Street
Birmingham B3 2PB, UK..

ISBN 978-1-84951-518-4

www.packtpub.com

Cover Image by Rakesh Shejwal (shejwal.rakesh@gmail.com)

Credits

Authors
Odili Charles Opute
Oded Nissan

Reviewers
Venkatesh D. Chitnis
Geoff Froud
Andreas Winkler

Acquisition Editor
Usha Iyer

Lead Technical Editor
Susmita Panda

Technical Editor
Madhuri Das

Copy Editor
Brandt D'Mello

Project Coordinator
Joel Goveya

Proofreader
Maria Gould

Indexer
Tejal Soni

Graphics
Aditi Gajjar
Manu Joseph

Production Coordinator
Nilesh R. Mohite

Cover Work
Nilesh R. Mohite

About the Authors

Odili Charles Opute started his IT career with web technologies in 2003, after obtaining a degree in Computer Engineering from the University of Benin. Having successfully completed the Enterprise Java track in NIIT, Benin, he joined Digitanx Systems in 2006, where he led Java and Mobile development, in 2006. In 2007, he embraced the freelance game, consulting for several agencies and development shops while still experimenting with other non-Java technologies.

He later moved to Port Harcourt city, in late 2008, and joined XChequer, a vibrant startup hoping to change the mobile landscape in Africa with NFC-powered contactless payment solutions.

Whilst in XChequer, he was responsible for cutting-edge web solutions and led the development of the NFC prototypes. He currently works with the University of Benin as one of the webmasters, but with the specific responsibility of strategy, design, and integration, and as the development lead for the institution's online presence.

> This book has really come a long way. I want to thank God for making it a reality and to specially acknowledge my family for their support. This would also not be complete without mentioning Anita: thanks, honey, for your love and understanding.

Oded Nissan is a software architect working for leading companies in Israel as a Senior Software Architect. He has been working in the software industry for 18 years as a developer, architect, and development manager. He started working with Java technologies in 1999 and has worked with GWT for the past three years.

Oded has also worked as an instructor, teaching JEE technologies and the Spring framework. His interests include GWT, Android development, and software architecture.

Oded has an MBA in Information Systems from the Hebrew University in Jerusalem and a BA in Computer Science from the Open University in Israel.

About the Reviewers

Venkatesh D. Chitnis works as a software engineer in the area of decision management. Before moving on to decision management, he worked for product life cycle management software. His love for computer games in early childhood turned into a passion for computer programming as a profession. Venkatesh is a big proponent of open source technology/freeware for building commercial products. During his free time, he enjoys experimenting with the latest Java technologies, reading fiction, travelling, and playing with his one-and-a-half year old son.

Geoff Froud has been a software developer for over 20 years, with experience in many different industries, including satellite control, broadcasting, telecommunications, and finance. After many years of C++ development, Geoff's primary focus is on Java, GWT, and related technologies. Currently, he is Development Manager at 1View Solutions, which provides data integration solutions to the finance industry.

Andreas Winkler started his developer career during his study at the University of Applied Sciences in Berlin, Germany. There he studied Automation Engineering, with a focus on Software Developing. During his study, he began to work as a software developer for PLC systems. One task during this work was the porting of a C++ legacy application to Java, which started in 1998; the frontend of the new application was SWT-based.

After his graduation, he started his own company and development software solution for various customers. During this time, the company created this solution using cutting-edge technologies of the time. Especially with the start of development of the Web 2.0 and AJAX web pages, they switched their web-based application to a new level. The frontend developing started with the Sencha Ext JS and switched —for new applications —to Sencha GXT.

In 2010, he sold his company and switched to a new challenge, the introduction of the German healthcare card. This task was not focused on any AJAX frontend. But Andreas didn't lose his passion for the Sencha GXT framework, which he used to extend older projects.

www.PacktPub.com

Support files, eBooks, discount offers and more

You might want to visit `www.PacktPub.com` for support files and downloads related to your book.

Did you know that Packt offers eBook versions of every book published, with PDF and ePub files available? You can upgrade to the eBook version at `www.PacktPub.com` and as a print book customer, you are entitled to a discount on the eBook copy. Get in touch with us at `service@packtpub.com` for more details.

At `www.PacktPub.com`, you can also read a collection of free technical articles, sign up for a range of free newsletters and receive exclusive discounts and offers on Packt books and eBooks.

`http://PacktLib.PacktPub.com`

Do you need instant solutions to your IT questions? PacktLib is Packt's online digital book library. Here, you can access, read and search across Packt's entire library of books.

Why Subscribe?

- Fully searchable across every book published by Packt
- Copy and paste, print and bookmark content
- On demand and accessible via web browser

Free Access for Packt account holders

If you have an account with Packt at `www.PacktPub.com`, you can use this to access PacktLib today and view nine entirely free books. Simply use your login credentials for immediate access.

Table of Contents

Preface	**1**
Chapter 1: Playing with Panels and Windows	**7**
Introduction	7
Creating a basic window	8
Building windows that can be maximized, resized, dragged, and made modal	10
Creating dialog windows	13
Pre-empt users with messages	15
Building a window management system	18
Chapter 2: Playing Hide and Seek with Tabs	**25**
Introduction	25
Building tabbed content with custom tab icons	26
Creating bottom navigation tabs	29
Creating a tab panel with scrollable tab strip	30
Programmatically adding/removing a tab	33
Tab notification	35
Searching for, locating, and selecting a particular tab	40
Showing a tab strip for only two or more tabs	42
Chapter 3: Click-ware: Buttons, Toolbars, and Menus	**47**
Introduction	47
Creating buttons with text and icons	48
Aligning buttons	50
Creating on/off toggle buttons	52
Organizing actions with the menu and split buttons	55
Building a bar of tools	58
Crafting multi-column buttons in ToolBar	61
Binding a single action to several click-wares	64

Table of Contents

Chapter 4: Crafting UI Real Estate — 75
Introduction — 75
Organizing navigation with AccordionLayout — 77
Snapping components even when resized — 79
UI cardinality with BorderLayout — 82
Building a basic wizard with CardLayout — 85
RowLayout vertical and horizontal aligning — 92
Building grids with ColumnLayout — 94
Building DashBoards — 96

Chapter 5: Engaging Users with Forms and Data Input — 101
Introduction — 101
Building a simple form with basic validation — 102
Showing options with combos — 110
Customizing a combo's bound model — 113
Linking combos — 117
Capturing multiple input selection — 121
Simple FileUpload and processing — 124
Binding data into forms — 127
Building a better slider field — 134

Chapter 6: Data Hierarchy with Trees — 139
Introduction — 139
Building a basic tree — 140
Custom node labels — 144
Decorating trees with icons — 146
Augmenting trees with ContextMenu — 149
Building trees with checkbox selection — 152
Building asynchronous trees — 155
Custom sorting within trees — 158

Chapter 7: The Venerable Grid Component — 161
Introduction — 161
Basic grid: numbered rows, re-orderable columns — 162
Formatting cell data — 165
Grouping column headers — 168
Aggregating column data — 171
Easy record selection with checkboxes — 176
Entering validated data into a grid — 179
Automatic pagination in grids — 183
Data grouping in grids — 187
Custom rendering for grid groups — 189
Live data group summaries — 192

BeanModel grid	198
Intuitive record filtering	200

Chapter 8: Templates and Views — 205

Introduction	205
Formatting data with a basic template	206
Doing logic in templates	210
Doing math in templates	214
Custom ComboBox displays	217
Giving details with RowExpander	220

Chapter 9: Data Makeovers with Charts and Visualizations — 225

Introduction	225
Using a bar chart	226
Using a pie chart	230
Using a line chart	232
Using an area chart	235
Visualizing data from a component	238
Visualizing remote Data	244
Drawing on a canvas	248

Chapter 10: Drag-and-drop — 251

Introduction	251
Dragging any component	252
Simple DnD within components	255
DnD across components	259
DnD from desktop, with HTML5	265
Implementing custom DnD on tabs	269

Chapter 11: Advanced Tips — 275

Introduction	275
Client/server persistence setup	276
Client/server persistence	285
A novel UI with MVP, actions, and a bus	294
History and view transitions	300
Real-time server push	303

Chapter 12: Theming — 311

Introduction	311
Setting a default theme	312
Registering and using themes	313
Switching themes at runtime	315
Customizing a theme	317
Building a custom theme	319

Appendix A: Event Handling—Making Those GUIs Do Something — 321
- The event loop — 321
- Event handling 101 — 321
- Summary — 324

Appendix B: Custom Icons in GXT — 325
- GXT icons — 325
- Leveraging icons in the wild — 326

Appendix C: GWT-RPC — 329
- Components of the GWT RPC mechanism — 329
- GWT-RPC development steps — 330
- RPC data types — 331
- A simple example — 332
- Handling exceptions — 334
- Summary — 335

Appendix D: Jakarta Commons–FileUpload — 337
- Handling uploads — 338
- Tracking upload progress — 341

Index — 343

Preface

Get ready to build the next generation Gmail, Facebook, or Meebo, with HTML5 and Server Push, taking advantage of the power and versatility of Java using ExtGWT. Sencha ExtGWT takes GWT to the next level, giving you high performance widgets, feature rich templates and layouts, advanced charting, data loaders and stores, accessibility, and much more.

ExtGWT Rich Internet Application Cookbook will teach you to quickly build stunning functionality into your own apps, with ExtGWT.

This is a catalog of practical solutions to get your ExtGWT web app up and running in no time, with tips for persistence and best practices. You will begin by playing with panels, windows, and tabs, to learn the essentials. Next, you will engage with forms, buttons, toolbars, and menus, to build on your existing knowledge. Dealing with the UI and the trees will follow, to help you make stunning user interfaces. Then, you will be taught to work with Listview, Views, and Grids, the more complex problems. The book will then deal with charts, visualization, and drag-and-drop, to take you to the next level. Finally, you will wind up with serialization, persistence, and custom theming. And before you know it, you'll be an expert!

What this book covers

Chapter 1, Playing With Panels and Windows, deals with creating windows and different kinds of dialogs.

Chapter 2, Playing Hide and Seek with Tabs, explains how to create and manage tabs.

Chapter 3, Click-ware: Buttons, Toolbars, and Menus, describes how to create and align different types of buttons, how to create menus, and how to create toolbars and align buttons in toolbars.

Chapter 4, Crafting UI Real Estate, deals with the different layouts available in ExtGWT. Layouts such as AccordionLayout, BorderLayout, and CardLayout, as well as creating dashboards, are covered.

Chapter 5, Engaging Users with Forms and Data Input, deals with building forms, binding data into forms, and binding and retrieving remote data into a combobox.

Chapter 6, Data Hierarchy with Trees, introduces the Tree widget. The recipes in this chapter include building a tree, adding custom icons and context menus to the tree, adding checkbox selection to tree nodes, and building asynchronous trees.

Chapter 7, The Venerable Grid Component, presents ExtGWT's complex Grid component. The chapter's recipes demonstrate various features of this complex component, such as: formatting cell data, grouping data and headers, aggregating data, entering data into the grid, and data pagination.

Chapter 8, Templates and Views, introduces the Template component and its use for formatting data.

Chapter 9, Data Makeovers with Charts and Visualizations, deals with the various charts available in ExtGWT as well as drawing shapes with the Canvas class.

Chapter 10, Drag-and-drop, deals with the drag-and-drop mechanism available in ExtGWT as well as using a third-party library to do drag-and-drop, using HTML5.

Chapter 11, Advanced Tips, introduces various advanced topics, such as: using JPA (Java Persistence API) with GWT, using the MVP (model view presenter) pattern, and implementing a server-side push.

Chapter 12, Theming, explains how to use ExtGWT's existing UI themes, how to switch themes, and how to build a custom theme.

Appendix A, Event Handling—Making Those GUIs Do Something, explains ExtGWT's event-handling mechanism.

Appendix B, Custom Icons in GXT, explains how to add custom icons to your application.

Appendix C, GWT-RPC, describes GWT's RPC mechanism for client-server communication.

Appendix D, Jakarta Commons—FileUpload, demonstrates the use of Apache's FileUpload library for uploading files in a GWT application.

What you need for this book

To work with GWT, Java SDK needs to be installed. It can be downloaded from here:

http://www.oracle.com/technetwork/java/javase/downloads/index.html

The GWT SDK as well as the GWT Eclipse plugin can be downloaded from here:

https://developers.google.com/web-toolkit/download

Sencha's ExtGWT library can be downloaded from the following location:

http://dev.sencha.com/deploy/gxt-2.2.5.zip

(The code recipes for this book were developed and tested with GWT 2.4, Java JDK 1.7, and GXT 2.2.5).

Who this book is for

This book is intended for the intermediate to advanced Java developer who wants to build really cool and powerful web apps using cutting-edge Java technology and web standards. Knowledge of basic web technologies and a working GWT setup is needed. Basic knowledge of ExtGWT will be an advantage.

Conventions

In this book, you will find a number of styles of text that distinguish between different kinds of information. Here are some examples of these styles, and an explanation of their meaning.

Code words in text are shown as follows: "Configure basic settings, such as a title with setHeading() and an initial dimension with setSize()."

A block of code is set as follows:

```
@Override
public void onModuleLoad() {
  // create and set up window
  Window basicWindow = new Window();
  basicWindow.setHeading("GXT CookBook | Recipe One");
  basicWindow.setClosable(true);
  basicWindow.setSize(250, 50);
```

New terms and **important words** are shown in bold. Words that you see on the screen, in menus or dialog boxes for example, appear in the text like this: "our dialog will be configured to use the **OK** and **Cancel** buttons combination, allowing the user to accept or decline the action presented by the dialog".

> Warnings or important notes appear in a box like this.

> Tips and tricks appear like this.

Reader feedback

Feedback from our readers is always welcome. Let us know what you think about this book—what you liked or may have disliked. Reader feedback is important for us to develop titles that you really get the most out of.

To send us general feedback, simply send an e-mail to feedback@packtpub.com, and mention the book title via the subject of your message.

If there is a book that you need and would like to see us publish, please send us a note in the **SUGGEST A TITLE** form on www.packtpub.com or e-mail suggest@packtpub.com.

If there is a topic that you have expertise in and you are interested in either writing or contributing to a book, see our author guide on www.packtpub.com/authors.

Customer support

Now that you are the proud owner of a Packt book, we have a number of things to help you to get the most from your purchase.

Downloading the example code

You can download the example code files for all Packt books you have purchased from your account at http://www.PacktPub.com. If you purchased this book elsewhere, you can visit http://www.PacktPub.com/support and register to have the files e-mailed directly to you.

Errata

Although we have taken every care to ensure the accuracy of our content, mistakes do happen. If you find a mistake in one of our books—maybe a mistake in the text or the code—we would be grateful if you would report this to us. By doing so, you can save other readers from frustration and help us improve subsequent versions of this book. If you find any errata, please report them by visiting http://www.packtpub.com/support, selecting your book, clicking on the **errata submission form** link, and entering the details of your errata. Once your errata are verified, your submission will be accepted and the errata will be uploaded on our website, or added to any list of existing errata, under the Errata section of that title. Any existing errata can be viewed by selecting your title from http://www.packtpub.com/support.

Piracy

Piracy of copyright material on the Internet is an ongoing problem across all media. At Packt, we take the protection of our copyright and licenses very seriously. If you come across any illegal copies of our works, in any form, on the Internet, please provide us with the location address or website name immediately so that we can pursue a remedy.

Please contact us at copyright@packtpub.com with a link to the suspected pirated material.

We appreciate your help in protecting our authors, and our ability to bring you valuable content.

Questions

You can contact us at questions@packtpub.com if you are having a problem with any aspect of the book, and we will do our best to address it.

1
Playing with Panels and Windows

In this chapter we will cover:

- ▸ Creating a basic window
- ▸ Building windows that can be maximized, resized, dragged, and made modal
- ▸ Creating dialog windows
- ▸ Pre-empt users with messages
- ▸ Building a window management system

Introduction

Windows are top-level UI components, used mainly to access data in a way that accents the information being presented. We often think they are only used as a region of boxed data and controls overlaid on other UI components; although this is usually the case, I recommend that you begin thinking of them in a way that does not limit their usage to overlays.

Windows as UI controls became really cool in web development with the advent of Ajax, which in many ways makes web applications behave like multi-threaded operating systems—allowing asynchronous activities to continue in the background while the user is engaged with the active window. These new breeds of window widgets have quickly replaced the old-fashioned browser dialogs and DHTML hacks that were its forerunners.

Playing with Panels and Windows

Creating a basic window

We will create a barebones window, without all the bells and whistles, but with enough handling to give you a good footing for the next two recipes. Here, we will create a window to display information about this text and a close button on the top far right corner.

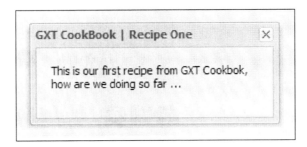

How to do it...

Our basic window should just take a few lines of code; we'll split these into segments for easy comprehension.

1. Instantiate the window with `new Window()`.
2. Configure basic settings, such as a title with `setHeading()` and an initial dimension with `setSize()`.
3. Add some content with `LayoutContainer`.
4. Invoke `show()` on the window object, to display it.

We can create a basic window using the following code:

```
@Override
public void onModuleLoad() {
  // create and set up window
  Window basicWindow = new Window();
  basicWindow.setHeading("GXT CookBook | Recipe One");
  basicWindow.setClosable(true);
  basicWindow.setSize(250, 50);
```

```
    // prepare content to show
    LayoutContainer textPanel = new VerticalPanel();
    textPanel.setStyleAttribute("padding", "15px");
    textPanel.addText("This is our first recipe from GXT Cookbook, how
are we doing so far ...");

    // place content on the window
    // and display it.
    basicWindow.add(textPanel);
    basicWindow.show();
}
```

How it works...

The code is broken up into three segments; the first part creates and sets up the window, the second part puts together the content to be shown, while the third part attaches the content built from the second part to the window and then displays it.

The window is instantiated, given a title/heading, made closable, and also given an initial dimension of 250 x 50 units. Next, we use `LayoutContainer` and one of its specialized subclasses, `VerticalPanel`, to set up our content area. `LayoutContainer` is just an empty container used to lay out arbitrary stuff within it, but the specialized `VerticalPanel` class ensures that our content is rendered in a top-to-bottom fashion, usually if we are displaying several contents anyway.

The way this line is coded, assigning a value of a subtype to a variable of a supertype, is worth noting—a good implementation pattern (the strategy pattern) that reduces brittleness in our code. As we coded the `LayoutContainer` interface with a `VerticalPanel` instance, we can just swap `VerticalPanel` with `HorizontalPanel` or our custom `OscilatorPanel`, and the rest of our code will not need to be altered!

The `textPanel.setStyleAttribute("padding", "15px")` method gives us some spacing so the text does not collide with its surrounding walls, the `basicWindow.add(textPanel)` method adds our `textPanel` to the window, while the `basicWindow.show()` method tells the window the time it (the window) got displayed.

Playing with Panels and Windows

Building windows that can be maximized, resized, dragged, and made modal

The previous recipe produced a simple window (well, ok, with some extra baggage!); now, we'll expand that to make a window that can be maximized (expanded to fill the browser's viewable area, usually called the viewport), resized (dragged with special arrow handles at the edges to expand it to any size), dragged (moved arbitrarily and placed anywhere on the screen), and made modal (prevents the user from interacting with any other element on the screen while it is still active).

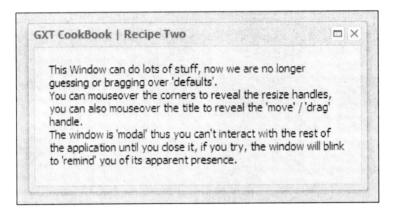

How to do it...

I am actually modifying the code template from the previous recipe, *Creating a basic window*, to create this one, so the code is very similar.

1. Create the window with `new Window()`.
2. Apply some basic settings to it with `setHeading()`, `setClosable(true)`, and `setSize()`.
3. Then add the extra features using `setDraggable(true)` to make it arbitrarily "draggable".
4. Use `setResizable(true)` to allow the user to drag its sides and corners to resize it.
5. Call `setMaximizable(true)` to enable it to expand to fill the viewport.
6. Use `setModal(true)` to make it a modal window, one that prevents interaction with the rest of the screen until the window is closed. If accompanied with `setBlinkModal(true)`, the window will blink if the user tries to anything outside the window without first closing it.

We can build a window with the "x" features using the following code:

```java
@Override
public void onModuleLoad() {
  // basic window setup
  Window xWindow = new Window();
  xWindow.setHeading("GXT CookBook | Recipe Two");
  xWindow.setClosable(true);
  xWindow.setSize(350, 170);

  // add the 'x' features
  xWindow.setDraggable(true);
  // actually defaults to true
  xWindow.setResizable(true);
  xWindow.setMaximizable(true);
  xWindow.setModal(true);
  xWindow.setBlinkModal(true);

  // constrain the maximize operation
  // such that when maximized the window
  // will expand to fill the box defined by
  // the dimensions of centerPanel instead
  // of the entire browser viewable area.
  // centerPanel is a standard GXT Panel
  xWindow.setContainer(centerPanel.getElement());

  // constrain drag actions to a specific
  // container (centerPanel, a standard GXT Panel)
  // instead of the browser's viewable area.
  // Thus you can't drag the window outside
  // the bounds of centerPanel.
  xWindow.getDraggable().setContainer(centerPanel);

  // prepare some content to show,
  // you've got to have something to show!
  LayoutContainer textPanel = new VerticalPanel();
  textPanel.setStyleAttribute("padding", "15px");
  StringBuilder msg = new StringBuilder();
  msg.append("This Window can do lots of stuff,");
  msg.append("now we are no longer guessing or ");
  msg.append("bragging over 'defaults'. <p>You can ");
  msg.append("move the mouse over the corners to ");
  msg.append("reveal the resize handles, ");
  msg.append("moving the mouse over the title also ");
```

```
        msg.append("reveals the 'move' / 'drag' handle.</p>");
        msg.append("<p>The window is 'modal' thus you can't interact ");
        msg.append("with the rest of the application until you close it, ");
        msg.append("if you try, the window will blink to ");
        msg.append("'remind' you of its apparent presence.</p>");
        textPanel.addText(msg.toString());

        // attach the content to
        // the window and show it
        xWindow.add(textPanel);
        xWindow.show();
    }
```

How it works...

The `Window` object is now assigned to a variable called `xWindow`. Among other things, its initial dimensions are set to something much bigger to make room, as more text is being displayed in this recipe.

The section denoted by the single line comment `add the 'x' features` is where we do all the stuff that really makes this window different with the "x" features (resizable, draggable, maximizable, and modal).

`setDraggable(true)` makes the window draggable, `setResizable(true)` makes it resizable (although this is the default behavior), `setMaximizable(true)` makes it maximizable, while `setModal(true)` makes it a modal window, so that you must close it before continuing to use the rest of the UI. You can pass `false` to any of these methods to disable that feature, for example, calling `setResizable(false)` will prevent the window from being resized.

Moving the mouse over the corners reveals the resize handles, while moving the mouse over the title reveals the "move"/"drag" handle.

About two years ago, while still actively developing with ExtJs, I created a plugin called `Ext.plugin.ModalNotice` that basically causes modal windows to blink if you attempt to do anything outside the window while it's still active; this was achieved by animating a show/hide sequence on the window. Many thanks to the community, because once the plugin was out, folks came up with better and more efficient ways (algorithms) to make the window blink. I am very glad that it made it into core. `xWindow.setBlinkModal(true)` will cause the modal window to blink, reminding you of its apparent presence and that you must deal with it before doing anything else.

There's more...

When it comes to resizing windows, sometimes you want to define constraints for the resize behavior. It makes sense to prevent resizing below a certain width and/or height, so that the window is still functional; you could achieve that with the `setMinWidth` and `setMinHeight` methods of the Window API.

Creating dialog windows

A **dialog** is a window derived from the `Window` class, thus it can participate in whatever routine a window can, but it can also do more. Dialogs are generally used to present information to the user, information for which feedback is expected, hence it has specialized button combination configurations that can be provided and used to get user feedback.

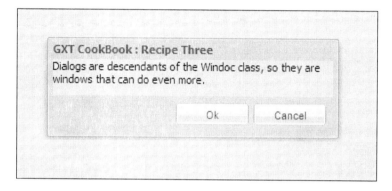

How to do it...

1. Create one dialog with `new Dialog()`.
2. Use its `addText()` method to place text content inside it.
3. Invoke its `show()` method to display it.

A dialog window can be generated using the following code:

```
@Override
public void onModuleLoad() {
  Dialog dialog = new Dialog();
  dialog.setBodyBorder(false);
  dialog.setClosable(false);
  dialog.setHideOnButtonClick(true);
  dialog.setButtons(Dialog.OKCANCEL);
  dialog.setScrollMode(Scroll.NONE);
  dialog.setHeading("GXT CookBook : Recipe Three");
```

Playing with Panels and Windows

```
      dialog.addText("Dialogs are descendants of the Window class, so they
are windows that can do even more.");
      dialog.show();

      SelectionListener<ButtonEvent> listener = new SelectionListener<But
tonEvent>() {
        @Override
        public void componentSelected(ButtonEvent evt) {
          String text = evt.getButton().getText();
          String format = "You clicked the {0} button";
          Info.display("Recipe Three", format, text);
        }
      };

      Button okBtn = dialog.getButtonById(Dialog.OK);
      okBtn.addSelectionListener(listener);

      Button cancelBtn = dialog.getButtonById(Dialog.CANCEL);
      cancelBtn.addSelectionListener(listener);

  }
```

How it works...

First, we instantiate a `Dialog` object from the constructor and assign it to the `dialog` variable. The `dialog.setBodyBorder(false)` ensures that the default blue border around the body of our content is not shown, while `dialog.setCloseable(false)` ensures that we don't have the standard window close button shown, because we want the user to interact and give feedback with the specialized buttons we'll be providing. This is why `dialog.setHideOnButtonClick(true)` is used to automatically hide the dialog (equivalent of an explicit `dialog.hide()` call) when any of the buttons are clicked.

`dialog.setButtons(DialogOKCANCEL)` specifies that our dialog will be configured to use the **OK** and **Cancel** buttons combination, allowing the user to accept or decline the action presented by the dialog. The `dialog.setScrollMode(Scroll.NONE)` is used to prevent scrolling within the content the dialog presents; this means that it must be properly sized else its contents may be clipped.

The `setHeading()` method from the `Window` class is used to specify the title shown on the header of the dialog, just as it does in standard windows, from which it inherits, while its specialized `dialog.addText()` method populates its content area with the text to be shown to the user. Once these are done, we are ready to show the dialog using the now familiar `show()` method.

The last segment of the code creates an instance of `SelectionListener`—which is a special listener that can be used with buttons—and attaches it to the buttons on our dialog, so that we can handle click actions (or selections) on them. When the button is clicked, the `componentSelected()` method of the listener gets called; although this is not required to display or render a dialog, it is very unlikely that you would have a dialog with dummy buttons. Saving the explanation of events and listeners for later, you can see that `dialog.getButtonById()` uses the special button ID of our configured buttons (`Dialog.OK` and `Dialog.CANCEL` button ID constants in the `Dialog` class) to return a reference to them. As we chose the `Dialog.OKCANCEL` combination, `dialog.getButtonById(Dialog.OK)` returns the **OK** button from the button set, allowing us to tweak it in whatever way we want, such as attaching our listener, which just shows a message stating which button was actually clicked. It does this with the help of the `Info` class, which displays a message in the bottom-right region of the browser for a specified amount of time.

Pre-empt users with messages

The GXT toolkit also has a `MessageBox` class. It is very similar in concept and functionality to the `Dialog` class, except for its convenience methods for specific displays and the icons associated with these displays (which can be achieved with the `Dialog` class too, but with a little hair-pulling). It's therefore safe for us to call them (both classes) *Dialogs*, especially considering them from a presentation perspective, but they are different.

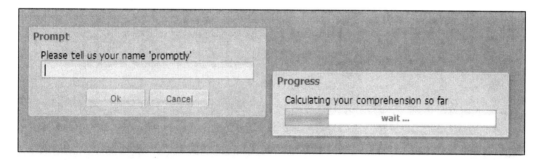

How to do it...

1. Call `MessageBox.alert()`, passing in a title, a message to show, and an optional listener as parameters, to display an alert dialog.

2. Call `MessageBox.confirm()`, passing in a title, a message to show, and an optional listener as parameters, to display a confirmation dialog.

Playing with Panels and Windows

3. Call `MessageBox.prompt()` with a title, a message to show, and an optional listener, to display a prompt dialog.

```
@Override
public void onModuleLoad() {
  // So we can handle your button clicks
  Listener<MessageBoxEvent> listener = new Listener<MessageBoxEvent>()
{
    @Override
    public void handleEvent(MessageBoxEvent evt) {
      Button btn = evt.getButtonClicked();
      Info.display("Recipe Four", "The '{0}' button was pressed", btn.
getText());

      MessageBoxType msgBoxType = evt.getMessageBox().getType();
      if(msgBoxType != null &&
          (msgBoxType.equals(MessageBoxType.PROMPT) ||
            msgBoxType.equals(MessageBoxType.MULTIPROMPT))){
        Info.display("Recipe Four : Prompt", evt.getValue());
      }
    }

  };

  // Show alert message
  MessageBox.alert("Alert", "Invalid Login Credentials", listener);

  // Show confirm message
  MessageBox.confirm("Confirm", "Do you intend to logout", listener);

  // Show prompt message
  MessageBox.prompt("Prompt", "Please tell us your name 'promptly'",
listener);

  // Show progress message
  final MessageBox pBar = MessageBox.progress("Progress", "Calculating
your comprehension so far", "wait ...");
  pBar.getProgressBar().auto();
  Timer pBarTimer = new Timer(){
    @Override
    public void run() {
      pBar.close();
    }
  };
  pBarTimer.schedule(5000);
}
```

How it works...

For clarity we have segmented our code; the first segment shows how we make a listener, simply to show an info window stating which `MessageBox` button was clicked—not to cover the concept of events and listeners, but just to see how listeners can be created and attached to `MessageBox` objects.

It turns out that using a `MessageBox` object is very easy once you have made up your mind which one to use. To alert the user (of course with a non-obtrusive widget, unlike the standard browser alert dialog, which *freezes* the entire application), we simply call `MessageBox.alert()`, passing three parameters—a title, a message to be displayed, and a callback (listener), to handle the user's click action on the **OK** button. This automatically gets displayed with an alert icon:

We use `MessageBox.confirm()` to pop up a confirm dialog, also requiring a title, a message, and a listener callback, as parameters. At the end of the call, we get a confirm dialog (as in the next screenshot) posing a question (ideally in response to a user action), which the user can respond to with either the **Yes** or **No** buttons:

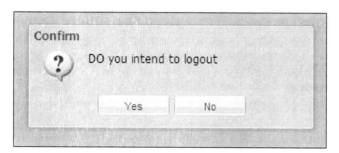

Playing with Panels and Windows

We also use `MessageBox.prompt()` to elicit input from the user (see the following screenshot). The call expects the three standard parameters—a title, a message, and a listener callback. The result of this call is a cool prompt dialog with a text field for a single line of text. Although we can allow multiline text entry, that would have required us to pass `true` as the third parameter, while our callback becomes the fourth parameter to the `MessageBox.confirm()` call.

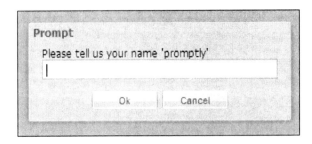

The `MessageBox` class is really handy, especially because of its ease and convenience. The idea of having a fully functional confirm or prompt dialog, kitted with icons and event listener support, and with just one line of code is quite amazing, don't you think?

Building a window management system

GXT windows are cool, they look great, and can be resized, dragged, maximized, and so on—we've seen how easy it is to achieve all this. Depending on your style and layout design, you probably use a lot of them in a GXT project. However, without a way to manage them, you'll soon become weary of their use.

A typical GXT app will have many windows; we want to build a system that can present them to us in a way (probably with a menu) so that we can elect to make use of a particular one, and if there are several already on screen, that one would be brought to the forefront. The system should allow us to hide and show them all with a single action, and also cascade them all (overlay them in a hierarchical fashion on the screen), so that you can see and identify the windows by their headings.

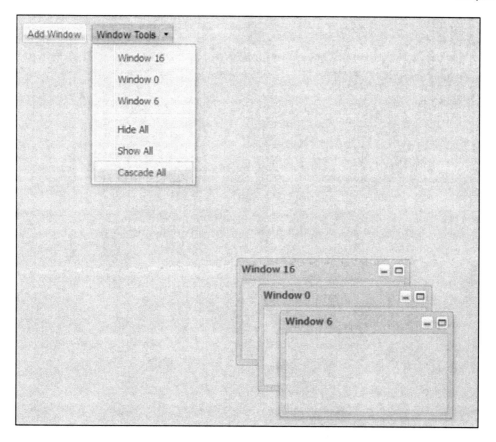

Finally, the system should allow us to minimize windows, as if saving them for future use. The previous screenshot shows a preview of our system in use. The **Add Window** button is used to create the windows for whom the ID and heading are set automatically with a randomly generated integer, thanks to the Random class from the com.google.gwt.user.client package. Once we have a set of windows to play with, we can apply our hide/show/cascade functionality on them. Note that each window that's created automatically has a menu entry inside the splitbutton; this is there so that you can click on any one at any time, to show that particular window and have it brought to the forefront.

Playing with Panels and Windows

How to do it...

Our code here is a little on the lengthy side but for obvious reasons, even at that, it's simple and straight to the point, once you get a hang of what it is doing.

```
@Override
public void onModuleLoad() {
  // set up some "global" variables
  final Menu toolMenu = new Menu();
  ButtonBar buttonBar = new ButtonBar();
  final WindowManager mgr = WindowManager.get();
  final List<Window> windowList = new ArrayList<Window>();

  final WindowListener windowListener = new WindowListener(){
    @Override
    public void windowMinimize(WindowEvent we) {
      final Window window = we.getWindow();

      // make a menu-item for this window,
      // but only once, so we'll search first
      boolean found = false;
      Iterator<Component> it = toolMenu.getItems().iterator();
      while (it.hasNext()) {
        Component cmp = (Component) it.next();
    if(cmp instanceof MenuItem){
        MenuItem item = (MenuItem) cmp;
          if(item.getText().equals(we.getWindow().getHeading())){
            found = true;
            break;
          }
        }
      }

      if(found == false){
        toolMenu.insert(new MenuItem(we.getWindow().getHeading(), new SelectionListener<MenuEvent>() {
          @Override
          public void componentSelected(MenuEvent ce) {
            if(!window.isVisible()){
              window.show();
            }
            mgr.bringToFront(window);
          }
        }), 0);
      }
```

```
      window.hide();
    }
  };

  // we'll use this to generate the windows
  Button addWindowBtn = new Button("Add Window", new SelectionListener
<ButtonEvent>() {
    @Override
    public void componentSelected(ButtonEvent evt) {
       int randInt = Random.nextInt(20);
       Window dummy = new Window();
       dummy.setClosable(false);
       dummy.setSize(200, 120);
       dummy.setMinimizable(true);
       dummy.setMaximizable(true);
       dummy.setId("win_" + randInt);
       dummy.setHeading("Window " + randInt);
       dummy.setContainer(GxtCookBk.getCenterPanel().getElement());
       dummy.addWindowListener(windowListener);

       dummy.show();
       windowList.add(dummy);
    }
  });
  buttonBar.add(addWindowBtn);
  toolMenu.add(new SeparatorMenuItem());

  // add the menu-items to handle hide/show/cascade all
  // hide-all is easy anyways
  toolMenu.add(new MenuItem("Hide All", new
SelectionListener<MenuEvent>() {
    @Override
    public void componentSelected(MenuEvent evt) {
       mgr.hideAll();
    }
  }));

  // show-all only works because we kept
  // a local list of the windows we've made
  toolMenu.add(new MenuItem("Show All", new
SelectionListener<MenuEvent>() {
    @Override
    public void componentSelected(MenuEvent evt) {
       // mgr.getWindows() || mgr.getStack() returns only visible
windows
```

Playing with Panels and Windows

```java
        // so we always have an empty list after calling mgr.hideAll()
        for(Window window : windowList){
          if(window != null && !window.isVisible()){
             window.show();
          }
        }
      }
    }
  }));
  // cascade is tricky, yeah.
  // cascade is implemented by positioning
  // the windows atop each other, but 25x29 pixels
  // "more" from the last one
  toolMenu.add(new MenuItem("Cascade All", new
SelectionListener<MenuEvent>() {
     @Override
     public void componentSelected(MenuEvent evt) {
       List<Window> windows = mgr.getWindows();
       Window reference = null;
       for (Window window : windows) {
         window.show();
         mgr.bringToFront(window);
         window.center();
         if(reference != null){
            window.setPosition(reference.getPosition(true).x + 25,
reference.getPosition(true).y + 29);
         }
         reference = window;
       }
     }
  }));

  // create a menu button and attach the menu to it
  Button toolBtn = new Button("Window Tools");    // correct book from
SplitButton to this
  toolBtn.setMenu(toolMenu);
  buttonBar.add(toolBtn);
  centerPanel.add(buttonBar, new FlowData(10));
}
```

How it works...

First, we set up some variables that we'll be using throughout this recipe. The first section does it for us; within those lines we create an instance `toolMenu` using the `new Menu()` method, this will contain items that we will click on, to execute actions on the windows. Secondly, an instance `buttonBar` is created using the `new ButtonBar()` method; this is just a bar to hold the buttons we'll be using—one button to create a new window when clicked and the other one to expose the menu made from the `toolMenu` instance. `WindowManager.get()` gives us the singleton `WindowManager` instance, with which we intend to do most of the interesting stuff in this recipe. We also instantiate a type-safe list of `Window` objects. Although the `WindowManager` class automatically keeps a register of windows internally, it usually contains only visible windows, so if we ever hide a window (we actually want you to easily hide all at once) we'll end up with no way to show them again; this is why we must keep our own list of the windows.

Next, we make an instance of `WindowListener`, to listen to and handle window events. Events are fired for every window-related action the user performs, whether it's a drag, resize, minimize, or maximize action. However, we are particularly interested in handling minimize gestures, so we'll only override the `windowMinimize()` method within our listener, which like all the other methods, will be called with a `WindowEvent` object, from where we can get a reference to the window that triggered the event and other context artifacts associated with it. These objects are created first because we will need them as the code progresses, and so you can get a grasp of the flow of the code easily.

In the `windowMinimize()` method of our `WindowListener` class (called when a window is minimized), first we obtain a reference to the minimized window and then we iterate over the menu items in `toolMenu`, investigating each to see if we can find a match between its text and the heading of the referenced window. If we find a match, we know that this window has been minimized before and a menu item already exists for it, with the heading of the window; if we don't find a match (`found` will remain false after the iteration), we know that the referenced window is being minimized for the first time, so we make a menu item for it by passing the referenced window's heading (as its label) and a `SelectionListener` instance. This will show up the referenced window and bring it to the front of other windows (if any), when the menu item is clicked/selected.

With our variables and `WindowListener` out of the way, we proceed to create an `addWindow` button, passing `Add Window` (as the label) and an anonymous `SelectionListener` instance, to handle click actions on it. Within the listener, we make a closable and maximizeable window using `Random.nextInt(20)`; we set its ID and heading automatically to a random integer not exceeding 20. We also set the listener of this window to the one created previously and make it minimizeable with `setMinimizable(true)`.

Playing with Panels and Windows

Recall that our `windowListener` instance is where we actually implement the minimize functionality (by hiding the window, having made a menu item for it), else we get nothing when the window is minimized. Once the window is created and shown, `windowList.add(dummy)` adds it to our register of windows; this is important if we want to implement a show-all feature.

At this point, the `addWindowBtn` button is all set up; we can now add it to the button bar, which is done with a call to `buttonBar.add(addWindowBtn)`.

The next code segment implements the hide all feature by adding a simple menu item to `toolMenu` and passing an anonymous `SelectionListener` instance; this newly added menu item calls `hideAll()` on our `WindowManager` object (`mgr.hideAll()`) to hide all visible windows. The show all feature is a little more involved, because there's no `showAll()` method (or anything similar) to call from the `WindowManager` object. Also, its internal list of windows only references windows that have not been previously hidden or closed. Hence, we iterate over our own list of windows kept in the `final ArrayList<Window> windowList` variable, conditionally calling `show()` on each.

So far, we've done everything except cascade all, which is intended to overlay the windows over each other in a hierarchy that allows us see their headings so that we can identify them. We do this by iterating over the list of windows from our `WindowManager` object; when we get a handle to a window from the list, we show it with `window.show()`. Then, we bring it to the forefront with `mgr.bringToFront(window)`, and next, center it with `window.center()`. If this is not the first window to be cascaded from the list, in which case `reference != null` will be `true`, we position it 25 pixels farther and 29 pixels lower than the previously cascaded window, which we are storing with the reference variable.

Now, what's left is to make our `SplitButton` button, attach the `toolMenu` instance to it, and then attach the button to the button bar from where it's available for user interaction.

2
Playing Hide and Seek with Tabs

In this chapter we will cover:

- Building tabbed content with custom tab icons
- Creating bottom navigation tabs
- Creating a tab panel with scrollable tab strip
- Programmatically adding/removing a tab
- Tab notification
- Searching for, locating, and selecting a particular tab
- Showing a tab strip for only two or more tabs

Introduction

Tabs are inspired by their use in filing cabinets, where they separate sections of files. Although they are not really different from a normal horizontal bar, the shape of the tabs makes the menu less boring and more visually distinguishable and intuitive.

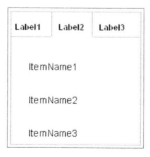

Playing Hide and Seek with Tabs

The most frequent use of tabs is in a horizontal menu. The tabs are then used to separate categorized information. Another use is to show a (partial) view of one object, for example, when showing a product page with sections about features, design, connectivity, and so on.

The information placed in the tab pane belongs to the selected tab and can have its own subnavigation. The currently selected category is highlighted by using a contrasting color, a shape, a size, or a typeface. It is best to create the needed contrast by using combinations, such as color and shape. Connecting the selected tab to the area underneath it, say by making both the area and the tab the same background color, the relationship is enforced even further.

Building tabbed content with custom tab icons

Organizing content into tabs is not only visually appealing but also helps to judiciously utilize UI real estate. The user can easily identify and navigate through the tabbed content by clicking on the title on any of the tabs; augmenting this with tooltips and icons gives a better visual cue for a tab, thus improving navigation.

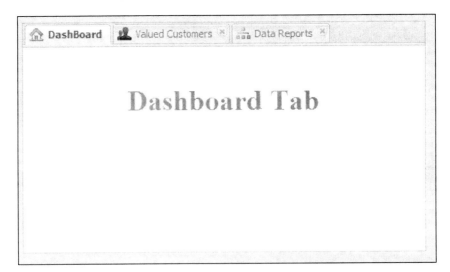

How to do it...

We will create a custom interface that extends `ImageBundle`. The `ImageBundle` is a GWT tag interface that is used to bundle several images into one big image, in order to optimize the delivery of the images over the network. We will call `ImageBundle` `Icons` and use it to encapsulate methods that return the icon images as instances of `AbstractImagePrototype`, which our tabs will gladly accept. Once this is done, every other thing is straightforward and produces a beautiful and interactive tab display.

Use the following code to perform this recipe:

```java
public interface Icons extends ImageBundle {
  AbstractImagePrototype people();
  AbstractImagePrototype home();
  AbstractImagePrototype orgchart();
}


TabPanel tabPanel = new TabPanel();
tabPanel.setHeight(250);
tabPanel.setWidth(450);
tabPanel.setCloseContextMenu(true);

/*
 * Our Icons interface extends ImageBundle and declares three methods,
 * each named with the exact name of an image placed in the same package
 * as the Icons interface. Having created the interface,
 * preferably in its own java file,
 * we proceed to used it with tabs and everywhere
 *     else AbstractImagePrototype icons are used in GXT.
 *
 */
Icons ICONS = GWT.create(Icons.class);

String title = "DashBoard";
TabItem homeTab = new TabItem(title);
homeTab.setIcon(ICONS.home());
homeTab.getHeader().setToolTip("Our " + title);
homeTab.add(new HtmlContainer("<h1>Dashboard Tab</h1>"));
tabPanel.add(homeTab);

title = "Valued Customers";
TabItem customersTab = new TabItem(title);
customersTab.setIcon(ICONS.people());
customersTab.getHeader().setToolTip("Our Really " + title);
customersTab.setClosable(true);
customersTab.add(new HtmlContainer("<h1>Customers Tab</h1>"));
tabPanel.add(customersTab);
```

Playing Hide and Seek with Tabs

```
    title = "Data Reports";
    TabItem reportsTab = new TabItem(title);
    reportsTab.setIcon(ICONS.orgchart());
    reportsTab.getHeader().setToolTip("The customer " + title);
    reportsTab.setClosable(true);
    reportsTab.add(new HtmlContainer("<h1>Reports Tab</h1>"));
    tabPanel.add(reportsTab);
    /*
     * GxtCookbk is the application's entry point class.
     * We access its main content panel using the
     * static GxtCookBk.getAppCenterPanel() call.
     * We add the tabPanel to the main content panel.
     */
    GxtCookBk.getAppCenterPanel().add(tabPanel);
```

How it works...

To begin using tabs, we must first instantiate the `TabPanel` class; this is the parent container for tabs, which are themselves instances of the `TabItem` class. After instantiation, the height of the `tabPanel` instance is set with `tabPanel.setHeight(450)`, which is followed by a call to enable the close context menu on the tabs, providing us with a handy context menu on the tab title, so that we can elect to close it (if it is closable) or close all the others that are closable. On the last line of that code section, we employ the GWT factory method, `GWT.create()`, to obtain an instance of our `Icons` interface; thus, we are ready to create `TabItem` objects (tabs), set icons and tooltips on them, and then attach them to the `tabPanel` container.

The next code section creates a **Dashboard** tab. We simply instantiate the `TabItem` class and assign it to `homeTab`, and then set its icon to `ICONS.home()` using `homeTab.setIcon(ICONS.home())`. This means that the image named `home` (a PNG, JPEG, or GIF file) will be set as this tab's icon. *Appendix B* explains how to create and use icons in GXT.

The next line of code sets a tooltip on the tab, with `homeTab.setToolTip()`, while `homeTab.getHeader().setToolTip()` sets the tooltip on the tab's title. I find it unnecessary to set two tooltips on a single tab as it can easily annoy the user, however I recommend the latter option, which allows the user to get hints on a tab by hovering on its title without leaving the currently selected tab being viewed. Next, we add an `HtmlContainer` instance (displays HTML) to the tab and then add the tab to the `tabPanel` instance.

The other tabs are built in a similar fashion, except we use a different icon and of course a different title, for each tab. The last line of code obtains our playground panel (it's just a `LayoutContainer` panel) and attaches the instance `tabPanel` to it, so that it can be shown. All tabs can be closed using the context menu (enabled by the `setCloseContextMenu()` call), except the first tab.

Creating bottom navigation tabs

Tabs are usually displayed at the top of the tab panel, however sometimes we might want to use a different tab position. GXT supports two different tab positions: top and bottom. In this recipe, we will show you how to create bottom navigation tabs.

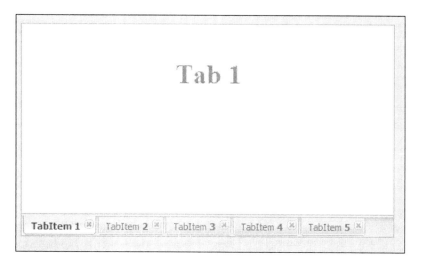

How to do it...

It turns out that this is achieved with just a single line of code...ok, not really!

The following code will create the bottom navigation tab:

```
TabPanel tabPanel = new TabPanel();
tabPanel.setHeight(450);
tabPanel.setCloseContextMenu(true);

// the magic line
tabPanel.setTabPosition(TabPanel.TabPosition.BOTTOM);

for(int i = 1; i <= 5; ++i){
  TabItem aTab = new TabItem("TabItem <b>" + i + "</b>");
  aTab.setClosable(true);
  aTab.add(new HtmlContainer("<h1>Tab " + i + "</h1>"));
  tabPanel.add(aTab);
}
/*
 * GxtCookbk is the application's entry point class.
 * We access its main content panel using the
```

Playing Hide and Seek with Tabs

```
 * static GxtCookBk.getAppCenterPanel() call.
 * We add the tabPanel to the main content panel.
 */
GxtCookBk.getAppCenterPanel().add(tabPanel);
```

How it works...

As usual, we instantiate the `TabPanel` class and set its height; we also enable the close context menu—which gives us a handy context menu from a tab's title bar—to either close that tab or all the others. Next, we pass `TabPanel.TabPosition.BOTTOM` to `tabPanel.setTabPosition()`, and this does it all.

Ok, so that we can have a complete example, we enter a loop and add five tabs to the tab panel, after making each tab closable and setting HTML content on it with `HtmlContainer`.

Finally, we attach the tab panel to our playground panel (a `LayoutContainer` panel) with `GxtCookBk.getAppCenterPanel().add(tabPanel)`. The `GxtCookBk` entry-point class sets up the main view port and main layout. The recipes are attached to the content area in the main layout.

Creating a tab panel with scrollable tab strip

The tab strip is the portion of the `TabPanel` class containing the titles or headings of the tabs that the user clicks on to navigate through the tabbed content. Although it is not generally considered good usability, sometimes we might need to have more tabs than the tab strip can display. Thanks to the GXT toolkit, we can scroll on the tab strip to solve this problem.

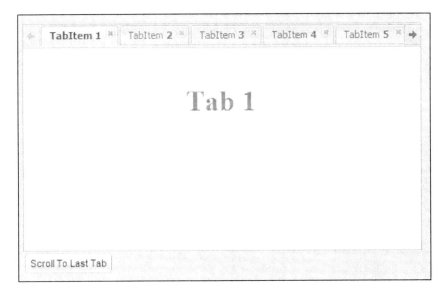

How to do it...

Enabling the tab strip scroll feature on a `TabPanel` instance is quite easy; even if you want the scroll operation animated, you are welcome to try it, it just takes a few (about three) lines of code to achieve this. We may also need to scroll to a particular tab, irrespective of which one is currently selected, instead of only scrolling sequentially to the left-hand side or right-hand side, till we either get to it or reach the end.

The following code will create a tab panel with scrollable tab strip:

```java
final TabPanel tabPanel = new TabPanel();
tabPanel.setHeight(250);
tabPanel.setWidth(450);
tabPanel.setTabScroll(true);
tabPanel.setAnimScroll(true);
tabPanel.setCloseContextMenu(true);

for(int i = 1; i <= 10; ++i){
  TabItem aTab = new TabItem("TabItem <b>" + i + "</b>");
  aTab.setClosable(true);
  aTab.add(new HtmlContainer("<h1>Tab " + i + "</h1>"));
  tabPanel.add(aTab);
}

ButtonBar buttonBar = new ButtonBar();
buttonBar.add(new ToggleButton("Scroll To Last Tab", new
SelectionListener<ButtonEvent>(){
  @Override
  public void componentSelected(ButtonEvent evt) {

    int index = 0;
    String title = "Scroll To Last Tab";
    ToggleButton btn = (ToggleButton) evt.getButton();
    if(btn.isPressed()){
      index = tabPanel.getItemCount()-1;
      title = "Scroll To First Tab";

    } else {
      title = "Scroll To Last Tab";
      index = 0;
    }
    TabItem target = tabPanel.getItem(index);
    if(tabPanel.getSelectedItem() != target){
      tabPanel.scrollToTab(target, true);
      tabPanel.setSelection(target);
```

```
            btn.setText(title);
        }
    }
}));

/*
 * GxtCookbk is the application's entry point class.
 * We access its main content panel using the
 * static GxtCookBk.getAppCenterPanel() call.
 * We add the tabPanel and the buttonBar to the main content panel.
 */

GxtCookBk.getAppCenterPanel().add(tabPanel);
GxtCookBk.getAppCenterPanel().add(buttonBar);
```

How it works...

We begin by setting the width and height on the instantiated `TabPanel` with `tabPanel.setWidth(450)` and `tabPanel.setHeight(250)`, respectively. `tabPanel.setTabScroll(true)` turns scrolling on, while `tabPanel.setAnimScroll(true)` augments the scroll with a fancy slide effect. The last line on the section, though not necessary for tab scrolling, enables the handy close context menu, used to either close a particular tab or all others.

The next segment of the code utilizes a loop to create 10 closable tabs (`TabItem` instances), each containing HTML content with the `HtmlContainer` class, and each attached to the instance of `TabPanel` class with `tabPanel.add(aTab)`.

Stopping at this point, we will have a tab strip allowing us to scroll to the left-hand side or the right-hand side, arbitrarily, until we reach the end. How about scrolling to a particular tab from where we are, programmatically, whether to the left-hand side or the right-hand side? That's what the last segment of the code achieves, by scrolling either to the first or last tab in the tab panel using a `ToggleButton` object.

Next, we create a `ButtonBar` instance that will hold a `ToggleButton` object. We instantiate the `ToggleButton` class and add a `SelectionListener` instance that will handle the button events.

Within the `componentSelected()` method of our anonymous listener, we set the ordinal position of the tab we are scrolling to and change the title.

We then perform the scroll by invoking `tabPanel.scrollToTab(target, true)` and `tabPanel.setSelection(target)`.

Programmatically adding/removing a tab

The GXT toolkit makes it really easy to add or remove a tab from a tab panel. Within code, however, there is a little twist to removing tabs, because in real-world use cases you'll want to do this conditionally. That is, you want to check for a precondition, in the absence of which you will reject or decline, or better still, cancel the request to remove (or close) a tab from its containing `TabPanel` object.

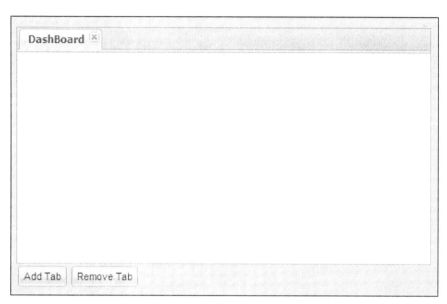

How to do it...

To properly see this in action, we will create two buttons, one that the user can click to add a tab and another to remove the currently selected tab (active tab). However, we will prevent the last tab from being removed; that way, our instance of `TabPanel` class will always have one tab, at least.

The following code programmatically adds/removes a tab from the instance of `TabPanel` class:

```
final TabPanel tabPanel = new TabPanel();
tabPanel.setHeight(250);
tabPanel.setWidth(450);
tabPanel.setCloseContextMenu(true);

TabItem homeTab = new TabItem("DashBoard");
homeTab.setClosable(true);
tabPanel.add(homeTab);
```

```java
ButtonBar btnBar = new ButtonBar();
btnBar.add(new Button("Add Tab", new SelectionListener<ButtonEvent>()
{
  @Override
  public void componentSelected(ButtonEvent evt) {
    TabItem tab = new TabItem("TabItem " + (tabPanel.getItemCount()+1));
    tab.setClosable(true);
    tabPanel.add(tab);
  }
}));
btnBar.add(new Button("Remove Tab", new SelectionListener<ButtonEvent>() {
  @Override
  public void componentSelected(ButtonEvent evt) {
    TabItem tab = tabPanel.getSelectedItem();
    if(tab.isClosable()){
      tabPanel.remove(tab);
    }

  }
}));

tabPanel.addListener(Events.BeforeRemove, new Listener<TabPanelEvent>() {
  @Override
  public void handleEvent(TabPanelEvent evt) {
    if(evt.getItem().getTabPanel().getItemCount() == 1){
      evt.setCancelled(true);
      MessageBox.alert("Error", "But there's only one tab left, Y remove it", null);
    }
  }

});

/*
 * GxtCookbk is the application's entry point class.
 * We access its main content panel using the
 * static GxtCookBk.getAppCenterPanel() call.
 * We add the tabPanel and the buttonBar to the main content panel.
 */
GxtCookBk.getAppCenterPanel().add(tabPanel);
GxtCookBk.getAppCenterPanel().add(btnBar);
```

How it works...

To begin, we instantiate the `TabPanel` class with the default constructor, and then we do some housekeeping on it, setting its height and width, and enabling the close context menu with `tabPanel.setCloseContextMenu(true)` so that we can easily close a particular tab or all others except that particular tab.

Next, we create an instance of `ButtonBar` and add the **Add Tab** button to it, giving it a `SelectionListener` object that will create a new `TabItem` instance and make it closable before adding it to the `TabPanel` instance represented by our final `tabPanel` variable. We also add a second button to the `ButtonBar` instance, which when clicked obtains the currently selected tab (active tab) with `tabPanel.getSelectedItem()` and invokes `tabPanel.remove(tab)` to remove it, after checking to see if it is closable.

So far, we can add as many tabs to the `TabPanel` instance as we want, and remove them one after the other until there's none left, but if we want to conditionally remove tabs, we must do one more thing before we can get it to work. The `TabPanel` class, like every GXT container, fires the `Events.BeforeRemove` event just before a `TabItem` object within it is removed. So, we listen for, and handle this event to implement our functionality. In our simple example, we use the `TabPanelEvent` object passed to our listener to investigate the number of items (tabs) left on the `TabPanel` instance. If there's only one tab left we reject/prevent the remove operation by calling `evt.setCancelled(true)`. It is just logical to display a message to the user explaining why we are declining their action at this point, so we display an alert message with `MessageBox.alert()`.

Although you may not be looking to stop the user from removing the last tab in a tab panel, consider a user trying to close a tab containing a `Grid` object with dirty fields, fields where changes have been made but not yet saved to the server.

Tab notification

Tab panels are designed to render related content, such that only one can be viewed at any given time. Despite all the benefits of this style of display, one is sometimes forced to point out that while viewing a particular tab that you are completely oblivious to whatever goes on in the other tabs. A nice and simple way to keep an eye on a tab while still viewing another is to *configure* the tab you are interested in to blink when something worthy of your attention occurs.

Consider a scenario where we have a tab panel with one of the tabs containing a `Grid` object, where we have edited fields and attempted to save the changes to the server. After initializing the save operation, and while the AJAX request is being handled by the server, we may decide to navigate from this tab to another one (or even leave the PC); if we do, we will have no way of knowing if the save operation fails on the server and the changes on the `Grid` object are persisted. As there's nothing that stops the user from assuming that all went well with the save operation (assuming you want something more than alerts), he/she may not return to the grid's tab, simply close shop, and end up losing a day's work.

Playing Hide and Seek with Tabs

Of course there are always many ways for solving problems in programming. So just another cool way I would recommend in this situation is to make the tab in question blink, like saying "Hey pal, may I have your attention please!"

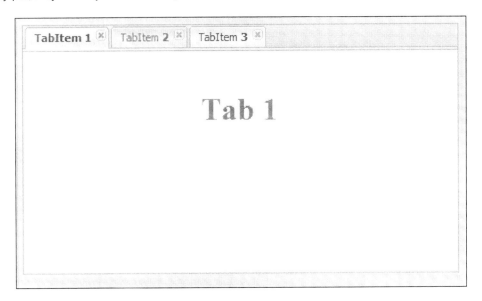

The screenshot captures the tab titled **TabItem3** in one of its blink transition states.

How to do it...

For this to work well without complicating our code, the blink feature is encapsulated in a subclass of the `TabItem` class, which we will consider in detail later. However, the usage is very similar to a normal `TabItem`.

To perform this recipe, use the following code:

```
// BlinkTabItem usage
final TabPanel tabPanel = new TabPanel();
tabPanel.setHeight(250);
tabPanel.setWidth(450);
tabPanel.setCloseContextMenu(true);

TabItem aTab;
for(int i = 1; i <= 3; ++i){
   aTab = new BlinkTabItem("TabItem <b>" + i + "</b>");
   aTab.setClosable(true);
   aTab.add(new HtmlContainer("<h1>Tab " + i + "</h1>"));
   tabPanel.add(aTab);
}
```

```java
GxtCookBk.getAppCenterPanel().add(tabPanel);

Timer wait = new Timer() {
  @Override
  public void run() {
    BlinkTabItem tab = (BlinkTabItem) tabPanel.getItem(2);
    tab.startBlinking();
  }
};
wait.schedule(2000);


// BlinkTabItem definition
public class BlinkTabItem extends TabItem {

  private Timer blinker;

  protected boolean blinking;
  protected int blinkInterval;

  public BlinkTabItem(){
    super();
    initBlink();
  }

  public BlinkTabItem(String text) {
    super(text);
    initBlink();
  }

  @Override
  protected void onRender(Element parent, int index){
    super.onRender(parent, index);
    this.getTabPanel().addListener(
    Events.Select, new Listener<TabPanelEvent>(){
      @Override
      public void handleEvent(TabPanelEvent be) {
        if(isBlinking()){
          stopBlinking();
        }
      }
    });
  }
```

```java
    private void initBlink(){
      blinking = false;
      blinkInterval = 800;
    }

    public boolean isBlinking() {
      return blinking;
    }

    public void stopBlinking() {
      blinker.cancel();
      blinking = false;
    }

    public void startBlinking(){
      startBlinking(blinkInterval);
    }

    public void startBlinking(int interval) {
      TabItem active = this.getTabPanel().getSelectedItem();
      if(isBlinking() || this.equals(active) || !header.isEnabled()){
        return;
      }

      final El headerEl = header.el();
      blinker = new Timer() {
        @Override
        public void run() {
          String style = "x-tab-strip-over";
          if(headerEl.hasStyleName(style)){
            headerEl.setStyleName(style, false);
          }else{
            headerEl.setStyleName(style, true);
          }
        }
      };
      blinker.scheduleRepeating(interval);
      blinking = true;
    }

}
```

How it works...

First, we create an instance of `TabPanel` class, and then we use a loop to create three `BlinkTabItem` tabs, and set them to show some basic HTML content with `HtmlContainer`, before adding them to the `TabPanel` object.

After adding the `tabPanel` instance (to show up on our screen with a call) to `GxtCookBk.getAppCenterPanel().add(tabPanel)`, we use the GWT simplified `Timer` class to schedule the last tab in the tab panel to start blinking after two seconds.

To see how the simple blink is implemented, let's take a look at the `BlinkTabItem` class, which is derived from `TabItem` and begins by declaring a private (internal) `Timer` that switches the visual states of the tab's title/header to implement the blink feature. This is immediately followed by a protected `Boolean` variable (`blinking`), used to check if the tab is currently blinking or not, and finally, a `protected int` variable is used as the default blink interval.

The next section shows the default constructor and another one that accepts a string, thus mirroring the constructors of the superclass. In our constructors, we make a call to `super()` and `super(text)`, appropriately, before initializing the blink variables with a call to `initBlink()`, in which we set `blinking` to `false` and `blinkInterval` to `800` milliseconds.

Besides providing an `isBlinking()` method, which is just a getter for the blinking variable, we define a `startBlinking()` method, which is just a call to the overloaded version of the same method that accepts a blink interval as an `int` parameter. It makes this call by passing the default blink interval that has been set in the `initBlink()` method.

Within the overloaded `startBlinking(int interval)` method, we check to see with the `if` statement, whether the tab is: already blinking, currently being viewed (it would not make sense to blink a tab you are already looking at!), or disabled. If any of these conditions evaluate to `true`, it's not sensible to continue. After passing the test, we obtain the `Element` type of the tab's header element, create a GWT `Timer` object, and override the run method to either add or remove the `x-tab-strip-over` CSS class from the tab's header element. The `x-tab-strip-over` CSS class is used by the GXT TabItem component as a CSS class for a selected tab; we simulate the blinking by adding and removing this style. The blinking will be done every 800 milliseconds (if the default blink interval is used), courtesy of `blinker.scheduleRepeating(interval)`. Lastly, we set `blinking` to `true`, to indicate that the tab is now blinking.

As we are creating a custom component, we need to override GXT's `onRender` method. In the `onRender` method, we listen for the `Events.Select` listener that gets fired by `TabPanel` when a tab is selected to be viewed. It will be annoying to allow a tab to continue blinking even after you've selected it, thus the listener simply investigates with `isBlinking()`, asking "is this tab blinking?", and if true, `stopBlinking()` is invoked, instructing the blink timer to cancel the routine and also setting the `blinking` variable to `false`.

Playing Hide and Seek with Tabs

Searching for, locating, and selecting a particular tab

Some things are implied, hence whenever there is a collection of items, such as tabs in a tab panel, searching is imminent. You may never need to implement a search box (as with Google), where the user is required to enter data with which you'll search for a tab, but it's likely that you will have a UI with a navigation tree on the side and a tab panel in the middle, with the intention of allowing the user to click on leaf nodes on the navigation tree, to open a new tab (or select it if already opened) in the tab panel. For such a navigation system to work, you must first search for the tab associated to the tree node clicked (there has to be some relation by configuration or customization), if found, we select it to make it the active tab, and if not found, we create a new tab and attach it to the tab panel. Problem solved!

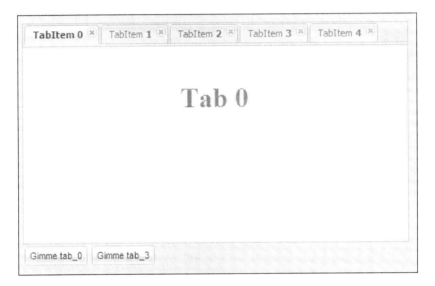

How to do it...

When working with tabs, the code structure seems to always follow a pattern; we create an instance of `TabPanel` class, set some configurations on it, and then we create, configure, and add a `TabItem` object to the instance of `TabPanel` class. To make our example simple to grasp, we would use buttons to get input for the tab to be searched for and selected, instead of a navigation tree.

To perform this recipe, use the following code:

```java
final TabPanel tabPanel = new TabPanel();
tabPanel.setHeight(250);
tabPanel.setWidth(450);
tabPanel.setCloseContextMenu(true);
for(int i = 0; i < 5; ++i){
  TabItem aTab = new TabItem("TabItem <b>" + i + "</b>");
  aTab.setItemId("tab_" + i);
  aTab.setClosable(true);
  aTab.add(new HtmlContainer("<h1>Tab " + i + "</h1>"));
  tabPanel.add(aTab);
}

SelectionListener<ButtonEvent> listener = new
SelectionListener<ButtonEvent>(){
  @Override
  public void componentSelected(ButtonEvent evt) {
    String btnId = evt.getButton().getItemId();
    String tabId = "tab" + btnId.substring(btnId.indexOf("_"), btnId.length());
    TabItem result = tabPanel.findItem(tabId, true);
    if(result != null){
      if(result.equals(tabPanel.getSelectedItem())){
        Info.display("Message", "already selected");
      }else{
        tabPanel.setSelection(result);
      }
    }
  }
};

ButtonBar buttonBar = new ButtonBar();
Button btn1 = new Button("Gimme tab_0", listener);
btn1.setItemId("btn_0");
buttonBar.add(btn1);

Button btn2 = new Button("Gimme tab_3", listener);
btn2.setItemId("btn_3");
```

Playing Hide and Seek with Tabs

How it works...

Our code begins with the classic instantiation of the `TabPanel` class, which is further configured with `setHeight()`, `setWidth()`, and `setCloseContextMenu()`, after which we enter a loop that creates five tabs (`TabItem`), each configured with an item ID (with `setItemId()`) in the format `tab_n`, where *n* is the value of the loop counter at any point in the iteration. As we are looping from zero (0) to five (5), the item ID set on the tab created in the first iteration is `tab_0`, while that of the last will be `tab_4`; this is what we will be using to identify the tab while performing the search. After making the tab closable and setting some HTML content on it using `HtmlContainer`, we add the tab to the tab panel.

The code proceeds to make a `SelectionListener` object to be passed to the buttons that you'd click to locate a tab. The listener is implemented to first get the button that was clicked; this is because there will be a relationship between this button's item ID and that of the tab we intend to locate. The item ID set on the button is in the format `btn_n`, where *n* is an integer.

After getting the button, the next line removes the substring `btn` from a button ID of, say, `btn_0` leaving out `_0`, which is then appended to `tab` and eventually evaluates to something like `tab_0` and is then assigned to the `tabId` string variable; this is our search key or phrase—or whatever you like to call it.

We then use the `tabPanel.findItem(tabId, true)` call to perform the search, passing in the `tabId` variable to search for, and `true` as the second parameter indicating that we want to include the tab's title in the search instead of only its item ID. If we find the tab (`result != null`) and it's the currently selected tab (`result.equals(tabPanel.getSelectedItem())`), we display a message saying **the tab you are looking for is already looking at you**, but if it's not the currently selected tab, we select it.

Having defined our `SelectionListener` object, we create a `ButtonBar` object—to which our buttons will be added—and finally create the buttons passing in the listener previously created. `btn1.setItemId("btn_0")` and `btn2.setItemId("btn_3")` set the item ID on the buttons. Thus, when the buttons are clicked, our system will search for tabs with the corresponding item ID, which will be `tab_0` and `tab_3`. The last two lines attach the `tabPanel` object and `buttonBar` object to the `LayoutContainer` instance.

Showing a tab strip for only two or more tabs

The tab strip is the portion of a tab panel where the tab titles or headers used for navigation are placed. It also plays host to the left-hand side and right-hand side scroll buttons on an instance of `TabPanel` class that is configured to allow scrolling on the tab strip. Sometimes, I find it counterintuitive and visually displeasing to have an instance of `TabPanel` class with only one `TabItem` object in it, yet the header of that single `TabItem` is still displayed.

It would be really cool to have an instance of TabPanel class that can be configured to only show the tab strip and—by proxy—its contained tab headers and scroll buttons, if and only if we have two or more tabs. After all, it's only then that you can navigate from one to the other, right!

How to do it...

Considering that we want clean code (always strive for clean and readable code; coding is poetry...) but without going overboard with details about how to make GXT plugins or extensions, we'll simply extend the TabPanel class into a class called WiseStripTabPanel, to contain our algorithm for a wiser and smarter tab strip.

To perform this recipe, use the following code:

```
// WiseStripTabPanel usage
final TabPanel tabPanel = new WiseStripTabPanel();
tabPanel.setHeight(250);
tabPanel.setWidth(450);
tabPanel.setCloseContextMenu(true);

TabItem homeTab = new TabItem("DashBoard");
homeTab.add(new HtmlContainer("<h1>DashBoard Tab</h1>"));
tabPanel.add(homeTab);
```

Playing Hide and Seek with Tabs

```java
ButtonBar btnBar = new ButtonBar();
btnBar.add(new Button("Add Tab", new SelectionListener<ButtonEvent>()
{
  @Override
  public void componentSelected(ButtonEvent evt) {
    int pos = tabPanel.getItemCount()+1;
    TabItem tab = new TabItem("TabItem " + pos);
    tab.add(new HtmlContainer("<h1>Tab " + pos + "</h1>"));
    tab.setClosable(true);
    tabPanel.add(tab);
  }
}));
btnBar.add(new Button("Remove Tab", new SelectionListener<ButtonEve
nt>() {
  @Override
  public void componentSelected(ButtonEvent evt) {
    TabItem tab = tabPanel.getSelectedItem();
    if(tab.isClosable()){
      tabPanel.remove(tab);
    }

  }
}));

GxtCookBk.getAppCenterPanel().add(tabPanel);
GxtCookBk.getAppCenterPanel().add(btnBar);

// WiseStripTabPanel definition
public class WiseStripTabPanel extends TabPanel {

  public WiseStripTabPanel(){
    super();
  }

  @Override
  protected void onRender(Element parent, int index){
    super.onRender(parent, index);

    hideTabStrip();
    addListener(Events.Add, new Listener<TabPanelEvent>() {
      @Override
      public void handleEvent(TabPanelEvent evt) {
        if(getItemCount() >= 2){
          showTabStrip();
```

```
          }
        }
      });
      addListener(Events.Remove, new Listener<TabPanelEvent>() {
        @Override
        public void handleEvent(TabPanelEvent evt) {
          if(getItemCount() == 1){
            hideTabStrip();
          }
        }
      });
  }

  private void hideTabStrip() {
    TabItem lastMan = getItem(0);
    String cls = ".x-tab-strip-wrap";
    El stripWrap = lastMan.getHeader().el().findParent(cls, 10);
    stripWrap.hide();
  }

  private void showTabStrip() {
    TabItem lastMan = getItem(0);
    String cls = ".x-tab-strip-wrap";
    El stripWrap = lastMan.getHeader().el().findParent(cls, 10);
    stripWrap.show();
  }

}
```

How it works...

Our code usage is very similar to that of a standard `TabPanel` class and it provides two buttons that allow the user to add or remove tabs to see how the tab strip behaves.

First, we instantiate the `WiseStripTabPanel` class (we'll look into this class later) and assign it to a `TabPanel` variable (after all, we'll be using the `TabPanel` interface, nothing more). After setting the height and width, and enabling the close context menu on the `tabPanel` instance, the next section makes a tab, provides HTML content for it, and attaches it to the `tabPanel` instance; this is so that the system starts up with at least one `TabItem` object while waiting for the user to click on the buttons to add more or remove any tabs.

Playing Hide and Seek with Tabs

Next, we make a `ButtonBar` object to hold the buttons, the first of which is created with a `SelectionListener` instance that is implemented to simply add (to the `tabPanel` instance) a closable tab showing HTML content, while the other button, when clicked, will get the currently active tab and request to remove it after checking to see that it is closable in the first place.

The next logical step is to append our `tabPanel` and `buttonBar` instances to the UI, and this is done with `GxtCookBk.getAppCenterPanel().add(tabPanel)` and `GxtCookBk.getAppCenterPanel().add(btnBar)`. You will observe that, apart from the first line (where we instantiate the tab panel), nothing else in this code (so far) suggests that we are using a custom class derived from `TabPanel`, which is why we assigned the instantiated object to a `TabPanel` variable, more like we are coding to the `TabPanel` interface but with a `WiseStripTabPanel` instance.

The `WiseStripTabPanel` class turns out to be quite simple, the most important part being the overridden `onRender` method. In this method, we call `hideTabStrip()` to first hide the tab strip (which we implemented in the `hideTabStrip()` method by getting the first tab on the tab panel), locating the strip wrapper element with its CSS class name, and invoking the `hide()` method on it.

After this initial hide call on the `onRender` method, we listen for `Events.Add`, which gets fired when a container (this custom tab panel) adds a child component (tabs) and handles the event by calling the `showTabStrip()` method, if and only if we now have two or more children (tabs).

The `showTabStrip()` method does the direct opposite of the earlier `hideTabStrip()` method; it simply locates the strip wrapper element with its CSS class name and invokes the `show()` method on it.

Finally, the last part of the `onRender()` method adds a listener to `Events.Remove`, which gets fired when a child component (tab) is removed from its container (this custom tab panel). The listener simply calls our `hideTabStrip()` method to hide the tab strip, if there's only one child component (tab) left on this tab panel container, after the remove operation.

The summary of the operations of the `WiseStripTabPanel` class is that when it is rendered, it first hides the tab strip (if there's just one tab), and then it listens for add operations and shows the tab strip when two or more tabs have been added. Conversely, it listens for remove operations and hides the tab strip, if there's only one tab left.

3
Click-ware: Buttons, Toolbars, and Menus

In this chapter we will cover the following points:

- Creating buttons with text and icons
- Aligning buttons
- Creating on/off toggle buttons
- Organizing actions using the menu and split buttons
- Building a bar of tools
- Crafting multi-column buttons in toolbar
- Binding a single action to several Click-wares

Introduction

The web has rapidly evolved from the early beginnings of static HTML pages with GIF animations to fully-fledged web apps, now powered by HTML5/CSS3 and built with solid tools and APIs such as GWT. The `XMLHttpRequest` object in modern browsers and powerful UI toolkits make it possible for developers to craft web apps that look and behave like rich desktop apps, thereby increasing the enthusiasm, interaction, and engagement of web surfers.

It is a fact that the expectation of web users has significantly increased from mere "window shopping" (look around a website by navigating from page to page with URLs) to an outright demand for better looks, effective user interaction, and instant gratification, courtesy of an increased engagement surface area made possible by many forms of widgets they can interact with (click-and-drag) to get things done while putting an application to use.

Click-ware: Buttons, Toolbars, and Menus

Humans appreciate choice and gravitate towards it, because this concept is plausible for user engagement in web apps; we'll give them better options instead of plain old HTML links and forms that are often drab.

Creating buttons with text and icons

Buttons are often simple widgets that allow the user to execute an action by clicking on it, such as submitting an HTML form with its **Submit** button. However, we can do more with buttons nowadays beyond form submission; we can even give them a complete makeover with the various text, icon, and alignment options available with a `GXT` button.

How to do it...

A `GXT` button is a very simple widget; without all the bells and whistles it is a one-liner.

```
ButtonBar btnBar = new ButtonBar();
Icons ICONS = GWT.create(Icons.class);

// Text button
Button textBtn = new Button("Btn Text");
textBtn.setToolTip("This is a simple text button");
btnBar.add(textBtn);

// Icon button
Button iconBtn = new Button();
iconBtn.setIcon(ICONS.people());
btnBar.add(iconBtn);

// Text and Icon button
Button mixedBtn = new Button("Mixed Btn", ICONS.orgchart());
btnBar.add(mixedBtn);

// Real world button
SelectionListener<ButtonEvent> listener = new SelectionListener<ButtonEvent>() {
  @Override
  public void componentSelected(ButtonEvent evt) {
    Info.display("Message", "Clicked - " + evt.getButton().getText());
  }
};
```

```
Button realBtn = new Button("Home Btn", ICONS.home(), listener);
btnBar.add(realBtn);

GxtCookBk.getAppCenterPanel().add(btnBar);
/*
 * GxtCookbk is the application's entry point class.
 * We access its main content panel using the
 * static GxtCookBk.getAppCenterPanel() call.
 * We add the ButtonBar to the main content panel.
 */
GxtCookBk.getAppCenterPanel().add(btnBar);
```

How it works...

The code begins with the creation of `ButtonBar`, which is a container (its indirect superclass) used to lay out buttons horizontally; we will be placing the buttons in this bar. Next, we instantiate the `Icons` object using the GWT factory system `GWT.create()` and assign it to the variable named as `ICONS` (see *Appendix B, Custom Icons in GXT*, for details on this). We are now ready to create our buttons.

We now create three buttons; the first button `textBtn`, is a simple button containing only text. The next button `iconBtn` has no text and is only assigned an icon. The last button, `mixedBtn` contains both text and an icon. We add each button to `ButtonBar`.

The last button in this recipe is a real button, of course the buttons we've looked at so far are dummies, and they do nothing when clicked.

To make a real button that will do something when clicked, we create a `Listener` object, specifically `SelectionListener` since we are dealing with a GXT button (it can be "selected"), and then pass it to the button either with an appropriate constructor or with the `addSelectionListener()` method. *Appendix A, Event Handling—Making Those GUIs Do Something*, demystifies event handling; you should take a moment to read up on it if you are not yet familiar with the concept.

We can now instantiate the real button giving it a label, an icon, and a listener, using `new Button("Real Btn", ICONS.home(), listener)`. Once created, our button can be added to `ButtonBar` as usual, bringing us to the last line which just adds our `btnBar` to `LayoutContainer` on the screen, more like serving the dish we just prepared!

There's more...

A GXT button can be configured to show up in several scales (sizes) and with several alignments for the label and icon. These and more will be covered as we proceed in this chapter.

Click-ware: Buttons, Toolbars, and Menus

Aligning buttons

Buttons are usually placed next to each other in a horizontal fashion (rarely vertically which often requires a special layout), and by default at the middle (centre) of their section within the container they provide actions for. If we can only present buttons this way in our apps, then they'll look down-right boring no matter what they can do. Thankfully, `GXT` gives us more options for alignment.

How to do it...

I want to show how to snap buttons to the left-hand side or right-hand side in `ContentPanel` and it only takes one line to configure it.

```
/*
 * We create a content panel and size it.
 */
ContentPanel ctPanel = new ContentPanel(new FitLayout());
ctPanel.setSize(450, 200);
ctPanel.setFrame(true);
```

```
/*
 * remove the header from the ContentPanel
 */
ctPanel.setHeaderVisible(false);
/*
 * set the ContentPanel's background and margin using CSS.
 */
ctPanel.setStyleAttribute("marginBottom", "15px");
ctPanel.setStyleAttribute("backgroundColor", "white");

/*
 * Create an inner container for the text.
 */
LayoutContainer inner = new LayoutContainer();
inner.setStyleAttribute("backgroundColor", "white");
inner.addText("<h1>Align to left</h1>");
inner.setBorders(true);
/*
 * add the inner container to the ContentPanel.
 */
ctPanel.add(inner);

/*
 * Add the buttons to the ContentPanel
 * and align them to the left.
 */
ctPanel.addButton(new Button("Ok"));
ctPanel.addButton(new Button("Cancel"));
ctPanel.setButtonAlign(HorizontalAlignment.LEFT);

/*
 * GxtCookbk is the application's entry point class.
 * We access its main content panel using the
 * static GxtCookBk.getAppCenterPanel() call.
 * We add the ContentPanel to the main content panel.
 */
GxtCookBk.getAppCenterPanel().add(ctPanel);
```

Click-ware: Buttons, Toolbars, and Menus

How it works...

We are doing our alignment from within `ContentPanel` which is a specialized panel (container) having top and bottom toolbars, along with separate header, body, and footer sections, so the code begins by creating one which is configured with `FitLayout`. (`FitLayout` is a layout which contains only one widget and expands that widget to fit the entire container.) The section continues with configurations on the created `ContentPanel`; we turn off the `ContentPanel` header and set arbitrary CSS styling on it (padding in this case) with `setStyleAttribute()`.

We next create an inner panel containing some HTML text and add it to `ContentPanel`.

Now the main stuff; we add two buttons to our `ctPanel ContentPanel` and use `setButtonAlignment()` that takes any of the three (`LEFT`, `CENTER`, or `RIGHT`) options of `HorizontalAlignment` to configure the alignment of the buttons. As we want left alignment, we give it `HorizontalAlignment.LEFT`. The `ctPanel ContentPanel` is ready to be served up so we add it to the screen with `GxtCookBk.getAppCenterPanel().add(ctPanel)`.

The second segment of the code does the same thing as the one we just covered except that it uses `HorizontalAlignment.RIGHT` to configure the buttons to align rightwards. As the default setup aligns buttons to the center, we are only showing the other two possibilities and I can say that under the hood `GXT` is simply doing the equivalent of `ctPanel.getButtonBar().setAlignment()` giving it center, left, or right `HorizontalAlignment`.

Creating on/off toggle buttons

Standard buttons do not have the ability to represent and communicate state, apart from the enabled/disabled state of course. Users often want to be able to turn on/off (toggle) a feature (for example, expand/collapse a tree-like structure) with the push of one button, not two separate buttons for the on/off states, but one button that can visually give cues whether the feature is switched on or switched off. I almost named this recipe "Contextual switching" but realized it would make me sound like medical pros who are often good in saving life but so bad in naming thing (consider osteoporosis), so I thought again.

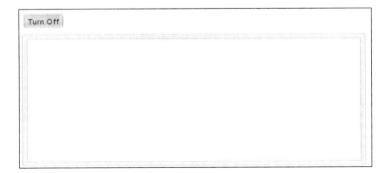

How to do it...

Contextual switching (well you can't nail me now, after all I've explained it) in GXT is done with the aid of `ToggleButton`, a specialized derivative of button that we can use to demonstrate switching over the expand/collapse feature of `ContentPanel`.

```java
/*
 * We create a content panel and size it.
 */
final ContentPanel ctPanel = new ContentPanel(new FitLayout());
ctPanel.setSize(450, 200);
ctPanel.setFrame(true);
ctPanel.setCollapsible(true);
ctPanel.setHeaderVisible(false);
/*
 * set the ContentPanel's margin using CSS.
 */
ctPanel.setStyleAttribute("marginTop", "8px");

final LayoutContainer innerPanel = new LayoutContainer();
innerPanel.setBorders(true);
innerPanel.setStyleAttribute("backgroundColor", "white");

ctPanel.add(innerPanel);
ctPanel.collapse();

/*
 * create a ButtonBar.
 */
ButtonBar buttonBar = new ButtonBar();
/*
 * create the ToggleButton
 */
ToggleButton toggleBtn = new ToggleButton("Turn On", new SelectionList
ener<ButtonEvent>() {
  @Override
  public void componentSelected(ButtonEvent evt) {
    ToggleButton btn = (ToggleButton) evt.getButton();
    String text = "Turn On";
    if(btn.isPressed()){
      text = "Turn Off";
      ctPanel.expand();
    }else{
      innerPanel.addText("<h1>Switching Off ...</h1>");
      innerPanel.layout();
```

Click-ware: Buttons, Toolbars, and Menus

```
          new Timer() {
            @Override
            public void run() {
              innerPanel.removeAll();
                ctPanel.collapse();
            }
          }.schedule(1500);
        }
        btn.setText(text);
      }
  });
  /*
   * add the ToggleButton to the ButtonBar.
   */
  buttonBar.add(toggleBtn);
  /*
   * GxtCookbk is the application's entry point class.
   * We access its main content panel using the
   * static GxtCookBk.getAppCenterPanel() call.
   * We add the ButtonBar and the ContentPanel to the main content
  panel.
   */
  GxtCookBk.getAppCenterPanel().add(buttonBar);
  GxtCookBk.getAppCenterPanel().add(ctPanel);
```

How it works...

Remember, we want to switch between the collapse and expand states of `ContentPanel`, so we have to make one, right. The `FitLayout` given to the `ContentPanel` during construction expands its content to fit the available space. After instantiation, we further configure its dimensions with `setSize()`, give it beautiful round borders with `setFrame(true)`, make it collapsible (else we can't switch anything!) with `setCollapsible(true)`, turn off the header section, and give it additional padding.

After creating `LayoutContainer` (the content region for our `ctPanel`) and configuring it to have a white background, we attach it to `ContentPanel` with `ctPanel.add(cntPanel)` and then we initially collapse `ContentPanel` with `ctPanel.collapse(.)` so that you'll have to use `ToggleButton` to expand it (switch it on). Let's set up `ToggleButton`.

We need `ButtonBar` to hold the button so we make one, and afterwards we create `ToggleButton` with a constructor passing in the initial label and `SelectionListener` to handle click events. You should read *Appendix A* if you are not familiar with events and event handling.

Within the `componentSelected()` method of the listener we first obtain a reference to the clicked button from the passed in `ButtonEvent` object so that we can set the right label (or tooltip) on it to communicate its state depending on if the feature is on or off. The next line initializes the variable used to set the button's label to "Turn On", this variable's value will eventually (after setting it correctly using some flags) communicate the action the user should take with `ToggleButton` afterwards, relative to its current state which is determined by the next line.

`btn.isPressed()` is used to determine the button's state (which can either be pressed or not pressed). The method is defined in the `ToggleButton` class and not in its `Button` superclass, hence it's cast in the first line within the listener.

So when the button's state is pressed, we set the text variable to *Turn Off* and expand `ContentPanel`, else the text variable remains as *Turn On* and all we really have to do is collapse `ContentPanel`, but I am doing more. Ok, I am just showing a message saying "Hey, this dude is switching off" and using a timer from `com.google.gwt.user.client` to delay the collapse call so you'll have time to see the fancy warning before `ContentPanel` gets collapsed.

Since our text variable would have been set correctly with the outplay of the conditional if/else block, we can just set it on the button.

Organizing actions with the menu and split buttons

One of the challenges in UI design, specifically interaction design and how it turns out to impact user experience, is properly managing UI artifacts (widgets) such that they are compact and pleasing on the eye but easy and handy to use. So how do you put together buttons that do related things? If you have similar things to create or related reports to show and you place them (as buttons) all on `ButtonBar`, you'll soon run out of space. Even if you have enough space, there'll be this monotony about their presentation that will make them boring.

This is the sort of thing that the **Menu Button** and **Split Button** are designed for, helping you present an array of related actions with a drop-down (well depending on the alignment) menu when the button is clicked.

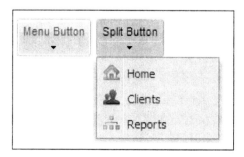

Click-ware: Buttons, Toolbars, and Menus

How to do it...

The menu button is actually just a button, and the same can be said of the split button except that it has custom handling and styling.

```java
// Give us icons
Icons ICONS = GWT.create(Icons.class);

// Listen for clicks on the menu items
SelectionListener<MenuEvent> menuListener = new
SelectionListener<MenuEvent>() {
  @Override
  public void componentSelected(MenuEvent evt) {
    MenuItem item = (MenuItem) evt.getItem();
    Info.display("Message", "You clicked - " + item.getText());
  }
};

// Setup the menu
Menu btnMenu1 = new Menu();
Menu btnMenu2 = new Menu();

btnMenu1.add(new MenuItem("Home", ICONS.home(), menuListener));
btnMenu2.add(new MenuItem("Home", ICONS.home(), menuListener));

btnMenu1.add(new MenuItem("Clients", ICONS.people(), menuListener));
btnMenu2.add(new MenuItem("Clients", ICONS.people(), menuListener));

btnMenu1.add(new MenuItem("Reports", ICONS.orgchart(), menuListener));
btnMenu2.add(new MenuItem("Reports", ICONS.orgchart(), menuListener));

// Setup the buttons
ButtonBar btnBar = new ButtonBar();
Button menuBtn = new Button("Menu Button");
menuBtn.setMenu(btnMenu1);
menuBtn.setArrowAlign(ButtonArrowAlign.BOTTOM);
btnBar.add(menuBtn);

Button splitBtn = new SplitButton("Split Button", new SelectionListener<ButtonEvent>() {
  @Override
  public void componentSelected(ButtonEvent evt) {
    Info.display("Message", "This is the default action, click on the arrow to reveal others");
  }
```

```
});
splitBtn.setMenu(btnMenu2);
splitBtn.setArrowAlign(ButtonArrowAlign.BOTTOM);
btnBar.add(splitBtn);

/*
 * GxtCookbk is the application's entry point class.
 * We access its main content panel using the
 * static GxtCookBk.getAppCenterPanel() call.
 * We add the ButtonBar to the main content panel.
 */
GxtCookBk.getAppCenterPanel().add(btnBar);
```

How it works...

We'll be using some icons so we use the static GWT factory instantiation mechanism to create an object from our `Icons` interface. Next, we create `SelectionListener` to handle clicks on the actions we want to present in the menus from the buttons (see *Appendix A* for details on event handling). The listener simply obtains the item clicked, casts it to `MenuItem` (a clickable item in a menu) because the call to `evt.getItem()` actually returns a component, and then displays a message with the label on `MenuItem`.

The following code segment, designated by the comment *setup menu* creates two menus using the default constructor `new Menu()`, one for the menu button and the other for the split button. We then add items to each menu with `new MenuItem()` passing in a label, an icon, and the listener just created.

We now build the buttons by first creating a `ButtonBar` to hold them. The menu button is instantiated with the normal `Button` constructor and assigned to a `Button` variable, so it is absolutely just a `Button` we've designated `menuBtn`. The magic that makes it a menu button is the next line, `menuBtn.setMenu(btnMenu)`, and to make it look radically different from the buttons in earlier recipes I applied a bottom alignment to the arrows that will show up on the button.

After adding `menuBtn` to the `ButtonBar`, we create the split button with the `SplitButton` constructor, passing in a label and a listener that just displays a message; more on this particular listener shortly. Notice that the `SplitButton` object is also assigned to a `Button` variable named as `splitBtn`, much the same way as `menuBtn` was done. This is just to demonstrate that the `setMenu()` method is actually defined in the `Button` class, so we also use it on the next line to assign `btnMenu2` to `splitBtn`. The arrow alignment is set to `HorizontalAlignment.BOTTOM` to create some sort of sameness between the two buttons. All is now set, and we can add `splitBtn` to `btnBar` and then add `btnBar` to the screen.

Click-ware: Buttons, Toolbars, and Menus

Just to recap, to create a menu button just set up a menu with the actions to present as `MenuItem` and assign the menu to a standard `Button` (or its subclass of course) reference with `setMenu()`, while for a split button you'll have to create a `SplitButton` object and since it is derived from `Button` you can also call `setMenu()` on it to provide its collection of actions as a menu too. There is, however, a subtle difference between these two button setups, not only does the SplitButton differ visually (the arrow is always separated with an etched line), its menu only shows up if you click on its arrow, that's why I passed an anonymous `SelectionListener` to the `SplitButton` constructor to show that a separate action can be tied to normal button clicks on it, which is different from clicking the arrow.

Clicking the menu button reveals its menu so the arrow is actually just a visual cue saying "there are more options here", if we had passed a listener to the `Button` constructor used to instantiate the `menuBtn` object then it will be executed at the same time its menu pops up, certainly not what you want.

Building a bar of tools

Ok it's actually a toolbar of tools or better still components, not like a chocolate bar or candy bar of tools which would not be so tasty after all. So how do you build a toolbar of components (mainly buttons anyway), with sections delimited by separators and the likes, common with real toolbars. Well, `ToolBar` is basically a container to place components in some sort of order and layout, so that there's one place the user can access actions to be performed on the content being viewed.

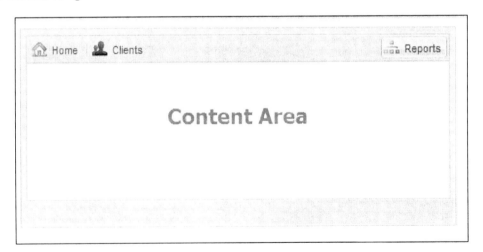

How to do it...

Create a `ToolBar` widget, create some buttons, and add the buttons to the toolbar. The toolbar component can then be added to a `ContentPanel`.

```
ToolBar tBar = new ToolBar();
Icons ICONS = GWT.create(Icons.class);

// Add the buttons
Button homeBtn = new Button("Home", ICONS.home());
tBar.add(homeBtn);

tBar.add(new SeparatorToolItem());
Button clientsBtn = new Button("Clients", ICONS.people());
tBar.add(clientsBtn);

tBar.add(new FillToolItem());
Button reportsBtn = new Button("Reports", ICONS.orgchart());
tBar.add(reportsBtn);

// Build the container
ContentPanel ctPanel = new ContentPanel();
ctPanel.setSize(450, 200);
ctPanel.setFrame(true);
ctPanel.setHeaderVisible(false);

LayoutContainer inner = new LayoutContainer();
inner.setStyleAttribute("backgroundColor", "white");
inner.addText("<h1>Content Area</h1>");
inner.setBorders(true);
ctPanel.add(inner);
ctPanel.setTopComponent(tBar);

/*
 * GxtCookbk is the application's entry point class.
 * We access its main content panel using the
 * static GxtCookBk.getAppCenterPanel() call.
 * We add the ContentPanel to the main content panel.
 */
GxtCookBk.getAppCenterPanel().add(ctPanel);
```

Click-ware: Buttons, Toolbars, and Menus

How it works...

We begin by creating `ToolBar` using `new ToolBar()` and then we also create an `Icons` object with `GWT.create()` (see *Appendix B* for details on Icons).

`homeBtn` is created with a `"Home"` label and `ICONS.home()` as its icon before adding it to `ToolBar` with `tBar.add(homeBtn)`, it's therefore a Button instantiated (further configured if you like) and then added to `ToolBar` as many recipes in this chapter have done with ButtonBar (which interestingly extends `ToolBar`!). The remainder of that section creates two additional buttons and adds them to the bar, but you'll notice that we also added a special separator component (a vertical etched line used to delimit sections) with `new SeparatorToolItem()` and later on we added another special component; this time `FillToolItem` is used to fill up space so that what gets added after it will show up at the end of `ToolBar`.

To put `tBar` to use, we'll have to attach it to `ContentPanel` (or a derived class) because they have been wired to use toolbars, in fact you can attach two toolbars to `ContentPanel` using its `setTopComponent()` and `setBottomComponent()` methods. After creating and configuring `ctPanel`, we add a styled `LayoutContainer` to it and then finally we do the most important task with `ctPanel.setTopComponent(tBar)` which says `ctPanel` toolbar is `tBar` and should be placed on the top.

There's more...

A `GXT` `ToolBar` overflows its items into a pull-out menu when its container (`ContentPanel` derivatives) is resized such that `ToolBar` no longer has enough space to render all the items at once, this feature is enabled by default and is controlled with its `setEnableOverflow()` method. Secondly, `ToolBar` is a first class container so you can add any component to it, not just buttons; a `TextField` for search is a very good example. This is, however, not a license to place `GridPanel` in it, if you do I'll deny ever knowing you!

Chapter 3

Crafting multi-column buttons in ToolBar

I am a not a huge fan of Microsoft but I love the new tab and toolbar styles in the recent incarnate of their popular office suite. It's such a delight that these beautiful UI structures have found their way into the web, courtesy of the innovation of APIs such as GXT. Now you can have a toolbar that departs from the norm of being a plain horizontal strip of humdrum buttons that's maybe spiced up a little with 16 X 16 icons, to one that can have a group labeled, say *File*, with all the (or most plausible) *File* buttons placed within it, and have some of those buttons rendered in a fashion that accentuates their importance (or usefulness) over others in the same group.

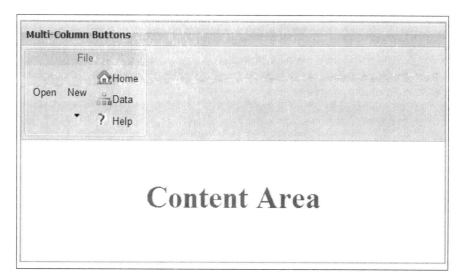

How to do it...

Apart from using `ButtonGroup` and its accompanying classes during configuration, a multi-column `ToolBar` is used much the same way as you may have probably seen before.

```
ToolBar tBar = new ToolBar();
/*
 * create a ButtonGroup with 3 rows.
 */
ButtonGroup group = new ButtonGroup(3);
group.setHeading("File");

/*
 * add the ButtonGroup to the ToolBar
 */
tBar.add(group);
```

```java
/*
 * make a layout that will span 3 rows.
 * This will be used to make the Open and New
 * Buttons span 3 rows.
 */
TableData data = new TableData();
data.setRowspan(3);

/*
 * create the Open button
 * and add it to the group
 */
Button openBtn = new Button("Open");
openBtn.setScale(ButtonScale.LARGE);
openBtn.setIconAlign(IconAlign.TOP);
openBtn.addStyleName("x-btn-as-arrow");
group.add(openBtn, data);


/*
 * create the New button
 * and add it to the group
 */
Button createBtn = new Button("New");
createBtn.setScale(ButtonScale.LARGE);
createBtn.setIconAlign(IconAlign.TOP);
createBtn.setArrowAlign(ButtonArrowAlign.BOTTOM);

/*
* create the menu and assign it to the New button.
*/
Menu subMenu = new Menu();
subMenu.add(new MenuItem("Gwt Module"));
subMenu.add(new MenuItem("Gwt Project"));
subMenu.add(new MenuItem("Gwt RPC Service"));
createBtn.setMenu(subMenu);
group.add(createBtn, data);

/*
 * add the icons.
 */
Icons ICONS = GWT.create(Icons.class);
group.add(new Button("Home", ICONS.home()));
group.add(new Button("Data", ICONS.orgchart()));
group.add(new Button("Help", ICONS.help()));
```

```
/*
 * Build the container
 */
ContentPanel ctPanel = new ContentPanel();
ctPanel.setSize(450, 250);
ctPanel.setBorders(true);
ctPanel.setHeading("Multi-Column Buttons");

/*
 * create an inner panel with some text.
 */
LayoutContainer inner = new LayoutContainer();
inner.setStyleAttribute("backgroundColor", "white");
inner.addText("<h1>Content Area</h1>");
ctPanel.add(inner);
ctPanel.setTopComponent(tBar);

/*
 * GxtCookbk is the application's entry point class.
 * We access its main content panel using the
 * static GxtCookBk.getAppCenterPanel() call.
 * We add the ContentPanel to the main content panel.
 */
GxtCookBk.getAppCenterPanel().add(ctPanel);
```

How it works...

After instantiating `ToolBar` with its default (and only) constructor we create `ButtonGroup`, which is a special `ContentPanel` for showing groups of components within a `ToolBar`. Our `ButtonGroup` is instantiated with three rows, given a heading of `"File"`, and added to `ToolBar` with the usual `tBar.add(group)`.

Next, we create a `TableData` object, usually used to specify data for `TableLayout` (the same layout used within `ButtonGroup`; more on layouts in the following chapters) and we configure the `TableData` object to span three rows using `data.setRowspan(3)` and then proceed to begin a new section of code that set up buttons for `ToolBar`.

The first button, `openBtn`, is instantiated with a label and an icon from a special icon system I've built (see *Appendix B*); its size (or scale) is set to be large by calling `setScale` with `ButtonScale.LARGE`, its icon will show up at the top as a result of `setIconAlign(IconAlign.TOP)`, and the `"x-btn-as-arrow"` CSS class (a GXT CSS class used for the `Button` component) added to this button with the `addStyleName()` method ensures that the button renders well (its label's positioning) since it's going to be standing beside another button exposing a menu with an arrow. The last line in this section adds the button to the group (not `ToolBar`) with `group.add(openBtn, data)`.

Click-ware: Buttons, Toolbars, and Menus

The next button, `createBtn`, is set up as the previous one, but in addition we configured its menu arrow to point downwards with `ButtonArrowAlign.BOTTOM` passed to a call to `setArrowAlign()`, and we added a Menu to it using `createBtn.setMenu(submenu)` so that when the button gets clicked the menu shows up.

The remaining three buttons are created as default buttons (just label and icons, no special bells) and added to `ButtonGroup` like the previous heavily configured ones.

Lastly, the code created a `ContentPanel`, to which `ToolBar` is added with `ctPanel.setTopComponent(tBar)`, and then the recipe is served to the screen using `GxtCookBk.getAppCenterPanel().add(ctPanel)`.

Binding a single action to several click-wares

The many great web UI toolkits that we use and have come to love seem to miss out one very important implementation detail that their desktop counterparts do so well, and that is the ability to bind an action (what a user can do; for example, edit profile) to multiple UI widgets so that the action is propagated across all bound widgets, while separating the action logic from the view logic.

Consider a scenario where you want to have an interface containing a top level menu, a `ToolBar`, and a context menu, all having a "help" tool (`Button` in `ToolBar` and `MenuItem` in `Menu`); you'll have to create three different widgets bound to three separate listeners just to implement this single tool.

What happens when the number goes up to 10? It means 10 widgets but 30 listeners, right? Even if the listeners are just a facade to the actual code that handles the click events, it will still be difficult to write and a nightmare to maintain.

Well, maybe we can further collapse the listeners (too many listeners, without the use of an event bus, produce unreadable spaghetti code and can affect UI performance.) after all they are mostly `SelectionListener` objects. So one generic listener for `ButtonEvent` from the `Button` tools and another generic listener for `MenuEvent` from the `MenuItem` tools, brings our problem space to 10 widgets and two generic (but with a lot of casting and convoluted if/else statements) listeners.

 An event bus in GWT dispatches events to interested components. It supports decoupling by allowing components to interact without have direct references to each other.

This may work but will not scale, is not robust, and is certainly not extendable. More importantly, you have no way (or will have to hack one soon) to propagate states across all the widgets used for a feature. So if you need to disable/enable the "help" feature, you'll need to locate the widget references (10 features mean 30 widgets and their listeners which means many references, your memory will be out soon!) and invoke the disable/enable method on them one after the other.

It's just a matter of time before you (not just your code) break down in despair from such chaotic hacks!

An action represents and encapsulates the configuration, state, and logic that can be shared and bound to several actionable widgets, such that the label, icon, and listener set on the action are served to the widgets (in many ways the action is a proxy, or a mediator, or better still an adapter for the widgets). When we disable the action all bound widgets, no matter how many or where they are on the screen (even those not yet rendered), get disabled automatically.

Given a system such as this, we can begin to conceive more powerful use cases, such as the ability to perform a sort of dependent action from a different UI context.

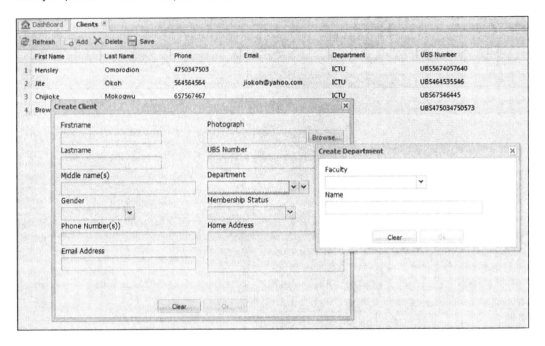

Imagine that you provide consulting to clients (individuals managing projects) from a yet to be known set of aid organizations; on the clients view you'll click on a *create client* button to add a new record, only to discover that the specified aid organization is not in the selected list. Now, you'll have to exit your current view and probably return later after adding the new aid organization from the Organizations view, how sad. On the *create client* form, we can simply put an *add organization* button and bind it to the action that a typical *create organization* button on the Organizations view would be bound to, such that when the button on the *create client* form is clicked we are able to execute the *create organization* routine even if the Organizations view is not open!

I think I've built enough argument for an action framework; stick around, let's build one.

How to do it...

We certainly need a couple of custom interfaces and we also need to extend existing widgets to allow them to leverage our actions framework. We need `ActionListener`, `ActionAware`, `Action`, `ActionButton`, and `ActionMenu`.

// ActionListener

```java
public interface ActionListener {
  public void runAction();

  public void actionPerformed();
}
```

// ActionAware

```java
public interface ActionAware extends ActionListener {
  public void setName(String name);

  public String getName();

  public void setTitle(String title);

  public String getTitle();

  public void setIcon(AbstractImagePrototype icon);

  public AbstractImagePrototype getIcon();

  public void setTip(ToolTipConfig tipCfg);

  public ToolTipConfig getTip();

  public void setEnabled(boolean b);

  public boolean isEnabled();

  public void addChangeListener(ChangeListener... listener);

  public void removeChangeListener(ChangeListener... listener);
}
```

// **Action**

```java
public abstract class Action extends BaseModel
implements ActionAware {

    protected String name;
    protected String title;
    protected ToolTipConfig tipCfg;
    protected boolean enabled = true;
    protected AbstractImagePrototype icon;

    public Action() {}

    public Action(String title) {
        setTitle(title);
    }

    public Action(String title, AbstractImagePrototype icon){
        this(title);
        setIcon(icon);
    }

    public Action(String title, AbstractImagePrototype icon,
      ToolTipConfig tip){
        this(title, icon);
        setTip(tip);
    }

    @Override
    public boolean isEnabled() {
        return enabled;
    }

    @Override
    public void setEnabled(boolean newValue) {
        boolean oldValue = this.enabled;

        if (oldValue != newValue) {
            this.enabled = newValue;
            notifyPropertyChanged("enabled", newValue,
              oldValue);
        }
    }
```

```java
    @Override
    public AbstractImagePrototype getIcon() {
        return icon;
    }

    @Override
    public ToolTipConfig getTip() {
        return tipCfg;
    }


    @Override
    public final void setIcon(AbstractImagePrototype icon) {
        this.icon = icon;
    }

    @Override
    public final void setTip(ToolTipConfig tipCfg) {
        this.tipCfg = tipCfg;
    }

    @Override
    public String getTitle() {
        return title;
    }

    @Override
    public final void setTitle(String title) {
        this.title = title;
    }

    @Override
    public void setName(String name) {
        this.name = name;
    }

    @Override
    public String getName() {
        return name;
    }

    @Override
    public void runAction() {
        this.actionPerformed();
    }

}
```

// **ActionButton**

```java
public class ActionButton extends Button {

  public ActionButton(final Action action) {
    super(action.getTitle(), action.getIcon());

    setToolTip(action.getTip());
    setEnabled(action.isEnabled());

    addSelectionListener(
new SelectionListener<ButtonEvent>() {
      @Override
      public void componentSelected(ButtonEvent evt) {
        action.actionPerformed();
      }
    });

    // make sure changes in the "enabled" state of
    // the action are propagated to the Button
    action.addChangeListener(new ChangeListener() {
      @Override
      public void modelChanged(ChangeEvent event)
        PropertyChangeEvent evt =
(PropertyChangeEvent) event;
        if (evt.getName().equals("enabled")) {
          boolean enabled = (Boolean) evt.getNewValue();
          setEnabled(enabled);
        }
      }
    });

  }
}
```

// **ActionMenu**

```java
public class ActionMenu extends Menu {

  public boolean add(final Action action) {

    final MenuItem item = new MenuItem(action.getTitle(), action.getIcon());

    item.setToolTip(action.getTip());
    item.setEnabled(action.isEnabled());
```

```
      item.addSelectionListener(new SelectionListener<MenuEvent>() {
        @Override
        public void componentSelected(MenuEvent evt) {
          action.actionPerformed();
        }
      });

      // make sure changes in the "enabled" state of
      // the action are propagated to the MenuItem
      action.addChangeListener(new ChangeListener() {
        @Override
        public void modelChanged(ChangeEvent event) {
          PropertyChangeEvent evt = (PropertyChangeEvent) event;
          if (evt.getName().equals("enabled")) {
            boolean enabled = (Boolean) evt.getNewValue();
            item.setEnabled(enabled);
          }
        }
      });

      return add(item);

}

// Client code
ToolBar tBar = new ToolBar();
ActionMenu ctxMenu = new ActionMenu();
Icons ICONS = GWT.create(Icons.class);

// Setup the 'actions'
Action homeActn = new Action("Home", ICONS.home()) {
  @Override
  public void actionPerformed() {
    Info.display("Message", "The 'Home' Action");
  }
};

Action clientsActn = new Action("Clients", ICONS.people()) {
  @Override
  public void actionPerformed() {
    Info.display("Message", "The 'Clients' Action");
  }
};
```

```java
Action reportsActn = new Action("Reports", ICONS.orgchart()) {
  @Override
  public void actionPerformed() {
    Info.display("Message", "The 'Reports' Action");
  }
};

// Bind widgets
Button homeBtn = new ActionButton(homeActn);
tBar.add(homeBtn);
ctxMenu.add(homeActn);

tBar.add(new SeparatorToolItem());
Button clientsBtn = new ActionButton(clientsActn);
tBar.add(clientsBtn);
ctxMenu.add(clientsActn);

tBar.add(new FillToolItem());
Button reportsBtn = new ActionButton(reportsActn);
tBar.add(reportsBtn);
ctxMenu.add(reportsActn);

// Build the container
ContentPanel ctPanel = new ContentPanel();
ctPanel.setSize(450, 200);
ctPanel.setFrame(true);
ctPanel.setHeaderVisible(false);

LayoutContainer inner = new LayoutContainer();
inner.setStyleAttribute("backgroundColor", "white");
inner.addText("<h1>Content Area</h1>");
inner.setBorders(true);
ctPanel.add(inner);

ctPanel.setTopComponent(tBar);
inner.setContextMenu(ctxMenu);

// some tests!
clientsBtn.setText("");
reportsActn.setEnabled(false);
```

```
/*
 * GxtCookbk is the application's entry point class.
 * We access its main content panel using the
 * static GxtCookBk.getAppCenterPanel() call.
 * We add the ContentPanel to the main content panel.
 */
GxtCookBk.getAppCenterPanel().add(ctPanel);
```

How it works...

Wow, that was some code. Maybe a class diagram will help in understanding it.

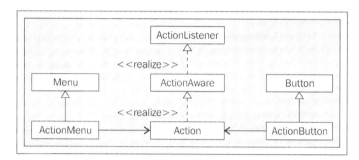

Our code, which is segmented with comments, begins with the definition of an **ActionListener** interface declaring two methods. actionPerformed() will be invoked by the standard event delegation system when the bound widgets are clicked while runAction() is intended to be used to remotely invoke the implementing **Action**.

The **ActionAware** interface extends **ActionListener** and gives meat to the system by defining the methods that widgets can tie into proxy stuff such as label, icon, and tooltip. Apart from support for the enabled state, it also defines the add/remove ChangeListener method pair which is implemented to propagate changes from the **Action** to their bound widgets.

Next we define the abstract **Action** class, extending BaseModel and implementing **ActionAware** interface. This is the class that really drives the system for which extensibility is achieved with the earlier two interfaces. **Action** starts by defining some variables to hold state and several constructors to initialize them. The second constructor, for example, initializes the **Action** with a label, and an icon, same to be used by a bound widget, while the rest of the code is laid out with regular getters and setters.

Of particular note is the setEnabled() method which utilizes our property change support (courtesy **ActionAware**) to propagate the enabled state, and the overridden runAction() method (courtesy **ActionListener**) that just forwards the call to actionPerformed() which must be implemented by users of this abstract **Action** class. In other words, actionPerformed() is what you'll override to provide code to execute by all bound widgets, while runAction() is a remote control to your actionable code, got it!

Ok, we've got to create extensions for the **Button** and **Menu** item so they can use our new mechanism. **ActionButton** extends the standard GXT **Button** class and accepts an action through its constructor. In its `SelectionListener`, **ActionButton** invokes the `actionPerformed()` method on the **Action**. Lastly, **ActionButton** adds `ChangeListener` to the action so that the button is notified whenever the action's state changes, hence it can update itself too.

ActionMenu does pretty much the same thing; it extends the standard GXT **Menu** class, it overloads the `add()` method to accept an **Action** class and in this method adds a `MenuItem` that is configured with the label, icon, and tooltip of the action. Then, it adds `SelectionListener` to the `MenuItem` that calls the action's `actionPerformed()` method. **ActionMenu** rounds up by listening for property changes (enabled) on the action so it can reflect it.

The last portion of the code (designated "client code") puts the system to use; we create a `ToolBar`, and a `ActionMenu`, and initialize `Icons` with `GWT.create()`. With these we build several actions implementing their `actionPerformed()` method to simply display a message stating what action was invoked.

The `Bind widgets` section builds a `Button` with an `Action`, attaches it to `ToolBar` and also attaches the same action to `ActionMenu`. After creating and decorating `ContentPanel (ctPanel)` and adding the `LayoutContainer (inner)` content region inside it, we attach the toolbar and context menu to them respectively with `ctPanel.setTopcomponent(tBar)` and `inner.setContextMenu(ctxMenu)`.

Just to see how we are doing, let's run some tests. `clientBtn.setText("")` turns off the label on the second button added to the toolbar just to prove that we can further customize our widgets without affecting the bound action, while `reportsActn.setEnabled(false)` disables that action which should equally disable the `Button` and `MenuItem` bound to it.

There's more...

This is a simple implementation; we ought to have an `ActionEvent` object (probably derived from `ComponentEvent`) that will be passed during the processing of the action especially when we need to know which widget out of the bound lot is initiating this action. We equally need it to pass/persist state with custom parameters especially since we may be executing the action outside its natural context.

We need `ActionManager`, a central place to manage and profile all actions. A simple use case is to disable certain actions on a current or remote view during an RPC request; we don't want a user clicking *edit*, *delete*, or *save* during a save operation.

The remote action execution is very cool and when collapsed into one line its call can be something similar to `LoanView.get().actionsManager().perform(ACTN_ADD_LOAN)` and this requires some real plumbing. More on these in later chapters.

4
Crafting UI Real Estate

In this chapter we will cover the following topics:

- Organizing navigation with AccordionLayout
- Snapping components even when resized
- UI cardinality with BorderLayout
- Building a basic wizard with CardLayout
- RowLayout vertical and horizontal aligning
- Building grids with ColumnLayout
- Building DashBoards

Introduction

Layouts are a fundamental part of the GXT library. They provide the ability to create flexible and beautiful application UIs easily. However, with this power comes a level of complexity. A solid understanding of layouts is the key to using the library effectively.

With GWT Panels, the panel itself is responsible for creating the panel's markup and inserting its children at the appropriate location, and creating appropriate markup as changes are made. Unlike GWT Panels, `LayoutContainer` (a concrete GXT container with support for layouts) does not physically connect its child components to the container's **DOM**. The **Document Object Model** is used to represent an HTML document in a tree-like structure in the browser's memory. We can dynamically change the content of the HTML page by manipulating the DOM. Rather, it is the job of the layout to both build the internal structure of the container, and to connect its child widgets.

Crafting UI Real Estate

In order for a GXT container's HTML to be rendered, the container's `layout()` method must execute. This is different from GWT panels, in which the HTML is rendered when the components are attached to the panel. There are several ways in which the layout can execute. For now, let's go with the simplest case in which the layout executes when the container is attached. **Attached** is a GWT term that indicates that the widget is part of the browser's DOM. Attaching and detaching could be a subject on its own, so let's just assume it means *when the widget is added to and removed from the page*.

When we add a container to `RootPanel` (for example, `RootPanel.get().add(container)`), the container will be attached, and the container's layout will execute, generating the needed HTML markup. If we add another component to the now rendered container, (`container.add(new Label("New Item"))`) we will have to manually execute/refresh the container (`container.layout()`) for the additions (as well as removals) to be effected. This sort of Lazy-Rendering is the default behavior of GXT as of 2.2.3 with GXT 3 planning to use the same approach as GWT itself.

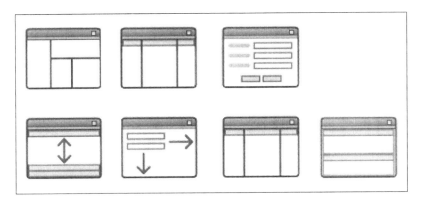

Many GXT layouts can be used in conjunction with `LayoutData`, which are configuration objects assigned to each child widget within a container, and provides the layout object with additional information to be used when executing the layout.

Aside from a layout being executed when the container is attached, or when `layout()` is called manually on the container, there are two other ways in which a layout will be executed. After a container executes its layout, it looks and sees if any of its children are containers. When it finds a child container, it then executes its layout. So as long as there is a chain of containers, the execution of layouts will cascade to the child containers. This is a very important concept as you can lay out a top-level container, and the child containers will have a chance to adjust their layouts as well.

A container's layout will also execute when its size is adjusted. This is default behavior, and can be disabled. This is another important concept as it means that if a container's size is changed, the layout has a chance to update based on the container's new size.

Organizing navigation with AccordionLayout

Aptly named after the musical instrument, `AccordionLayout` is GXT's implementation of the popular accordion structures found in many UI toolkits. It is a `FitLayout` (child is expanded or sized to fit the dimension of its container) that is implemented to render child components (must be `ContentPanel`) as mutually exclusively collapsible sections whose headings are always visible.

You can expand and collapse a section with either the collapse tool (default) or by clicking on its heading if the collapse tool has been disabled.

An important point to note with `AccordionLayout` is that it only takes `ContentPanel` items and only one (defaults to the first) is viewable (expanded) at a given time.

How to do it...

All we really need to do is set `AccordionLayout` as the layout for a container and then add `ContentPanel` child items to the container, with each `ContentPanel` having an appropriate heading.

```java
    public HtmlContainer makeLinks(String[] links){
      StringBuilder sb = new StringBuilder("<ul class='accordion-list'>");
      for (String link : links) {
        sb.append("<li>").append(link).append("</li>");
      }
```

```java
        sb.append("</ul>");
        HtmlContainer html = new HtmlContainer(sb.toString());
        return html;
    }

    // create the accordion
    ContentPanel accordionCt = new ContentPanel();
    accordionCt.setSize(180, 200);
    accordionCt.setHeading("Navigation");
    accordionCt.setBodyBorder(false);
    accordionCt.setLayout(new AccordionLayout());

    // add the products panel
    ContentPanel panel = new ContentPanel();
    panel.setHeading("Products");
    accordionCt.add(panel);

    // put links into "products"
    String[] links = new String[]{"view", "create", "search"};
    panel.add(makeLinks(links));

    // add the sales panel
    panel = new ContentPanel();
    panel.setHeading("Sales");
    accordionCt.add(panel);

    // put links into "sales"
    links = new String[]{"orders", "returns", "invoices"};
    panel.add(makeLinks(links));

    // add the reports panel
    panel = new ContentPanel();
    panel.setHeading("Reports");
    accordionCt.add(panel);

    // put links into "reports"
    links = new String[]{"summary", "stock", "Ad-hoc"};
    panel.add(makeLinks(links));

    // add the issues panel
    panel = new ContentPanel();
    // setAnimCollapse(false);
    panel.setHeading("Issues");
    panel.setBodyStyle("padding:10px;");
    panel.addText("<p>we don't have any <i>issues</i> right ...<p>");
    accordionCt.add(panel);

    GxtCookBk.getAppCenterPanel().add(accordionCt);
```

How it works...

First we define a `makeLinks()` convenience method that takes in an array of string literals which it formats as an unordered HTML list using `StringBuilder`, and then returned as the contents on `HtmlContainer`. This is what we finally present within the `ContentPanel` objects rendered with `AccordionLayout`.

With that out of the way, we initialize `accordionCt` as `ContentPanel` configured to occupy a dimension of 180 by 200 (`setSize()`), given a title of `"Navigation"` with `setHeading()`, and with inner borders turned off with `setBodyBorder(false)`; and lastly we set its layout to new `AccordionLayout()` using `accordionCt.setLayout()`. Next we create a `products ContentPanel` and employ our earlier defined `makeLinks()` method to generate `HtmlContainer` of an unordered list which we then add to the panel with `panel.add(makeLinks(links))`. We also do the same for a `sales` and `reports ContentPanel` all of which gets added to our `AccordionLayout` panel with `accordionCt.add(panel)`.

The `issues` panel is slightly different from the others because rather than adding a list of strings (links) we set a message on it (it's a panel, you can do anything with it!) rightly saying that there are no issues with this recipe.

There's more...

By default the `ContentPanel` items rendered with `AccordionLayout` can be toggled (expanded/collapsed) with the tool button on the far right of its heading or by just clicking anywhere on the title/heading bar. If the tool button is hidden with `accordionLayout.setHideCollapseTool(true)` then `accordionLayout.setTitleCollapse()` must not be given `false` (default is `true`) else you can't go from one panel to the other within the `AccordionLayout` container.

An alternative to using `AccordionLayout` is to expand and collapse a panel as a component is clicked. Note that we used this approach in *Chapter 3, Click-ware: Buttons, Toolbars, and Menus*, in the *Creating on/off toggle buttons* recipe.

Snapping components even when resized

Having your UI components maintain their sanity when the browser window or their container is resized without any effort from the coder is bliss. GXT provides `AnchorLayout` which enables contained components to anchor relatively to a container's dimensions, maintaining the anchor rules even when the container is resized.

Crafting UI Real Estate

The components rendered with `AnchorLayout` are sized with an anchor-spec which is a string of two values used for horizontal and vertical anchoring respectively. The values which can be expressed as percentages or offsets or even both, determine how a component is anchored to its container. A value of *100% 50%* would render a component the complete width of its container and half its height, if only one value is provided in the anchor-spec it is assumed to be the width while the height will default to auto.

Similarly, an anchor-spec of *-30 -120* would render the component using the complete width of its container minus 30 pixels and the complete height of its container minus 120 pixels, and if only one offset value is given it is assumed to be the right edge offset value while the bottom offset value will default to zero. A hybrid offset value of *-80 70%* would render the width offset from the container's right edge by 80 pixels and 70 percent of the container's height.

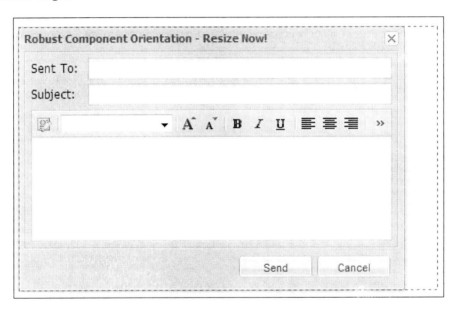

How to do it...

We simply add fields to `FormPanel` specifying the anchoring rule for the field with `FormData` instance (`FormData` extends `AnchorData`) which will be used by the `AnchorLayout` implementation (`FormLayout`) that `FormPanel` has.

```
// create a window
Window window = new Window();
window.setPlain(true);
window.setSize(400, 265);
window.setHeading("Robust Component Anchoring - Resize Now!");
window.setLayout(new FitLayout());
```

```
// create a FormPanel
FormPanel form = new FormPanel();
form.setBorders(false);
form.setBodyBorder(false);
form.setLabelWidth(55);
form.setPadding(5);
form.setHeaderVisible(false);

// add TextField to the form
TextField<String> field = new TextField<String>();
field.setFieldLabel("Sent To");
form.add(field, new FormData("100%"));

// add TextField to the form
field = new TextField<String>();
field.setFieldLabel("Subject");
form.add(field, new FormData("100%"));
// add HtmlEditor to the form
HtmlEditor html = new HtmlEditor();
html.setHideLabel(true);
form.add(html, new FormData("100% -53"));

// add the buttons and the form to the window.
window.addButton(new Button("Send"));
window.addButton(new Button("Cancel"));
window.add(form);

// show the window
window.show();
```

How it works...

We begin by creating a GXT window (so we can easily demonstrate resizing) and then we add `FormPanel` to it. `FormPanel` uses `FormLayout` which is actually a glorified `AnchorLayout`. This is a useful layout for laying out form-related components by auto-aligning them.

When adding a field to `FormPanel`, there is no need to explicitly add a label for the field, as we set the field's label using the field's `setFieldLabel()` method and the label is automatically added and aligned by the layout.

Next, we just add `Field` widgets to our `FormPanel`, providing the anchor-spec with `FormData` which is also `AnchorData` in disguise.

Crafting UI Real Estate

The two `TextField` widgets are given a one-valued anchoring-spec of *100%* meaning they would occupy the whole width of their container (`FormPanel`) but with a height of *auto*, while the `HtmlEditor` field whose label is hidden with `html.setHideLabel(true)` will also occupy the entire available width of the container just like the previous fields, but would have a height of the container's height minus 53 pixels.

A trial will convince you, resize the window and see!

UI cardinality with BorderLayout

It is almost natural for web developers to organize their UIs into regions; for example, header (top or north), footer (bottom or south), say navigation or adverts (left and right or east and west), and the center which is for serious stuff. As a result of this need, many UI toolkits have come up with all sorts of imaginable ways to help developers easily divide up the browser or a container into regions which they can further nest to conjure truly complex UI arrangements.

`BorderLayout` is GXT's simple yet powerful solution to what the web has been trying to solve with HTML tables and CSS grids. It allows components to be added to a container with `LayoutRegion` which can be `NORTH`, `EAST`, `SOUTH`, `WEST`, or `CENTER`. The only catch to using this layout is that if it has only one child component then it must be placed in the center region with `LayoutRegion.CENTER`.

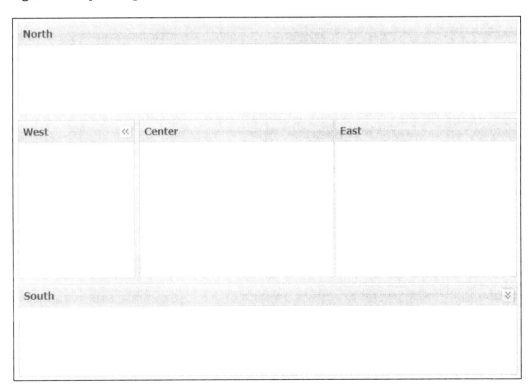

How to do it...

We simply set the layout of a container to `BorderLayout` and then add child components to it specifying a region with `LayoutRegion` encapsulated within `BorderLayoutData` which can have other settings such as `Margins`.

```
// create the main panel
ContentPanel mainView = new ContentPanel();
mainView.setSize(550, 380);
mainView.setHeaderVisible(false);
mainView.setBodyBorder(false);
mainView.setLayout(new BorderLayout());

// set up west-side
ContentPanel panel = new ContentPanel();
panel.setHeading("West");
BorderLayoutData westData = new BorderLayoutData(
    LayoutRegion.WEST);
westData.setSize(130);
westData.setMinSize(100);
westData.setMaxSize(180);
westData.setSplit(true);
westData.setCollapsible(true);
westData.setMargins(new Margins(0, 5, 0, 0));
mainView.add(panel, westData);

// set up center
panel = new ContentPanel();
panel.setHeading("Center");
panel.setStyleAttribute("background", "#fff");
BorderLayoutData centerData = new BorderLayoutData(
    LayoutRegion.CENTER);
centerData.setMargins(new Margins(5));
mainView.add(panel, centerData);

// set up north-side
panel = new ContentPanel();
panel.setHeading("North");
BorderLayoutData northData = new BorderLayoutData(LayoutRegion.
NORTH,100);
northData.setCollapsible(true);
northData.setFloatable(true);
northData.setHideCollapseTool(true);
northData.setSplit(true);
northData.setMargins(new Margins(0, 0, 5, 0));
mainView.add(panel, northData);
```

Crafting UI Real Estate

```
 //set up east-side
 panel = new ContentPanel();
 panel.setHeading("East");
 BorderLayoutData eastData = new BorderLayoutData(
       LayoutRegion.EAST);
  centerData.setMargins(new Margins(0, 0, 0, 5));
 mainView.add(panel, eastData);

 // set up south-side
 panel = new ContentPanel();
 panel.setHeading("South");
 BorderLayoutData southData = new BorderLayoutData(LayoutRegion.SOUTH,
100);
 southData.setSplit(true);
 southData.setCollapsible(true);
 southData.setFloatable(true);
 southData.setMargins(new Margins(5, 0, 0, 0));
 mainView.add(panel, southData);

/*
 * GxtCookbk is the application's entry point class.
 * We access its main content panel using the
 * static GxtCookBk.getAppCenterPanel() call.
 * We add our viewPort to the main content panel.
 */
GxtCookBk.getAppCenterPanel().add(mainView);
```

How it works...

First we create our container object as a `ContentPanel` assigned to `mainView` and then we give it the cardinal layout using `mainView.setLayout(new BorderLayout())`.

We create a "west-side" `ContentPanel` and then we initialize `westData` with new `BorderLayoutData()` passing in `LayoutRegion.WEST`. On `westData` we set a width, minimum width and maximum width using `setSize()`, `setMinSize()`, and `setMaxSize()` respectively, thus ensuring that this region is expandable within those limits but also because it can be resized by dragging the split bar. Resizing is supported by calling `westData.setSplit(true)`.

We also make it collapsible so that it can be minimized by pressing the minimize arrow on the top of the panel and then give it some surrounding space with `setMargins()`, controlling its top, right, bottom, and left margins. The panel is then added to `mainView` using the `westData LayoutData`.

Remember, we must provide a center region to `BorderLayout`, so we add `ContentPanel` to the center using `centerData` initialized as a `BorderLayoutData` with `LayoutRegion.CENTER` and given an all-round margin of 5 pixels.

Next, we add east, south, and north regions to `mainView`, by creating `ContentPanel`, a new `BorderLayoutData()` class and adding both the panel and the `BorderLayout` instance to the `mainView` panel.

Building a basic wizard with CardLayout

Wizards have become common place (except the ones in Harry Potter); they allow us to complete complex tasks in simple intuitive steps and can be as simple as just a sequence of navigable steps or as complex as having steps dynamically added from an RPC call based on a selection in a previous step.

The good news is that `CardLayout` can be used to build a basic wizard, devoid of all the bells and whistles that your imagination can conjure. `CardLayout` renders the child components of a container such that only one component is fitted or visible (`CardLayout` extends `FitLayout`) in the container at a time. The only way to move from one child component to the next is by calling `setActiveItem()` on the layout, giving it the component to display while the others stay hidden.

The drawback to this whole thing is that `CardLayout` itself does not provide a mechanism for handling navigation between the components it is rendering, nor does the supposedly handy `CardPanel` that GXT provides does this. Thankfully, building a real `WizardPanel` with basic navigation is trivial and that's what we set out to achieve here.

How to do it...

This one is a little bit involved, but all we are doing is simply defining an API with the `Wizard` interface which is then implemented in `WizardPanel`. `WizardPanel` uses `CardLayout` and does almost everything with the `getActiveItem()` and `setActiveItem()` methods of the `CardLayout` API.

```java
/**
 * implement FormPanel as a wizard in WizardPanel.
 */
public class WizardPanel extends FormPanel {
  enum DIR{
    NEXT, BACK
  }

  private Button nextBtn, prevBtn;
  protected CardLayout cardLayout;
  protected FormButtonBinding btnBind;
  protected List<LayoutContainer> cards;


  /**
   * constructor for WizardPanel
   */
  public WizardPanel() {
    super();
    // create a CardLayout.
    cardLayout = new CardLayout();
    setLayout(cardLayout);
    cards = new ArrayList<LayoutContainer>();
    setButtonAlign(HorizontalAlignment.RIGHT);

    // add a Back button
    prevBtn = new Button("Back", new SelectionListener<ButtonEvent>()
{
      @Override
      public void componentSelected(ButtonEvent ce) {
        navigate(DIR.BACK);
      }
    });
    // disable the Back button and add it to the panel.
    prevBtn.setEnabled(false);
    addButton(prevBtn);
```

```java
      // create the Next button.
      nextBtn = new Button("Next", new SelectionListener<ButtonEvent>()
    {
        @Override
        public void componentSelected(ButtonEvent ce) {
          navigate(DIR.NEXT);
        }
      });
      btnBind = new FormButtonBinding(this);
      btnBind.addButton(nextBtn);
      addButton(nextBtn);
    }

    public Button getNextBtn() {
      return nextBtn;
    }

    public Button getPrevBtn() {
      return prevBtn;
    }

    /**
     * check if there is a next card.
     * @return true if there is a next card.
     */
    public boolean hasNext() {
      boolean has = false;
      LayoutContainer active = getActive();
      if(!cards.isEmpty() && cards.indexOf(active)+1 < cards.size()){
        has = true;
      }
      return has;
    }

    /**
     * check if there is a previous card.
     * @return true if there is a previous card.
     */
    public boolean hasPrevious() {
      boolean has = false;
      LayoutContainer active = getActive();
      if(!cards.isEmpty() && cards.indexOf(active) >= 1){
        has = true;
      }
      return has;
    }
```

```java
/**
 * get the next card.
 * @return LayoutContainer the next card.
 */
public LayoutContainer getNext() {
  LayoutContainer active = getActive();
  LayoutContainer next = cards.get( cards.indexOf(active)+1 );
  return next;
}

/**
 * get the previous card.
 * @return LayoutContainer the previous card.
 */
public LayoutContainer getPrevious() {
  LayoutContainer active = getActive();
  LayoutContainer next = cards.get( cards.indexOf(active)-1 );
  return next;
}

/**
 * navigate between the cards according to the DIR
 * @param dir DIR enum.
 */
public void navigate(DIR dir) {
  LayoutContainer target = null;
  if(DIR.NEXT.equals(dir)){
    target = getNext();
  } else if(DIR.BACK.equals(dir)){
    target = getPrevious();
  }

  cardLayout.setActiveItem(target);

  // don't confuse our navigation sequence
  boolean hasNext = hasNext();
  if(hasNext){
    btnBind.startMonitoring();
  }else{
    btnBind.stopMonitoring();
  }
  getNextBtn().setEnabled(hasNext);
  getPrevBtn().setEnabled(hasPrevious());
}
```

```java
  /**
   * add a card to the panel
   * @param card the card to add.
   */
  public void addCard(LayoutContainer card) {
    cards.add(card);
    add(card);
  }


  /**
   * add a list of cards.
   * @param cards List of cards.
   */
  public void addCards(List<LayoutContainer> cards) {
    for (LayoutContainer card : cards) {
      addCard(card);
    }
  }


  /**
   * get the active card
   * @return LayoutContainer the active card.
   */
  public LayoutContainer getActive() {
    LayoutContainer active = (LayoutContainer) cardLayout.
getActiveItem();
    return active;
  }

  @Override
  public boolean isValid(boolean preventMark) {
    boolean valid = true;
    for (Field<?> f : getFields()) {
      if (f.isRendered() && f.isVisible() && !f.isValid(preventMark))
{
        valid = false;
      }
    }
    return valid;
  }


}
```

```java
// create a WizardPanel
WizardPanel wizardPanel = new WizardPanel();
wizardPanel.setSize(450, 300);
wizardPanel.setHeading("GXT Wizard");
wizardPanel.setStyleAttribute("background", "#fff");

// create the first card.
LayoutContainer card = new LayoutContainer();
card.addText("<h1>Please click Next to sign in ..</h1>");
// add card to the panel.
wizardPanel.addCard(card);

// create the second card.
card = new LayoutContainer(new FormLayout());
card.addText("<h1>Enter your login details below</h1>");

// create username field and add it to the card.
TextField<String> usrName = new TextField<String>();
usrName.setName("username");
usrName.setAllowBlank(false);
usrName.setFieldLabel("Username");
card.add(usrName);

// create the password field and add it to the card.
TextField<String> pswd = new TextField<String>();
pswd.setName("pswd");
pswd.setPassword(true);
pswd.setAllowBlank(false);
pswd.setFieldLabel("Password");
card.add(pswd);
wizardPanel.addCard(card);

card = new LayoutContainer();
card.addText("<h1>Welcome to GXT WizardPanel!</h1>");
// add card to the panel
wizardPanel.addCard(card);

/*
 * GxtCookbk is the application's entry point class.
 * We access its main content panel using the
 * static GxtCookBk.getAppCenterPanel() call.
 * We add our panel to the main content panel.
 */
GxtCookBk.getAppCenterPanel().add(wizardPanel);
```

How it works...

`WizardPanel` defines `hasNext()` and `hasPrevious()` methods both of which will return true or false indicating if there is a next or previous component to navigate to. It also defines a `navigate()` method which expects a `NEXT` or `BACK` direction from its `DIR` enum which indicates the direction of the navigation.

`getNext()`, `getActive()`, and `getPrevious()` methods all of which return `LayoutContainer` are used to do actual navigation.

Finally, it provides `addCard()` and `addCards()` methods which respectively accepts a `LayoutContainer` or list of `LayoutContainer` objects allowing us to easily add components to the wizard.

The `WizardPanel` constructor creates `CardLayout` and sets it as the layout to be used by the panel. It then creates an `ArrayList` to hold the card which will be added to the panel and creates the *Next* and *Back* buttons and binds them to the `navigate()` method, so they implement the forward and backward navigation.

`WizardPanel` provides the `getActive()` method to simply return the active component of the `CardLayout` as a `LayoutContainer`. `hasNext()` then returns true only if there are items beyond the active one from its list of cards and `hasPrevious()` only returns true if the active card is not the first one.

`getNext()` and `getPrevious()` first obtain the currently visible card with `getActive()` and then returns the next or previous card relative to the active card respectively.

The crux of `WizardPanel` is its `navigate()` method, which uses a conditional block to set the target `LayoutContainer` to the value of either `getNext()` or `getPrevious()` depending on the direction of navigation as represented by the `dir` argument. The second conditional block is used to stop validation of the form when we reach the *end* of the wizard otherwise the *next* button will remain enabled even when there are no more *next* steps to navigate to.

The last two lines of the `navigate()` method are used to enable/disable the *next* and *previous* navigation buttons based on the outcome of `hasNext()` and `hasPrevious()` respectively.

A very important override of `WizardPanel` is the `isValid()` method from its `FormPanel` superclass. It is implemented to only check validation rules for rendered and visible fields (those in current card), otherwise we would not be able to leave the wizard's first step and move to the wizard's second step because there happens to be a mandatory field in the second step which we have not even gotten to yet and will not be able to navigate to.

Using `WizardPanel` is as easy as using a standard GXT panel; we instantiate it with `new WizardPanel()` and then add components to it with its `addCard()` or `addCards()` methods.

Crafting UI Real Estate

RowLayout vertical and horizontal aligning

`RowLayout` renders a container's components in a single vertical or horizontal row. It is very flexible and allows configurable options for height, width, and margins for each child component.

`RowLayout` supports both pixel and percentage based measurement values using a `RowData` (`LayoutData`) object. A value from `0` to `1` (inclusive) is treated as a percentage while values greater than `1` are treated as pixels. However, the size of a component will be determined from the component itself (computed size) if given a `RowData` value of `-1`, for either the height or the width (but not both), thus allowing the component to decide its size and not the layout.

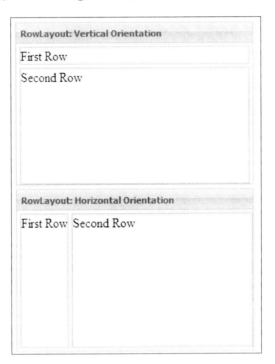

How to do it...

We simply set `RowLayout` as the layout for a container and then add child components to the container, providing a `RowData` object during the `add` operation. `RowData` will eventually determine how the components are rendered and sized in rows.

```
// create a ContentPanel with RowLayout
ContentPanel panel = new ContentPanel();
panel.setSize(400, 300);
panel.setHeading("RowLayout: Vertical Orientation");
panel.setLayout(new RowLayout());
```

```
Text item1 = new Text("First Row");
item1.setBorders(true);
Text item2 = new Text("Second Row");
item2.setBorders(true);

// add the rows
panel.add(item1, new RowData(1, -1, new Margins(4)));
panel.add(item2, new RowData(1, 1, new Margins(0, 4, 0, 4)));

/*
 * GxtCookbk is the application's entry point class.
 * We access its main content panel using the
 * static GxtCookBk.getAppCenterPanel() call.
 * We add our panel to the main content panel,
 * specifying a margin of * 5 pixels for all
 * dimentions of the panel
 */GxtCookBk.getAppCenterPanel().add(panel, new FlowData(5));

// create a ContentPanel with RowLayoutpanel = new ContentPanel();
panel.setSize(400, 300);
panel.setHeading("RowLayout: Horizontal Orientation");
panel.setLayout(new RowLayout(Orientation.HORIZONTAL));

item1 = new Text("First Row");
item1.setBorders(true);
item2 = new Text("Second Row");
item2.setBorders(true);

// add the rows
panel.add(item1, new RowData(-1, 1, new Margins(4)));
panel.add(item2, new RowData(1, 1, new Margins(4, 0, 4, 0)));

/*
 * GxtCookbk is the application's entry point class.
 * We access its main content panel using the
 * static GxtCookBk.getAppCenterPanel() call.
 * We add our panel to the main content panel,
 * specifying a margin of * 5 pixels for all
 * dimentions of the panel
 */GxtCookBk.getAppCenterPanel().add(panel, new FlowData(5));
```

Crafting UI Real Estate

How it works...

We begin by creating a ContentPanel with a RowLayout with the default Orientation.VERTICAL to render components vertically.

Next, we create two borderless `Text` widgets which are then added to the panel. The first `Text` is added with `RowData` indicating that `item1` will occupy 100 percent of its container's width but will have a height that is determined by its contents and will also have a margin of four pixels around it. `item2` will occupy 100 percent of the width of the container as well as 100 percent of what is left of its container's height after the height of `item1` has been computed. It will have a margin of four pixels for its left and right borders.

We also demonstrate the horizontal rendering of `RowLayout` with the second `ContentPanel` whose `RowLayout` is explicitly given `Orientation.HORIZONTAL`. The two (re-initialized) borderless `Text` widgets are also added to it but this time `item1` will have a computed width of 100 percent of the container height and four pixel surrounding margin while `item2` gets 100 percent of the available container width (of course after `item1` width is determined) and 100 percent of the container height, with four pixel top and bottom margin but zero pixel right and left margin.

Building grids with ColumnLayout

`ColumnLayout` positions and sizes a container's children horizontally, with each component specifying how much of the container's available width it will take up. This width specification which can be expressed in pixels or as a percentage is encapsulated as a `ColumnData` object, the child widgets are then sized by `ColumnData` and positioned in horizontal columns. If you need to render components in a small number of horizontal blocks, such as a three column (left, middle, and right) segmented form, then `ColumnLayout` is your best bet.

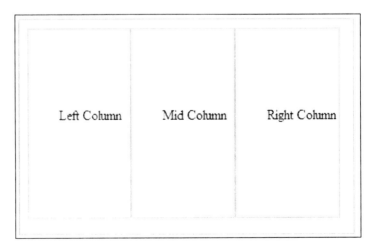

How to do it...

Set `ColumnLayout` as the layout for a container and then add components to the container providing a `ColumnData` object during the add operation that will specify how much of the container's width the component will occupy.

 The sum of the values given to `ColumnData` during all the add operations on the container should be less or equal to 1 (for percentage values) or less or equal to the width of the container, otherwise you could get some really bizarre overlapping on the child components.

```
LayoutContainer main = new LayoutContainer(new ColumnLayout());
main.setBorders(true);
main.setSize(400, 250);
main.setStyleAttribute("padding", "10px");

LayoutContainer panel = new LayoutContainer(new CenterLayout());
panel.setHeight(220);
panel.setBorders(true);
panel.add(new Html("Left Column"));
main.add(panel, new ColumnData(.33));

panel = new LayoutContainer(new CenterLayout());
panel.setHeight(220);
panel.setBorders(true);
panel.add(new Html("Mid Column"));
main.add(panel, new ColumnData(.33));

panel = new LayoutContainer(new CenterLayout());
panel.setHeight(220);
panel.setBorders(true);
panel.add(new Html("Right Column"));
main.add(panel, new ColumnData(.33));

GxtCookBk.getAppCenterPanel().add(main);
```

Crafting UI Real Estate

How it works...

Using `ColumnLayout` turns out to be quite simple. We create the container as a `LayoutContainer` object assigned to main but initialized with `new columnLayout()` as the constructor argument.

After some cosmetic configurations on `main`, we proceed to create the child components as `LayoutContainer` panels initialized with `CenterLayout`. `CenterLayout` is not a requirement for `ColumnLayout`, it is just used here on the panel objects so that the HTML widgets added to them will be centered instead of snapping to the top-left corner.

Our example code simply creates three `LayoutContainer` panels, each having a height of 220 pixels (`ColumnLayout` does not handle height of its components) and a width of 33 percent of the container's width. We could have easily used a pixel value with `main.add(panel, new columnData(120))`, in which case that panel will take up 120 pixels of horizontal space within main.

Building DashBoards

The discovery and further exploitation of the `XMLHTTPRequest` object (`xhr`) leads to single-page style web apps such as **Gmail** wherein the user can do just about everything the app offers within that single webpage without refreshing the browser. The idea of a UI where several portions of an application can be mashed up into draggable panes is not totally new to web ninjas; the JSR 258, which is called **portlet specification**, is an enterprise scale attempt at dashboards.

However, the rich UI toolkits of today, **XHR** in the modern browser and **Web2.x** communication systems (**JSON, JSONP, GWT RPC, Comet, WebSockets**, and so on) all combine to make building dash boards (**Portal/Portlets**) less painful and more fun.

Consider having to build a dashboard with several closable, collapsible, draggable, and re-orderable views/panes on it, with one view showing the current users' **Facebook** activity stream, the other showing recent 50 mails from Gmail and yet another showing the user's latest updates from **Twitter**, such that from a single console (dashboard) the user is able to peruse his or her (fair) share of today's organized privacy invasion.

Chapter 4

The GXT Portal and Portlet classes are specialized UI containers that you can employ to create a dashboard interface. However, it has nothing to do with the JSR 258 Portlet specification.

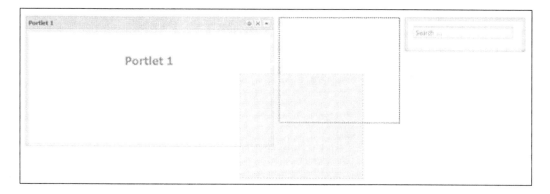

How to do it...

Simply create a `Portal` initializing it with the number of columns it will have, then configure the width of the columns and add `Portlet` components to `Portal`, each having a heading, and specify which of the columns in `Portal` it should initially (because it will eventually be dragged) show up in.

```
private void configurePortlet(final ContentPanel portlet) {
  portlet.setCollapsible(true);
  portlet.setAnimCollapse(false);
  portlet.setStyleName("x-window-tc", true);
  portlet.getHeader().addTool(new ToolButton("x-tool-gear"));

  ToolButton closeTb = new ToolButton("x-tool-close", new SelectionLis
tener<IconButtonEvent>(){
    @Override
    public void componentSelected(IconButtonEvent evt) {
      portlet.removeFromParent();
    }
  });
  portlet.getHeader().addTool(closeTb);
}
// create the Portal
Portal portal = new Portal(3);
portal.setColumnWidth(0, .50);
portal.setColumnWidth(1, .25);
portal.setColumnWidth(2, .25);
portal.setStyleAttribute("backgroundColor", "white");
```

```
// create Portlet
Portlet portlet = new Portlet();
portlet.setHeight(250);
configurePortlet(portlet);
portlet.setHeading("Portlet 1");
portlet.addText("<h1>Portlet 1</h1>");
// add portlet to the portal
portal.add(portlet, 0);

// create Portlet
portlet = new Portlet();
portlet.setHeight(200);
configurePortlet(portlet);
portlet.setHeading("Portlet 2");
portlet.addText("<h1>Portlet 2</h1>");
// portlet to the portal
portal.add(portlet, 1);
// create Portlet
portlet = new Portlet();
portlet.setHeight(65);
portlet.setHeaderVisible(false);
portlet.setLayout(new FormLayout());

// create and add search field to the portlet.
TextField<String> search = new TextField<String>();
search.setHideLabel(true);
search.setEmptyText("Search ...");
search.setStyleAttribute("padding", "10px 0 0 10px");
portlet.add(search);
// add portlet to the portal
portal.add(portlet, 2);

/*
 * GxtCookbk is the application's entry point class.
 * We access its main content panel using the
 * static GxtCookBk.getAppCenterPanel() call.
 * We add our portlet to the main content panel.
 */
GxtCookBk.getAppCenterPanel().add(portal);
```

How it works...

We begin by instantiating our dashboard container with `new Portal(3)`, meaning it will have three horizontal regions. Internally, the `Portal` constructor (as we have invoked it) will place three `LayoutContainer` panels horizontally using `ColumnLayout`; each of these panels in turn use a vertically oriented `RowLayout` to render the views/panes (`Portlet`) that will be added to `Portal`.

After the `Portal` instantiation, we use `setColumnWidth()` to size the three internal `LayoutContainer` panels, giving the first one 50 percent width while the second and third both get 25 percent width each.

We then create a `Portlet`, which is a specialized `ContentPanel` for use in a `Portal`. Our `configurePortlet()` helper method is then invoked with the just created `Portlet` from where we make it collapsible, turn off the collapse animation, and add a dummy *settings* `ToolButton`. We also add a *close* `ToolButton` which is used to remove the `Portlet` from its container (`Portal`).

After setting a heading and some text on `Portlet`, we add it to the first column (`LayoutContainer`) of the `Portal` using `portal.add(portlet, 0)`. The second portlet is much the same as the first except that it has a height of 200 pixels and it is added to the second column in the portal. The third portlet however is 65 pixels high, has no header bar (therefore cannot be dragged or closed even if we had used `configurePortlet()` on it), and uses a `FormLayout`.

The third portlet shows that we can do anything with `Portlet` as we can with `ContentPanel` which it actually is, so we give it `TextField` that looks like a search box because we hide its label component using the setHideLabel() method, which provides an elegant alternative to using a TextField with a label, as we usually do in forms.

5
Engaging Users with Forms and Data Input

In this chapter we will cover the following points:

- Building a simple form with basic validation
- Showing options with combos
- Customizing a combo's bound model
- Linking combos
- Capturing multiple input selection
- Simple FileUpload and processing
- Binding data into forms
- A better slider field

Introduction

Forms are the most popular way of making web pages interactive. If you've been on the Internet for a while, you've probably filled out a number of online forms. Forms are used to obtain information from visitors, and like forms on paper, a form on a web page allows the user to enter the requested information and submit it for processing (fortunately, forms on a web page are processed much faster).

While other elements within a web application give style and meaning to what is being viewed, a form adds interactivity such as taking orders, surveys, user registration, and more.

Engaging Users with Forms and Data Input

A standard web form has two parts: the HTML frontend and a backend form processor. The HTML frontend part handles the presentation while the backend handles the form submissions (such as saving the form submissions into a database, sending e-mails, and so on).

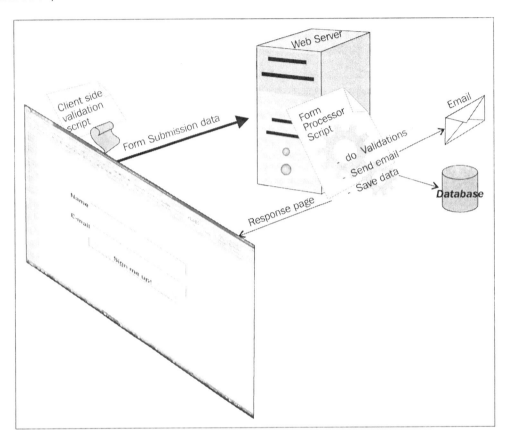

The GXT `FormPanel` does exceedingly more than its often bare HTML counterpart (watch out for **HTML5**), providing richer input widgets, better layouts, tighter validation, and asynchronous (as well as plain old synchronous) submission handling.

Building a simple form with basic validation

Anyone with more than basic knowledge of HTML and the web probably knows that the standard HTML form element provides a decent level of functionality for data entry and processing. However, it really comes out shy in the layout of input elements and validation of data entries, thus requiring all sorts of JavaScript and DOM hacks.

Chapter 5

The GXT `FormPanel` not only provides a very rich collection of input controls, but also has a mechanism for adopting other UI widgets into form input controls (`AdapterField`) and mashing several fields together to compose new ones (`MultiField`). With a GXT `FormPanel` and its `Field` implementations, you also get in-built validation enforcement and you can layout your fields in any fashion your want.

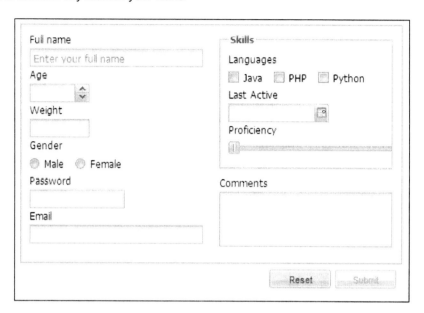

How to do it...

All we really have to do is make `FormPanel` and add several `Field` implementations to it using any layout we want.

```
// basic form configuration
final FormPanel formPanel = new FormPanel();
formPanel.setSize(465, 320);
formPanel.setHeaderVisible(false);
formPanel.setStyleAttribute("backgroundColor", "#fff");

// set up layout structure
FormData formData = new FormData("100%");
LayoutContainer main = new LayoutContainer(new ColumnLayout());

FormLayout formLayout = new FormLayout(LabelAlign.TOP);
formLayout.setLabelSeparator("");
LayoutContainer left = new LayoutContainer(formLayout);
left.setStyleAttribute("paddingRight", "10px");
main.add(left, new ColumnData(.5));
```

```java
formLayout = new FormLayout(LabelAlign.TOP);
formLayout.setLabelSeparator("");
LayoutContainer right = new LayoutContainer(formLayout);
right.setStyleAttribute("paddingLeft", "10px");
main.add(right, new ColumnData(.5));

// set up text field
TextField<String> name = new TextField<String>();
name.setName("name");
name.setMinLength(4);
name.setMaxLength(35);
name.setAllowBlank(false);
name.setMessageTarget("tooltip");
name.setFieldLabel("Full name");
name.setEmptyText("Enter your full name");
left.add(name, formData);

// set up spinner field
SpinnerField age = new SpinnerField();
age.setName("age");
age.setMinValue(18);
age.setMaxValue(50);
age.setFieldLabel("Age");
age.setAllowBlank(false);
age.setAllowDecimals(false);
age.setAllowNegative(false);
age.setMessageTarget("tooltip");
age.setPropertyEditorType(Integer.class);
age.setFormat(NumberFormat.getFormat("00"));
left.add(age, new FormData("35%"));

// set up number field
NumberField weight = new NumberField();
weight.setFieldLabel("Weight");
weight.setName("weight");
weight.setAllowNegative(false);
weight.setAllowDecimals(true);
weight.setMinValue(35);
weight.setMaxValue(150);
weight.setMessageTarget("tooltip");
weight.setPropertyEditorType(Double.class);
weight.setFormat(NumberFormat.getFormat("00.0"));
left.add(weight, new FormData("35%"));
```

```java
// set up radio buttons
RadioGroup genderGrp = new RadioGroup("gender");
genderGrp.setFieldLabel("Gender");
Radio maleRd = new Radio();
maleRd.setBoxLabel("Male");
genderGrp.add(maleRd);
Radio femaleRd = new Radio();
femaleRd.setBoxLabel("Female");
genderGrp.add(femaleRd);
genderGrp.setMessageTarget("tooltip");
left.add(genderGrp, formData);

// text field for password entry
TextField<String> pswd = new TextField<String>();
pswd.setName("pswd");
pswd.setPassword(true);
pswd.setMinLength(8);
pswd.setAllowBlank(false);
pswd.setFieldLabel("Password");
pswd.setMessageTarget("tooltip");
left.add(pswd, new FormData("55%"));

// text field for e-mail entry
TextField<String> email = new TextField<String>();
email.setName("email");
email.setAllowBlank(false);
email.setMessageTarget("tooltip");
email.setRegex("^(\\w+)([\\-+.][\\w]+)*@(\\w[\\-\\w]*\\.){1,5}([A-Za-z]){2,6}$");
email.getMessages().setRegexText("Invalid Email Address");
email.setFieldLabel("Email");
left.add(email, formData);

// group fields with fieldset
FieldSet skills = new FieldSet();
formLayout = new FormLayout(LabelAlign.TOP);
formLayout.setLabelSeparator("");
skills.setLayout(formLayout);
skills.setHeading("Skills");
right.add(skills, formData);

// set up checkboxes
CheckBoxGroup langGrp = new CheckBoxGroup();
langGrp.setFieldLabel("Languages");
skills.add(langGrp);
```

```
CheckBox javaBox = new CheckBox();
javaBox.setName("lang");
javaBox.setBoxLabel("Java");
langGrp.add(javaBox);

CheckBox phpBox = new CheckBox();
phpBox.setName("lang");
phpBox.setBoxLabel("PHP");
langGrp.add(phpBox);

CheckBox pythonBox = new CheckBox();
pythonBox.setName("lang");
pythonBox.setBoxLabel("Python");
langGrp.add(pythonBox);

// set up datefield
DateField lastActive = new DateField();
Date minVal = new Date(new DateWrapper(2005, 0, 1).getTime());
lastActive.setMinValue(minVal);
lastActive.setMaxValue(new Date());
lastActive.setName("lastactive");
lastActive.setFieldLabel("Last Active");
lastActive.getPropertyEditor().setFormat(DateTimeFormat.getFormat("d
MMM, yyyy"));
skills.add(lastActive, new FormData("65%"));

// set up slider field
Slider slider = new Slider();
slider.setMinValue(0);
slider.setMaxValue(100);
slider.setValue(0);
slider.setIncrement(10);
slider.setMessage("{0} %");

SliderField sliderField = new SliderField(slider);
sliderField.setName("skill_level");
sliderField.setFieldLabel("Proficiency");
skills.add(sliderField);

// set up textarea
TextArea comments = new TextArea();
comments.setName("comments");
comments.setHeight(65);
comments.setAllowBlank(false);
comments.setFieldLabel("Comments");
comments.setMessageTarget("tooltip");
comments.setPreventScrollbars(true);
right.add(comments, formData);
```

```
formPanel.add(main, formData);

// buttons and validation enforcement
Button resetBtn = new Button("Reset", new SelectionListener<ButtonEve
nt>() {
  @Override
  public void componentSelected(ButtonEvent evt) {
    formPanel.reset();
  }
});
formPanel.addButton(resetBtn);

Button submitBtn = new Button("Submit", new SelectionListener<ButtonE
vent>() {
  @Override
  public void componentSelected(ButtonEvent evt) {}
});
formPanel.addButton(submitBtn);

FormButtonBinding btnBinder = new FormButtonBinding(formPanel);
btnBinder.addButton(submitBtn);

// serve it up now!
GxtCookBk.getAppCenterPanel().add(formPanel);
```

How it works...

To begin working with a form in GXT, we instantiate `FormPanel` and add fields and buttons to it. `FormPanel` extends `ContentPanel` and therefore is a first class GXT panel inheriting all the capabilities (methods events, rendering, styling) of `ContentPanel`, hence after instantiating `formPanel` we configure its size with `setSize()`, turn off the header pane with `setHeaderVisible()`, and give it a white background with `setStyleAttribute()`. By default, `FormPanel` uses `FormLayout` to render its field in a top to bottom fashion, but nothing stops us from using `ColumnLayout` (renders items vertically in horizontal blocks) to create a more structured outline for the fields. So we create `LayoutContainer` (main) with `ColumnLayout` and then we add to this container two additional `LayoutContainer` (left and right), each configured with `FormLayout` (otherwise we can't render fields properly) that will place labels above fields (`LabelAlign.Top`) and separated from the fields by a black space instead of a colon (`setLabelSeparator("")`).

We then add the two inner containers to the main container.

Engaging Users with Forms and Data Input

The section denoted with the comment `setup text field` begins the code segment where we create the fields starting with `TextField`. After instantiating the field with new `TextField<Sting>()` which is assigned to name, we call `setName()` to set its name attribute as in HTML forms and we set the maximum and minimum entry length to `35` and `4` respectively. As part of the validation constraints for this field, we also make it mandatory with `setAllowBlank(false)` and cause validation error messages to show up as fancy tooltips using `setMessageTarget("tooltip")` which can also take `"title"`, `"side"`, and `"none"`. The next two lines set the field's label and its default text (well not really default since it disappears when you click on it or tab into it) after which we add it to the form by adding it to the left column using `left.add(name, formData)`.

Next, we create and configure controlled numeric input with a spinner, which we instantiate with `new SpinnerField()` and assign it to age. After setting the field's name, we set its valid input range with `setMinvalue()` and `setMaxValue()`, and make it mandatory using `setAllowBlank(false)`. Since age is never 2.5 or -3 years we also turn off decimals and negatives by passing `false` to `setAllowDecimals()` and `setAllowNegative()` and later on we seal the integer processing of this field with `setPropertyEditorType(Integer.class)`.

Common with other number field types, we set the rendering or formatting of its numeric value by passing a `NumberFormat` to `age.setFormat()` and then it gets added to occupy 35 percent of its column with `left.add(age, new FormData("35%"))`. The next field is a `NumberField` and it's set up conceptually much the same way as our just reviewed `SpinnerField`. The weight `NumberField` has a label, name, which will not accept negative values (or do you weigh -20) and will not accept values lesser than 35 or greater than 150. Since we are dealing with real numbers this time, we set its property editor type and number format appropriately with `setPropertyEditorType(Double.class)` and pass in `NumberFormat.getFormat("00.0")` to `setFormat()`.

`RadioGroup` is a `MultiField` used to present radio buttons in a `FormPanel`. We instantiate `genderGrp` with `new RadioGroup("gender")` and set its label to `"Gender"` and then add two radio buttons, representing male and female. Note, that putting these two radio buttons in the same `RadioGroup`, causes them to be mutually exclusive, which is exactly what we want in this case.

As there's no `EmailField` but support for regular expression validation checks on the `TextField` class, we can construct a field for e-mail entry (as well as for phone number, URL, and so on) by passing a regular expression string (many on the Internet) to `setRegex()` and using `getMessages().setRegexText()` to configure the error message that will show up if the data entry does not match the expression pattern.

Up next, we demonstrate how to group related fields together with the aid of `FieldSet`, which we instantiate and configure to render child items with a `FormLayout` because `FieldSet` extends `LayoutContainer` which does not automatically render form fields properly even when it (`FieldSet`) is placed within a `FormPanel`; this is not so smart you know! After setting its heading and adding it to the right column of the form, we proceed to add fields to it just as we've been doing with the earlier containers.

The first items added to our skills `FieldSet` is a set of three `CheckBox` items organized by a "Languages" `CheckBoxGroup` (another `MultiField`), the individual `CheckBox` items themselves are given the same name of `"lang"` (short for language!) and their corresponding labels with `setName()` and `setBoxLabel()` respectively before being added to the `langGroup CheckBoxGroup`. Checkboxes are not mutually exclusive, so we add them to the `CheckBoxGroup` for layout purposes only.

Although not shown in this code, you can set a radio or checkbox to be selected or checked by calling `setValue(true)` on it, and you can also get the selected radio from a `RadioGroup` using its `getValue()` method or the selected `CheckBox` items in a `CheckBoxGroup` using its `getValues()` method.

Next in `FieldSet` is a `DateField` configured to only accept dates between January 1, 2005 and the current date using its `setMinValue()` and `setMaxValue()` methods, we also show how to set up a custom formatting for the date value by passing a `DateFormat` to the `setFormat()` method of the `DateTimePropertyEditor` object of `DateField` gotten with its `setPropertyEditor()` method.

The skills `FieldSet` ends with `SliderField` constructed with `Slider` which is configured to slide from 0 (`setMinValue()`) to 100 (`setMaxValue()`) in 10 steps (`setIncrement()`) and a default value of 0. As the user slides the thumb of the slider, a formatted tooltip message (`setMessage("{0} %")`) shows the slider's current value. Lastly, we introduce multi-line text entry using a `TextArea` field, configured to be mandatory, to span a height of 65()px and to disable scrollbars (`setPreventScrollBars(true)`). We can now add the main panel to `FormPanel` to finalize our layout structure.

To conclude this recipe we add two buttons, a reset button whose click listener calls `formPanel.reset()` to reset the form fields, and a dummy submit button. Well, the submit button is not so dummy after all because it prevents you from attempting to submit the form (by being disabled) until you have entered accurate data; this is done with `FormButtonBinding` constructed with our `formPanel` and bound to the submit button with `btnBinder.addButtom(submitBtn)`.

Engaging Users with Forms and Data Input

Showing options with combos

We certainly can present options for selection to users using a collection of radio or checkbox fields, but these do not scale with large numbers. Consider having a user select one out of the many states in the US or one out of the very many languages in the world today. Not only does a combo save space with its compact list of the options overlaid above the rest of the UI, it also turns out to be very powerful and flexible because of how it is composed—the options are presented from a store (queryable, sortable, can be filtered, and so on) which is in turn populated with a loader that can be configured dynamically with parameters thereby tuning the load operation to return, say, a rang or subset of the original/total available options.

How to do it...

The GXT `ComboBox` is a `TriggerField` implementation that displays the `ModelData` items from its bound `ListStore` with a `ListView` when the trigger (arrow button) is clicked.

```
// set up form
final FormPanel formPanel = new FormPanel();
formPanel.setSize(300, 220);
formPanel.setLabelSeparator("");
formPanel.setHeaderVisible(false);
formPanel.setStyleAttribute("backgroundColor", "#fff");

// Make RPC call via a proxy
final RemoteGatewayAsync rpcService = (RemoteGatewayAsync) GWT.
create(RemoteGateway.class);
RpcProxy<ListLoadResult<Customer>> rpcProxy = new RpcProxy<ListLoadRes
ult<Customer>>() {
    @Override
```

```java
    public void load(Object cfg, AsyncCallback<ListLoadResult<Custom
er>> callback) {
       rpcService.listCustomers((ListLoadConfig) cfg, callback);
    }
};

// set up the store
ListLoader<ListLoadResult<ModelData>> loader = new BaseListLoader<List
LoadResult<ModelData>>(rpcProxy, new BeanModelReader());
final ListStore<BeanModel> customerStore = new
ListStore<BeanModel>(loader);

// set up the combo
ComboBox<BeanModel> customer = new ComboBox<BeanModel>();
customer.setValueField("id");
customer.setDisplayField("name");
customer.setName("customer");
customer.setFieldLabel("Customer");
customer.setAllowBlank(false);
customer.setMessageTarget("tooltip");
customer.setTriggerAction(TriggerAction.ALL);
customer.setStore(customerStore);
customer.setLoadingText("loading please wait ...");
customer.setEmptyText("choose a customer ...");
formPanel.add(customer, new FormData("85%"));

// just a dummy
TextArea comments = new TextArea();
comments.setName("comments");
comments.setHeight(105);
comments.setAllowBlank(false);
comments.setFieldLabel("Comments");
comments.setMessageTarget("tooltip");
comments.setPreventScrollbars(true);
formPanel.add(comments, new FormData("100%"));

Button resetBtn = new Button("Reset", new SelectionListener<ButtonEve
nt>() {
  @Override
  public void componentSelected(ButtonEvent evt) {
    formPanel.reset();
  }
});
formPanel.addButton(resetBtn);

// serve it
GxtCookBk.getAppCenterPanel().add(formPanel);
```

Engaging Users with Forms and Data Input

How it works...

We first need to understand the GXT data model concept. GXT provides a framework for passing data between client and server, and binding data models to UI components. Typically, we will make a call to the server, pass the data model to the client, and bind the data model to the UI components. In its simplest form, we can use the GXT framework to pass data from client to server, by having our data model objects extend the `BaseModel` class, which implements the `ModelData` interface. The `BaseModel` class stores its properties internally using a `HashMap` and provides getters and setters for accessing those properties. GXT components such as `Grids` and `ComboBoxes` are designed to interact with data model objects which extend `BaseModel`. However, we will usually want to avoid coupling server-side code to the GXT framework, so we will prefer to avoid having our server-side objects extend the `BaseModel` class. We can of course create **POJO** (**Plain Old Java Object**) objects on the server side and convert them to objects extending `BaseModel` on the client side. However, GXT provides a more elegant solution. We can use the `BeanModelTag` interface to mark our POJO class as a BeanModel. We can then use `BeanModelReader` in order to convert our objects into `BeanModel` objects that can be used by the UI components. This approach is used by the recipe, while our data model objects still depend on GXT's `BeanModelTag` interface, we can still use POJOs and convert our existing POJOs to work with the GXT framework by simply adding this marker interface. Another approach is to use a POJO object as our data model and generate a `BeanModel` from it using a factory, which allows us to decouple server-side code from GXT. This requires creating an interface that extends the `BeanModelMarker` interface and adding a `@Bean` annotation to our interface that specifies our POJO.

The following example demonstrates using the latter approach:

```
@Bean(Customer.class)
interface CustomerBeanModel extends BeanModelMarker {
}

BeanModelFactory factory = BeanModelLookup.get().getFactory(Customer.class);
// get customer POJO
Customer c = getCustomer();
BeanModel mode = factory.createModel(c);
```

Now we can turn to our recipe's code.

The code begins by creating a `FormPanel` which is given some cosmetic (`setSize()`, `setLabelSeparator()`, `setHeaderVisible()`, `setStyleAttribute()`) rather than functional tuning and then we make a `RpcProxy`. As the combo will be loading data across the wire (it can use local data too) we need to create a store with a loader which in turn needs an `RpcProxy` and a `BeanModelReader`.

First, we create `rpcService` by casting the return value of `GWT.create(RemoteGateway.class)` to `RemoteGatewayAsync`, where `RemoteGateway` and `RemoteGatewayAsync` are our synchronous and asynchronous RPC interfaces respectively. See *Appendix C, GWT-RPC*, for details on GWT RPC and its usage in GXT.

Next, we initialize `rpcProxy` from a parameterized new `RpcProxy()` call, calling our remote `listCustomers()` method on `rpcService` within the overridden `load()` method that the abstract `RpcProxy` class inherits from `DataProxy` interface. We then create a loader from `BaseListLoader` giving it `rpcProxy` and a reader (`BeanModelReader`) that can read beans/POJOs which implement the GXT `BeanModelTag` interface. With the proxy and loader constructed, we can now create a `ListStore` that can contain `BeanModelTag` beans/POJOs using `new ListStore<BeanModel>(loader)`.

The combo field itself is simple to create, using `new ComboBox<BeanModel>()`, meaning this combo will handle bean models or beans, a requirement that the customer POJO meets by implementing the GXT `BeanModelTag`. `setValueField("id")` indicates that the `id` field of the `Customer` class will represent the value of a selection in the combo, while the `name` field of the `Customer` class is what we will be presented with (`setDisplayField("name")`) when trying to make the selection. `TriggerAction.All` passed to `setTriggerAction()` will cause the combo to display every available item in the store (`ComboBox` can be paged) which is set on the combo with `setStore(customerStore)`.

After setting the waiting message during a `load` operation with `setLoadText()`, and the `"default"`/`"initial"` text with `setEmptyText()` we add the combo to the form and then add a dummy un-scrollable `TextArea` to the form to make it look like a serious form. Finally, we add a reset button to allow you to play ([reset, select]) with the form till you understand the code!

Customizing a combo's bound model

`Gxt ComboBox` provides a powerful and compact way of allowing selection from a lot of beans or POJOs as described in the previous recipe. However, there are times we need to configure the models (`ModelData` instances) stored in the combo's store by altering/formatting existing fields or adding totally new fields.

Consider a `Customer` POJO with a `firstname` and `lastname` field, no `fullname` field, but a `getFullName()` helper method that returns the concatenation of `getLastName()` and `getFirstName()`. How do we display the full names of the customers in the combo's drop-down list? As there's no `fullname` field in the `Customer` POJO (it is computed) what do we use in the combo's `setDisplayField()` configuration?

Engaging Users with Forms and Data Input

Even if there was a `fullname` field on the `Customer` POJO that is set somehow by some cryptic algorithm, how do we format it as uppercase or word-case in the combo's `ListView`? Well, we can do just that with a `ModelProcessor` which can be passed to the `ComboBox` with its `setModelProcessor()` method. A `ModelProcessor` is a callback class containing a method named `prepareData()` that gets called by `ComboBox` prior to rendering the `ComboBox` data. At this point `ComboBox` already has its `BeanModel` attached and it can manipulate the data in `BeanModel` prior to the data getting rendered by the component.

How to do it...

The GXT `ListView` is used by `ComboBox` to display items from its bound `ListStore`. `ListView` provides a `setModelProcessor()` method that takes a `ModelProcessor` object whose `prepareData()` method is called for every item in the store after they are loaded and before they are shown.

```
// set up form
final FormPanel formPanel = new FormPanel();
formPanel.setSize(300, 235);
formPanel.setLabelSeparator("");
formPanel.setHeaderVisible(false);
formPanel.setStyleAttribute("backgroundColor", "#fff");

// make RPC call via a proxy
final RemoteGatewayAsync rpcService = (RemoteGatewayAsync) GWT.create(RemoteGateway.class);
RpcProxy<ListLoadResult<Customer>> rpcProxy = new RpcProxy<ListLoadResult<Customer>>() {
    @Override
```

```java
      public void load(Object cfg, AsyncCallback<ListLoadResult<Custom
er>> callback) {
         rpcService.listCustomers((ListLoadConfig) cfg, callback);
      }
};

// set up store
ListLoader<ListLoadResult<ModelData>> loader = new BaseListLoader<List
LoadResult<ModelData>>(rpcProxy, new BeanModelReader());
final ListStore<BeanModel> customerStore = new
ListStore<BeanModel>(loader);

// set up combo
ComboBox<BeanModel> customer = new ComboBox<BeanModel>();
customer.setValueField("id");
customer.setName("customer");
customer.setFieldLabel("Customer");
customer.setAllowBlank(false);
customer.setMessageTarget("tooltip");
customer.setTriggerAction(TriggerAction.ALL);
customer.setStore(customerStore);
customer.setLoadingText("loading please wait ...");
customer.setEmptyText("choose a customer ...");
customer.setDisplayField("agegrpstr");

// customize the models
customer.getView().setModelProcessor(new ModelProcessor<BeanModel>() {
  @Override
  public BeanModel prepareData(BeanModel model) {
    Customer cust = (Customer) model.getBean();
    String group = "Adult";
    int age = cust.getAge();
    if(age >=20 && age <= 30){
      group = "Youth";
    } else if(age >=13 && age <= 19){
      group = "Teen";
    } else if(age >=3 && age <= 12){
      group = "Minor";
    }
    model.set("agegrp", group);
    model.set("agegrpstr", cust.getName() + " (" + group + ")");
    return model;
  }
});
formPanel.add(customer, new FormData("85%"));
```

```
// just a dummy
TextArea comments = new TextArea();
comments.setName("comments");
comments.setHeight(105);
comments.setAllowBlank(false);
comments.setFieldLabel("Comments");
comments.setMessageTarget("tooltip");
comments.setPreventScrollbars(true);
formPanel.add(comments, new FormData("100%"));

Button resetBtn = new Button("Reset", new SelectionListener<ButtonEve
nt>() {
  @Override
  public void componentSelected(ButtonEvent evt) {
    formPanel.reset();
  }
});
formPanel.addButton(resetBtn);

// serve it up
GxtCookBk.getAppCenterPanel().add(formPanel);
```

How it works...

Having created `FormPanel` with some basic (optional) configuration, we call the remote `listCustomers()` method on our RPC service from within an `rpcProxy`, then we create the `customerStore ListStore` with the `ListLoader` created using the `RpcProxy` and a `BeanModelReader`. See *Appendix C, GWT-RPC*, for details on GWT RPC.

The customer `ComboBox` is created and configured as usual, setting its value field, `name`, `label`, `trigger-action`, and `store` appropriately (see previous recipe). However, the call to `setDisplayField()` is given a value of `"agegrpstr"` even though the `Customer` POJO has no such field. The code segment `customize the models` shows how we use a `ModelProcessor` to add the computed age group to the model as `"agegrp"` and also a formatted string of the computed group prefixed with the customer's name, also set on the models but as `"agegrpstr"`, which is what our `setDisplayField()` configuration relies on when displaying the options in the combo.

After adding a dummy `TextArea` (just to complete the form), we add a standard reset button to the form and then serve it up to the display.

Linking combos

Perhaps more than once you have wanted to tie two or even more combo boxes together, such as for showing the countries in a continent, states in a particular country, languages within a locale, products within a category, students in a faculty, and so on, such that both of them would load all available data normally. But, if a selection has been made in the *parent* `Category` combo then the `Products` combo should only show *products* from the selected `Category`.

GXT's extensive array of widget lifecycle events can be employed to create this functionality. We can either craft this solution by preloading and populating both combos and then locally filtering the store of the *child* combo based on the selection made on the *parent* combo; or we can dynamically configure the loader of the *child* combo to load items from the server based on the selection made on the *parent* combo. For this recipe, we'll be opting for the latter solution.

How to do it...

If we want to load reviews for a selected customer, then we can listen for `selection` events on the customer combo and use the bound listener to configure the review combo (at runtime) to load reviews for the selected customer. Conversely, we can also listen for `beforeload` events on the review combo and use the bound listener to configure the review combo (at runtime) to load reviews for the selected customer or all reviews if there is no selection within the customer combo (or show an error if a customer selection must precede loading reviews).

```
// set up form
final FormPanel formPanel = new FormPanel();
formPanel.setSize(375, 185);
formPanel.setLabelSeparator("");
formPanel.setHeaderVisible(false);
formPanel.setStyleAttribute("backgroundColor", "#fff");
```

```
// make RPC calls
final RemoteGatewayAsync rpcService = (RemoteGatewayAsync) GWT.
create(RemoteGateway.class);

// proxy for customer RPC calls
RpcProxy<ListLoadResult<Customer>> custRpcProxy = new RpcProxy<ListLoa
dResult<Customer>>() {
    @Override
    public void load(Object cfg, AsyncCallback<ListLoadResult<Custom
er>> callback) {
        rpcService.listCustomers((ListLoadConfig) cfg, callback);
    }
};

// store for customer combo
ListLoader<ListLoadResult<ModelData>> custLoader = new BaseListLoader<
ListLoadResult<ModelData>>(custRpcProxy, new BeanModelReader());
ListStore<BeanModel> custStore = new ListStore<BeanModel>(custLoader);

// customer combo
final ComboBox<BeanModel> customerCombo = new ComboBox<BeanModel>();
customerCombo.setValueField("id");
customerCombo.setDisplayField("name");
customerCombo.setName("customer");
customerCombo.setFieldLabel("Customer");
customerCombo.setAllowBlank(false);
customerCombo.setMessageTarget("tooltip");
customerCombo.setTriggerAction(TriggerAction.ALL);
customerCombo.setStore(custStore);
customerCombo.setLoadingText("loading please wait ...");
customerCombo.setEmptyText("choose a customer ...");
formPanel.add(customerCombo, new FormData("75%"));

// proxy for review RPC calls
RpcProxy<ListLoadResult<Review>> revRpcProxy = new RpcProxy<ListLoadRe
sult<Review>>() {
    @Override
    public void load(Object cfg, AsyncCallback<ListLoadResult<Review>>
callback) {
        rpcService.listReviews((ListLoadConfig) cfg, callback);
    }
};

// store for review combo
BaseListLoader<ListLoadResult<ModelData>> revLoader = new BaseListLoad
er<ListLoadResult<ModelData>>(revRpcProxy, new BeanModelReader());
ListStore<BeanModel> revStore = new ListStore<BeanModel>(revLoader);
```

```
// review combo
final ComboBox<BeanModel> reviewCombo = new ComboBox<BeanModel>();
reviewCombo.setValueField("id");
reviewCombo.setDisplayField("title");
reviewCombo.setName("review");
reviewCombo.setFieldLabel("Review");
reviewCombo.setAllowBlank(false);
reviewCombo.setMessageTarget("tooltip");
reviewCombo.setTriggerAction(TriggerAction.ALL);
reviewCombo.setStore(revStore);
reviewCombo.setLoadingText("loading please wait ...");
reviewCombo.setEmptyText("choose a customer review ...");
reviewCombo.setUseQueryCache(false);
formPanel.add(reviewCombo, new FormData("95%"));

// always configure loader before it loads
revLoader.addLoadListener(new LoadListener(){
  @Override
  public void loaderBeforeLoad(LoadEvent evt) {
    super.loaderBeforeLoad(evt);
    if(customerCombo.isValid(true)){
      BeanModel model = customerCombo.getValue();
      Customer cust = (Customer) model.getBean();
      evt.<ModelData> getConfig().set("customer", cust.getId());
    }else{
      evt.<ModelData> getConfig().set("customer", null);
    }
  }
});

customerCombo.addSelectionChangedListener(new SelectionChangedListener
<BeanModel>() {
  @Override
  public void selectionChanged(SelectionChangedEvent<BeanModel> sel) {
    // Put the review combo in context.
    // Give the user a visual cue that he is about
    // to load reviews for this customer selection
    reviewCombo.clear();
    BeanModel model = sel.getSelectedItem();
    Customer cust = (Customer) model.getBean();
    reviewCombo.setEmptyText("choose a review for " + cust.getName());

    // kill two birds with one stone
    // we can do without the LoadListener added to revLoader
    // by un-commenting the next section
```

Engaging Users with Forms and Data Input

```
        /*
            ListLoadConfig cfg = (ListLoadConfig)       revLoader.
getLastConfig();
            cfg = (cfg == null ? new BasePagingLoadConfig() : cfg);
            cfg.set("customer", cust.getId());
            revLoader.useLoadConfig(cfg);
        */
      }
    });

    Button resetBtn = new Button("Reset", new SelectionListener<ButtonEve
nt>() {
      @Override
      public void componentSelected(ButtonEvent evt) {
        formPanel.reset();
      }
    });
    formPanel.addButton(resetBtn);

    // serve it up
    GxtCookBk.getAppCenterPanel().add(formPanel);
```

How it works...

First, we create and configure a `FormPanel` instance, after creating our RPC service object with `GWT.create(RemoteGateway.class)` we use it from the `custRpcProxy` RpcProxy object to invoke the remote `listCustomers()` method and then we create a `custStore` `ListStore` from a `Loader` configured with the `RpcProxy` created earlier. See *Appendix C, GWT-RPC,* for more details on GXT's use of GWT RPC.

Next, we create and configure `customerCombo` setting its name, label, value field, display field, and store appropriately (see the *Showing options with combos* recipe). We proceed to create a `RpcProxy`, `Loader`, and `ListStore` for the review combo much the same way we did for the customer combo. We also create and configure `reviewCombo`, setting its value field, display field, label, and store among other things. But of great importance to this recipe, we also turn off caching in `reviewCombo` by passing `false` to its `setUseQueryCache()` else its store will not always be queried for data.

Having created and configured our combos, we now need to set up the magic `Listener` objects on them. We add a `LoadListener` to the `Loader` of the review combo and override its `loaderBeforeLoad()` method which gets called just before the combo loads data from the server.

We had to disable caching using `setUseQueryCache(false)` otherwise this `beforeload` handler will only be called once!

In the `Listener`, we check to see if there is a selection on the `customerCombo` combo using `customerCombo.isvalid()`, if so we obtain the `Customer` object from the selection and then set it as a parameter on the `LoadConfig` object used during the combo's `load` operation. The server-side code can now watch out for this parameter and tune the results accordingly.

Although not necessary, we add a `SelectionListener` to `customerCombo`. We can achieve the linking from this listener too, but, here we just put the `reviewCombo` in context by setting in it a text that says "choose a review for Odili Charles" if the selected customer is Odili Charles.

The key point in this recipe is that our remote method takes a `ListLoadconfig` object as a parameter. This is how the dynamic load configurations get passed to the server for it to act accordingly. Also, we need to turn off query caching on the `review` combo.

Capturing multiple input selection

In an earlier recipe from this chapter, we stated why combos are generally better than checkboxes when we need to provide the user with an elaborate list of items to choose from. Well, the only drawback to that assertion is that while checkboxes are designed to allow multiple selections, the GXT `ComboBox` isn't, at least not without some sort of plugin. Thankfully, there are two ways (excluding the plugin approach) to solve this in GXT, the first is to use a `ListField` and the second is the `DualListField`, both of which provide multiple selections out-of-the-box.

`ListField` behaves like `HTML SELECT` element having the multiple attribute turned on, thus it allows the user to make multiple selections while holding the *Ctrl* (control) or *Shift* key. `DualListField` on the other hand is an implantation of GXT's `MultiField`, combining two `ListField` objects into one widget and allowing the user to select from one (source list) into the other (destination list) easily.

Engaging Users with Forms and Data Input

How to do it...

GXT provides a handy `ListField` widget that allows us to make multiple selections from a `ListStore` using a `ListField`, and `DualListfield` (an implementation of `MultiField`) combines two `ListField` widgets into a single field widget allowing us to select from a "source"/"available" list into a "destination"/"selected" list.

```java
// set up form
final FormPanel formPanel = new FormPanel();
formPanel.setSize(350, 250);
formPanel.setLabelSeparator("");
formPanel.setHeaderVisible(false);
formPanel.setStyleAttribute("backgroundColor", "#fff");

// make RPC calls via a proxy
final RemoteGatewayAsync rpcService = (RemoteGatewayAsync) GWT.create(RemoteGateway.class);
RpcProxy<ListLoadResult<Customer>> rpcProxy = new RpcProxy<ListLoadResult<Customer>>() {
    @Override
    public void load(Object cfg, AsyncCallback<ListLoadResult<Customer>> callback) {
        rpcService.listCustomers((ListLoadConfig) cfg, callback);
    }
};

// set up store
ListLoader<ListLoadResult<ModelData>> loader = new BaseListLoader<ListLoadResult<ModelData>>(rpcProxy, new BeanModelReader());
ListStore<BeanModel> customerStore = new ListStore<BeanModel>(loader);

// set up list field
final ListField<BeanModel> customers = new ListField<BeanModel>();
customers.setHeight(65);
customers.setName("customers");
customers.setValueField("id");
customers.setDisplayField("name");
customers.setFieldLabel("Customers");
customers.setMessageTarget("tooltip");
customers.setStore(customerStore);
formPanel.add(customers, new FormData("70%"));

// set up dual list field
DualListField<BeanModel> winners = new DualListField<BeanModel>();
winners.setMode(Mode.INSERT);
winners.setFieldLabel("Winners");
winners.setStyleAttribute("marginTop", "8px");
```

```
        ListField<BeanModel> srcList = winners.getFromList();
        srcList.setDisplayField("name");
    srcList.setStore(new ListStore<BeanModel>(loader));

    ListField<BeanModel> destList = winners.getToList();
    destList.setDisplayField("name");
    destList.setStore(new ListStore<BeanModel>());
    formPanel.add(winners, new FormData("98%"));

    Button resetBtn = new Button("Reset", new SelectionListener<ButtonEve
    nt>() {
      @Override
      public void componentSelected(ButtonEvent evt) {
        formPanel.reset();
      }
    });
    formPanel.addButton(resetBtn);

    // load all stores bound to this loader.
    // the first listfield and the "source"
    // listfield within the dual listfield will be loaded
    loader.load();

    // serve it up
    GxtCookBk.getAppCenterPanel().add(formPanel);
```

How it works...

First, we create a form with `new FormPanel()` and set some optional configuration on it. As we'll be using a `ListField` which is tied to a `Store` as a `ComboBox`, we create `customerStore` `ListStore` with a `ListLoader` which is itself created using a `RpcProxy` object that calls the remote `listCustomers()` methods on our RPC service object. See *Appendix C, GWT-RPC*, for details on how GXT uses GWT RPC.

Next up, we create the customers `ListField` and configure its height (100 default), name, value field, display field, label, and most importantly its store is set to the just created `customerStore`. After adding the `ListField` to the form, we then create a `DualListField` and among other configurations we set its mode to `Mode.INSERT` which means selections will be inserted and not appended to the destination list.

Having created the `DualListField`, we obtain its internal lists (two `ListField`) with `getFromList()` and `getToList()` so that they can be configured with the appropriate display name and store.

Engaging Users with Forms and Data Input

There's more...

Although `ListField` resembles `ComboBox` in concept and configuration, data is not automatically loaded into `ListField` as it does in `ComboBox` when the trigger button is clicked. Hence the explicit call to `loader.load()` which will cause the store associated with the loader to be populated with data from the server, and from which we can make as many selections as possible!

In order to get the selections from `ToList` we need to access it through `DualListField` and access its store to get the `BeanModel` objects:

```
ListField<BeanModel> destList = winners.getToList();
List<BeanModel> models = destList.getStore().getModels();
```

Simple FileUpload and processing

Building web applications that can handle file uploads is nothing new, but how do we do it in AJAX without the default (and ugly) HTML file field, and most of all without the page refreshing. GXT, like most other advanced UI toolkits, provides a richer form widget for handling file uploads on the client; the `FileUploadField` is the one-stop widget for doing validated file uploads to the server from where we can use any of the many Java APIs for processing.

How to do it...

It turns out that file uploads are handled well and easy to set up too. All we need to do is use the `FileUploadField` widget and (optionally) prevent malicious files with a validator, and GXT will do the rest from the client-side perspective. There are several Java APIs for server-side file upload handling, but the Commons IO and Commons FileUpload APIs from the very generous folks at Apache Foundation will suffice.

```java
// basic form configuration
final FormPanel formPanel = new FormPanel();
formPanel.setSize(300, 120);
formPanel.setLabelSeparator("");
formPanel.setHeaderVisible(false);
formPanel.setLabelAlign(LabelAlign.TOP);
formPanel.setStyleAttribute("backgroundColor", "#fff");

// configure form for file upload
formPanel.setMethod(Method.POST);
formPanel.setEncoding(Encoding.MULTIPART);
formPanel.setAction(GWT.getModuleBaseURL() + "uploadgateway");

// set up file upload field
FileUploadField fileField = new FileUploadField();
fileField.setName("gxtupload");
fileField.setAllowBlank(false);
fileField.setFieldLabel("Upload File (csv, xls)");

// only accept certain files
fileField.setValidator(new Validator() {
  @Override
  public String validate(Field<?> field, String value) {
    value = value.toLowerCase();
        String result = "Invalid File Type, Pls Be Serious";
        if(value.endsWith(".csv") || value.endsWith(".xls")){
           result = null;
        }
        return result;
  }
});
formPanel.add(fileField, new FormData("90%"));

// reset button
Button resetBtn = new Button("Reset", new SelectionListener<ButtonEvent>() {
  @Override
```

```java
      public void componentSelected(ButtonEvent evt) {
         formPanel.reset();
      }
   });
   formPanel.addButton(resetBtn);

   // submit the form
   Button submitBtn = new Button("Upload It", new SelectionListener<Butt
onEvent>() {
      @Override
      public void componentSelected(ButtonEvent evt) {
         formPanel.mask("Gimme a minute ...");
         formPanel.submit();
      }
   });
   formPanel.addButton(submitBtn);

   // bind the submit button to the "validity" of the form
   FormButtonBinding btnBinder = new FormButtonBinding(formPanel);
   btnBinder.addButton(submitBtn);

   // reset and unmask the form
   // after file upload
   formPanel.addListener(Events.Submit, new Listener<FormEvent>() {
      public void handleEvent(FormEvent evt) {
         formPanel.reset();
         formPanel.unmask();
      };
   });

   // serve it up
   GxtCookBk.getAppCenterPanel().add(formPanel);
```

How it works...

As with every form-based solution, we begin by creating `FormPanel`. Our code then sets some (cosmetic) configurations on the initialized `formPanel` object. The section designated as `configure form for file upload` is where we configure `formPanel` to be able to send files as part of a HTTP POST request to a server.

First, we set the HTTP request method to POST with setMethod(Method.POST) and then we set submission encoding to Encoding.MULTIPART. Finally, we set the URL. The form will submit its entries using formPanel.setAction(GWT.getModuleBaseURL()+ "uploadgateway" will result in a string such as "gxtcookbook/uploadgateway", this is the relative URL that our form submission will go to.

Having configured our form, we can now add the upload field using new FileUploadField(). We initialize fileField and then set its name (very important), label, and make it mandatory by passing false to setAllowBlank().

Going further, we set a validator on fileField with the TextField inherited setValidator() method. The validator's validate() method will participate in the validation of this field (and its parent form) but after other simple validations (for example, setAllowBlank()) have passed. On this field, we use the validator to restrict uploads to CSV or XLS files, otherwise nothing stops the user from uploading a Trojan to your server!

After adding a standard reset button, we also add a submit button labeled "Upload It" and given a SelectionListener such that when clicked the form is submitted with formPanel.submit() after masking it (to prevent further interactions on it, like the user clicking reset or even trying to submit it again!) with formPanel.mask("…"). Since the page is not refreshing nor are we been redirected to another URL (the one used in formPanel.setAction()), we reset and unmask the form after the file has been successfully uploaded. This is done from within a listener attached to the submit event (Events.Submit) of the form.

The URL set on the form with its setAction() method maps to (with servlet mapping in the web.xml file of the web app) our FileUploadServlet class on the server side which uses the Commons FileUpload API (see *Appendix D, Jakarta Commons - FileUpload*) to obtain a list of FileItem objects which are handed over to the handlefile() method of our FileUploadServlet which writes the file to the disk.

Binding data into forms

Standard HTML forms are very easy to fill-out and submit with entries either sent as URL encoded name/value pairs using HTTP GET or sent "behind the scenes" as part of HTTP payload using HTTP POST. Entering data into forms and submitting them with RPC in GXT is however more involved; this is primarily because the fields within a FormPanel can have values that are not simple such as strings or numbers but object representations (ModelData, BeanModel) that themselves cannot ordinarily be sent as name/value pairs but as a part of a stream of serialization tokens within the very capable RPC transport system.

Engaging Users with Forms and Data Input

Once I understood this, I shifted my expectations from basic HTML forms to the robust binding capabilities built into GXT forms. Binding allows you to capture complex data structures represented as object models on the server (with the right interfaces) that can be transported, used and, validated on the client side and vice-versa.

How to do it...

GXT provides a `FormBinding` class which extends the `Bindings` class to provide a two-way binding between models (`ModelData`) and form fields. However, we may need to implement a custom `FieldBinding` for certain form fields.

```
// configure form
final FormPanel formPanel = new FormPanel();
...

// make RPC calls via a proxy
final RemoteGatewayAsync rpcService = (RemoteGatewayAsync) GWT.
create(RemoteGateway.class);
RpcProxy<ListLoadResult<Customer>> custRpcProxy = new RpcProxy<ListLoa
dResult<Customer>>() {
    @Override
    public void load(Object cfg, AsyncCallback<ListLoadResult<Custom
er>> callback) {
```

```
            rpcService.listCustomers((ListLoadConfig) cfg, callback);
        }
};

// set up customers combo
ListLoader<ListLoadResult<ModelData>> custLoader = new BaseListLoader<
ListLoadResult<ModelData>>(custRpcProxy, new BeanModelReader());
ListStore<BeanModel> custStore = new ListStore<BeanModel>(custLoader);

final ComboBox<BeanModel> customerCB = new ComboBox<BeanModel>();
customerCB.setName("customer");
...
formPanel.add(customerCB, new FormData("90%"));

// bind these fields
TextField<String> name = new TextField<String>();
name.setName("name");
...

NumberField age = new NumberField();
age.setName("age");

...
formPanel.add(age, new FormData("45%"));

RpcProxy<ListLoadResult<Review>> revRpcProxy = new RpcProxy<ListLoadRe
sult<Review>>() {
    @Override
    public void load(Object cfg, AsyncCallback<ListLoadResult<Review>>
callback) {
        rpcService.listReviews((ListLoadConfig) cfg, callback);
    }
};

BaseListLoader<ListLoadResult<ModelData>> revLoader = new BaseListLoad
er<ListLoadResult<ModelData>>(revRpcProxy, new BeanModelReader());
ListStore<BeanModel> revStore = new ListStore<BeanModel>(revLoader);


final ListField<BeanModel> reviews = new ListField<BeanModel>();
reviews.setName("reviews");
...
reviewSet.add(reviews, new FormData("85%"));
```

Engaging Users with Forms and Data Input

```java
final TextArea comments = new TextArea();
comments.setName("comments");
...
reviewSet.add(comments, new FormData("90%"));

formPanel.add(reviewSet, new FormData("100%"));

// binding setup
final FormBinding formBind = new FormBinding(formPanel, true);
formBind.removeFieldBinding( formBind.getBinding(customerCB) );

// do actual binding
customerCB.addSelectionChangedListener(new SelectionChangedListener<B
eanModel>() {
  @Override
  public void selectionChanged(SelectionChangedEvent<BeanModel> evt) {
    final BeanModel model = evt.getSelectedItem();
    if(model != null){
      Scheduler.get().scheduleDeferred(new Scheduler.
ScheduledCommand(){
        @Override
        public void execute() {
          formBind.bind(model);
        }
      });
    }
  }
});

// custom binding for reviews listfield
final BeanModelFactory reviewModelFtry;
reviewModelFtry = BeanModelLookup.get().getFactory(Review.class);

FieldBinding reviewBinder = new FieldBinding(reviews, reviews.
getName());
reviewBinder.setConverter(new Converter() {
  @Override
  public Object convertFieldValue(Object value) {
    if (value instanceof ModelData) {
          ModelData val = (ModelData) value;
          return val.get(reviews.getValueField());
      } else {
          return value;
      }
  }
  @Override
  public Object convertModelValue(Object value) {
    if(value instanceof Collection<?>){
      List<Review> valList = new ArrayList<Review>(
(Collection<Review>) value );
```

```java
        List<BeanModel> models = reviewModelFtry.createModel(valList);
        reviews.setSelection(models);

        BeanModel model = models.get(0);
        int pos = reviews.getStore().indexOf(model);
        ListView<BeanModel> listView = reviews.getListView();
        if(pos < listView.getElements().size()){
           El.fly(listView.getElement(pos)).scrollIntoView(listView.
getElement(), false);
        }
        return model;
      }
      return null;
   }
});
formBind.addFieldBinding(reviewBinder);

// show the comment for a review
reviews.addSelectionChangedListener(new SelectionChangedListener<Bean
Model>() {
  @Override
  public void selectionChanged(SelectionChangedEvent<BeanModel> evt) {
    BeanModel selection = evt.getSelectedItem();
    if(selection != null){
      Review review = (Review) evt.getSelectedItem().getBean();
        comments.setValue(review.getBody());
    }
  }
});
reviews.getStore().getLoader().load();

// basic reset button
Button resetBtn = new Button("Reset", new SelectionListener<ButtonEve
nt>() {
  @Override
  public void componentSelected(ButtonEvent evt) {
    formPanel.reset();
  }
});
formPanel.addButton(resetBtn);

// send bound model down the wire
Button submitBtn = new Button("Submit", new SelectionListener<ButtonE
vent>() {
  @Override
  public void componentSelected(ButtonEvent evt) {
    BeanModel model = (BeanModel) formBind.getModel();
    Customer cust = (Customer) model.getBean();
```

Engaging Users with Forms and Data Input

```
      final MessageBox box = MessageBox.wait("Progress","Saving
Customer Please Wait...", "Saving...");
    rpcService.saveCustomer(cust, new AsyncCallback<Void>() {
      @Override
      public void onFailure(Throwable caught) {
        box.close();
        Info.display("Error", caught.getMessage());
      }

      @Override
      public void onSuccess(Void result) {
        box.close();
        Info.display("Message", "Saved!");
      }
    });
  }
});
formPanel.addButton(submitBtn);

// only submit form after validating
FormButtonBinding btnBinder = new FormButtonBinding(formPanel);
btnBinder.addButton(submitBtn);

// serve it up
GxtCookBk.getAppCenterPanel().add(formPanel);
```

How it works...

This example allows us to select a customer and have the name, age, and review (which is itself a first class JavaBeans object) show up in the appropriate fields (based on how they are named) for viewing or editing.

With some programming we can even go deep into the object graph of the bound `Customer` bean such that we are able to display the comment from a `Review` made by the `Customer` though the comment is not a bound property/field of `Customer`.

Our code begins by creating and configuring (although cosmetic) a `FormPanel` after which we initialize our RPC service using the `GWT.create()` factory. We then invoke the remote `listCustomers()` method the RPC service from within an `RpcProxy` object used to create a `ListLoader` and then the `custStore` `ListStore`. `custStore` is then used to create a text field only `ComboBox` (we hide the `trigger` component) which is used primarily to select the `Customer` object that is bound to the form. Therefore, the section designated by the comment `bind these fields` is where we create the `Field` objects we really want to bind.

First, we create a standard GXT `TextField` for the `name` property in the `Customer` object. Thus, the field is given the correct name by passing `"name"` to `setName()`. After adding it to the form, we also use a `NumberField` named `"age"` with `setName("age")` to bind to the `age` property of `Customer`.

Recall from *Appendix C, GWT-RPC*, that the `Serializable Customer` object has a `reviews` property that is a set of review objects. So, we create `revRpcProxy`, `revLoader`, and `revStore` with which we then create a `ListField` (instead of `ComboBox` so we can demonstrate custom `Binding`) to bind to the `reviews` property in `Customer`. Since `Review` implements `BeanModelTag`, our `ListField` can be defined and instantiated using `ListFiled<ModelData>` or `ListField<BeanModel>` and then its name set to `"reviews"` with `setName()`.

Finally, we add comments `TextArea` to the form, named as `"comments"` even though there is no `comments` property in `Customer`; the intention is to programmatically populate this field from the `Review` of a selected `Customer`. The binding setup is done by creating `formBind` with `new FormBinding(formPanel, true)`, meaning we want to bind the fields in `formPanel` automatically to a bean, but since our first `ComboBox` field is not part of the bind operation we exclude it with the line following the instantiation of `formBind` which is `formBind.removeFieldBinding(formBind.getBinding(customerCB))`.

Next, we demonstrate a custom binding for the reviews `ListField` by creating a `FieldBinding` object giving it the field we want to bind and its name (the binding link) after which we set up a `Converter` on the custom binding, that will be responsible for converting data/value between the `ListField` and the bound `BeanModel`. Within the converter, the `convertFieldValue(Object value)` method is used to convert the field's value before being set on the bound model object while the `convertModelValue(Object value)` converts the model's value before it is set on the field. Therefore, this is the method used to adapt the data that arrives from the server before it is shown on `ListField`.

In the section titled `do actual binding`, we attach a listener to the `Customer` `ComboBox` so that when you make a selection on it we extract the `BeanModel` of the selected `Customer` by calling `getSelectedItem()` on the `SelectionChangedEvent` object and then apply the model, or bind the model (if you prefer) to the form fields, having the same name as properties within the `BeanModel`. This is done on the `FormBinding` object with `formBind.bind(model)`.

Since we have the `comment` property not on the `Customer` bean but within the `review` property (a bean too) of the `Customer` bean, we can't expect automatic two-way binding for the comments `TextArea` in the form; so we do a "manual" bean-to-field binding for the `TextArea` under the section `show the comment for a review` by adding `SelectionChangedListener` to `reviews` and correctly setting its value to the body of the `Review` using `comments.setValue(review.getBody)`.

Engaging Users with Forms and Data Input

After manually loading the review's `Store` (we have to) and adding a standard reset button to `FormPanel`, we add a submit button within which we retrieve the bound `BeanModel` containing whatever edits/changes entered into the form fields (except the comments `TextArea` of course) and from it we get the actual mutated `Customer` object and invoke our remote `saveCustomer()` method with it to persist the changes!

To ensure that the form is really validated, we use a `FormButtonBinding` on the `submitBtn` Button so that it is only enabled when you've filled in data correctly.

We use a progress bar that will be displayed while the save action is being performed. We close the progress bar when our GWT RPC call returns (in the callback methods `Onsuccess()` and `OnFailure()`).

Building a better slider field

The GXT `SliderField` is beautiful and fun to use, it is passed a `Slider` and adapts it as an input widget for `FormPanel`. There is, however, one twist to its API that I think inhibits its use and it's the fact the you have very little control over the formatting of the tooltip message shown as you drag the slider's thumb back and forth.

As of GXT 2.2.3 you can only configure the tip message by setting a single string (one size fits all) with the `slider.setMessage()` method call; for example, `slider.setMessage("{0} inches tall")`. With this setup, you get the tooltip formatted like `"1 inches tall"`, `"2 inches tall"`, `"3 inches tall"`, and so on. Internally, `Slider` uses `Format.substitute(getMessage(), value)` such that the value of the slider is substituted into what has been set with `setMessage()` method.

If we have a `Slider` configured to slide from 1 to 5 and need to use it to implement, say, a rating control such that the value 1 could mean *Poor* and the value 5 could mean *Excellent*. The current API prevents us from doing that except with a subclass of `Slider`. Having to subclass `Slider` just to vary the algorithm for formatting its tooltip is not brilliant.

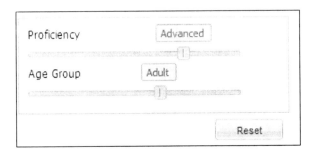

How to do it...

We will introduce a `TipRenderer` interface within our new `Slider` extension such that client code can implement this interface to vary the rendering of the `Slider value` tooltip.

```
// create Slider extension
public class XSlider extends Slider {

  public interface TipRenderer{
    String format(Slider slider, int value);
  }

   protected TipRenderer tipRenderer;

  public XSlider() {
    super();

    tipRenderer = new TipRenderer() {
      @Override
      public String format(Slider slider, int value) {
        return Format.substitute(getMessage(), value);
      }
    };
  }

  public void setTipRenderer(TipRenderer renderer){
    tipRenderer = renderer;
  }

  protected String onFormatValue(int value) {
    return tipRenderer.format(this, value);
  }
}


// configure form
final FormPanel formPanel = new FormPanel();
formPanel.setSize(300, 140);
formPanel.setLabelSeparator("");
formPanel.setHeaderVisible(false);
formPanel.setLabelAlign(LabelAlign.TOP);
formPanel.setStyleAttribute("backgroundColor", "#fff");
```

```
// single value detection
XSlider slider = new XSlider();
slider.setMinValue(1);
slider.setMaxValue(5);
slider.setValue(1);
slider.setIncrement(1);
slider.setTipRenderer(new XSlider.TipRenderer() {
  @Override
  public String format(Slider slider, int value) {
    String tip = "";
    switch (value) {
    case 1:
      tip = "Novice";
      break;
    case 2:
      tip = "Beginner";
      break;
    case 3:
      tip = "Intermediate";
      break;
    case 4:
      tip = "Advanced";
      break;
    case 5:
      tip = "Expert";
      break;
    }
    return tip;
  }
});

SliderField sliderField = new SliderField(slider);
sliderField.setName("skill_level");
sliderField.setFieldLabel("Proficiency");
formPanel.add(sliderField, new FormData("85%"));

// range value detection
slider = new XSlider();
slider.setMinValue(1);
slider.setMaxValue(50);
slider.setValue(1);
slider.setIncrement(1);
slider.setTipRenderer(new XSlider.TipRenderer() {
  @Override
```

```
    public String format(Slider slider, int value) {
      String tip = "";
      if(value >= 1 && value <= 12){
        tip = "Minor";
      } else if(value >= 13 && value <= 19){
        tip = "Teen";
      } else if(value >= 20 && value <= 30){
        tip = "Youth";
      } else if(value >= 31 && value <= 45){
        tip = "Adult";
      } else if(value >= 46){
        tip = "Mature Adult";
      }
      return tip;
    }
  });

  sliderField = new SliderField(slider);
  sliderField.setName("agegroup");
  sliderField.setFieldLabel("Age Group");
  formPanel.add(sliderField, new FormData("85%"));

  // basic reset button
  Button resetBtn = new Button("Reset", new SelectionListener<ButtonEve
  nt>() {
    @Override
    public void componentSelected(ButtonEvent evt) {
      formPanel.reset();
    }
  });
  formPanel.addButton(resetBtn);

  // serve it up
  GxtCookBk.getAppCenterPanel().add(formPanel);
```

How it works...

We needed a Slider API that can allow client code to implement the formatting algorithm in whatever way they please with the help of the **Strategy Pattern**. We introduced a TipRenderer interface with a format(Slider slider, int value) method which will return a string. The XSlider class now has a default TipRenderer that is implemented with the Format.substitute(getMessage(), value) invocation used in the current GXT Slider code, giving us a backwards compatible but flexible API.

Engaging Users with Forms and Data Input

In the examples shown in the code, the first creates an `XSlider` and configures it to slide from 1 through to 5 in increments of 1, and then we use the new `setTipRenderer()` method to configure it to render `Novice` if the value is 1, `Beginner` for 2, `Intermediate` for 3, `Advanced` for 4, and `Expert` for 5. Imagine doing this with the former `Slider.setMessage()` method?

In the second example, we show the flexibility of our Strategy Pattern implementation by trying to render a particular message for a range of values, so if the value of the `Slider` is between 13 and 19 the tooltip message will be `"Teen"` and it will be `"Mature Adult"` for a value equal to or greater than 46.

There's more...

Although our custom approach solves the rendering problems of the current GXT `Slider` implementation, it can be further simplified especially when dealing with ranges (like the second slider example). I would welcome a simplification of the `Slider` implementation in the next GXT version.

Here is my suggestions for simplifying the `Slider`:

```
Slider slider = new Slider();

slider.setRangeMessage(0, 12, "Minor");
slider.setRangeMessage(13, 19, "Teen");
slider.setRangeMessage(20, 30, "Youth");
slider.setRangeMessage(31, 45, "Adult");
slider.setRangeMessage(Slider.MORETHAN, 45, "Mature Adult");
```

This is not only simpler to code and easier on the eye (readable), but cuts the code drastically, requiring only five lines instead of 18 lines using `TipRenderer` (as it is right now, can be re-factored) to achieve the same effect.

6
Data Hierarchy with Trees

In this chapter we will cover:

- Building a basic tree
- Custom node labels
- Decorating trees with icons
- Augmenting trees with `ContextMenu`
- Building trees with checkbox selection
- Building asynchronous trees
- Custom sorting within trees

Introduction

A hierarchical data model is a data model in which the data is organized into a tree-like structure. The structure allows the representation of information using parent/child relationships; each parent can have many children but each child only has one parent. A tree structure is a way of representing the hierarchical nature of a structure in a graphical form. It is named a tree structure, because the classic representation resembles that of a tree, even though the chart is generally upside-down, compared to an actual tree, with the *root* at the top and the *leaves* at the bottom. A tree structure is conceptual and appears in several forms.

Data Hierarchy with Trees

The following diagram shows an example of a tree structure:

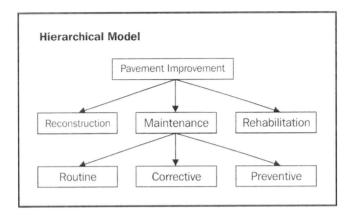

The following recipes will refer to terms belonging to the tree data structure.

If you are not familiar with the tree data structure or need to refresh your memory, please refer to the definition of the tree data structure at http://en.wikipedia.org/wiki/Tree_(data_structure).

Building a basic tree

The `TreePanel` class provides the API for working with trees in GXT, and it works much the same way as other store-based components. Once its `TreeStore` instance is populated with data and the `TreePanel` instance is attached to the DOM, we are ready to view the hierarchy of nodes that can either be a *parent* or a *leaf*.

The hierarchy of nodes is rendered as highlightable (setTrackMouseOver()) and clickable items, labelled either by passing a property name in the model (from the TreeStore instance) to the setDisplayProperty() method of the tree, or by passing a ModelStringProvider implementation to the setLabelProvider() method of the tree.

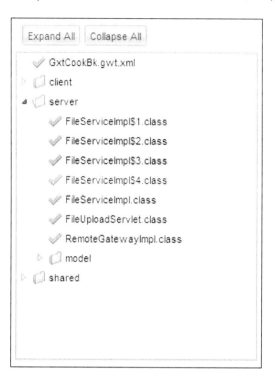

How to do it...

Besides the other things to enhance the comprehension of the code, we basically just have to create a TreeStore instance that is populated either locally with treeStore.add(), or automatically from remote data using an instance of the TreeLoader class. Once the store is set up and attached to the tree, we use setDisplayProperty() to determine how the nodes are labeled, and then we render the tree.

To perform this recipe, use the following code:

```
// Just for fun
final ButtonBar btnBar = new ButtonBar();
btnBar.disable();
GxtCookBk.getAppCenterPanel().add(btnBar, new FlowData(5));

// set up the store and tree
   final TreeStore<FileModel> store = new TreeStore<FileModel>();
```

Data Hierarchy with Trees

```java
    final TreePanel<FileModel> tree = new TreePanel<FileModel>(store);
    tree.setSize(265, 330);
    tree.setBorders(true);
    tree.setDisplayProperty("name");

// set leaf icon
Icons ICONS = GWT.create(Icons.class);
tree.getStyle().setLeafIcon(ICONS.tick());

// complete the fun buttons
Button expandBtn = new Button("Expand All", new SelectionListener<ButtonEvent>() {
  @Override
  public void componentSelected(ButtonEvent ce) {
    tree.expandAll();
  }
});
btnBar.add(expandBtn);

Button collapseBtn = new Button("Collapse All", new SelectionListener<ButtonEvent>() {
  @Override
  public void componentSelected(ButtonEvent ce) {
    tree.collapseAll();
  }
});
btnBar.add(collapseBtn);

// Populate tree from RPC call
final FileServiceAsync fileService = (FileServiceAsync) GWT.create(FileService.class);
AsyncCallback<List<FileModel>> callback = new AsyncCallback<List<FileModel>>() {

  @Override
  public void onSuccess(final List<FileModel> result) {
    Scheduler.get().scheduleDeferred(new ScheduledCommand() {
      @Override
      public void execute() {
        store.add(result, true);
        tree.unmask();
        btnBar.enable();
      }
    });
  }
```

```
      @Override
      public void onFailure(Throwable caught) {
        Info.display("Error", "Cannot Fetch Data for Tree!");
      }
    };

    tree.mask("Busy ...");
    fileService.getAll(null, callback);

    /*
     * GxtCookbk is the application's entry point class.
     * We access its main content panel using the
     * static GxtCookBk.getAppCenterPanel() call.
     * We add our tree to the main content panel.
     */
    GxtCookBk.getAppCenterPanel().add(tree);
```

How it works...

We create and render an initially disabled `ButtonBar` object, which will consist of a collapse and an expand button for collapsing/expanding all nodes in the `TreePanel` object.

Next, we create a `TreeStore` instance, parameterized with our custom `FileModel` class, which is just a `BaseTreeModel` (a `ModelData` class for trees) class extension that has `name` and `path` properties, and of course, getter/setter methods for them. Thus, the tree is intended to be used to show files in a directory. The `FileModel` class will be rendered as *leaf* nodes on the tree, while its `FolderModel` subclass will represent *parents* on the tree.

A parameterized `TreePanel` instance is then created, using the earlier `store` object, and then we set the display property of the tree nodes using `tree.setDisplayProperty("name")`, meaning the `name` property of each `FileModel` instance in the `store` object is what we want to display as nodes in the tree.

For the sake of beauty, we set the default leaf node icon to `ICONS.tick()`, using `tree.getstyle().setLeafIcon()`, but for demonstration, we add `expandBtn` and `collapseBtn` button instances to the `ButtonBar` object created earlier. Both of these are given `SelectionListener` handlers, which invoke `tree.expandAll()` and `tree.collapseAll()`, respectively.

After instantiating our clone of the GXT 2.2.3 `FileService` sample and masking the `TreePanel` instance with `tree.mask("Busy ..")`, we invoke the remote `getAll()` method, which we added to the `FileService` sample and implemented in the `FileServiceImpl` implementation, to get the contents within the `com/gxtcookbook/code` directory of our project codebase. The remote invocation is given an `AsynCallback` object, whose `onSuccess()` override adds the returned `FileModel` objects to the store, unmasks the tree, and enables the `ButtonBar` object.

Data Hierarchy with Trees

Note that, in the `onSuccess` callback, we add the returned `FileModel` objects to the store as a deferred command, by using GWT's `Scheduler` class. The deferred command mechanism in GWT is used to defer a code block, to be executed only after other browser event handlers have executed. We use this mechanism throughout the tree recipes, as rendering the tree with our `FileModel` objects could potentially be a heavy operation, and we want to give other event handlers a chance to run before executing this code block (remember that JavaScript is single-threaded).

Custom node labels

We can specify the node labels of a `TreePanel` instance by properly using its `setDisplayProperty()` method, giving it the name of a property from the `TreeStore` instance.. However, we may need to format this value (lowercase, uppercase, ellipsis, and so on), derive it from computation, or even display it from different properties of the model at different situations; this is where the `ModelStringProvider` interface comes to the rescue.

An implementation of the `ModelStringProvider` interface can be passed to the `TreePanel` class by using its `setLabelProvider()` method, and it will be used to determine how the label of nodes in the tree have been obtained.

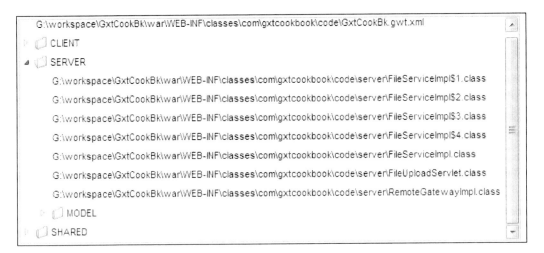

How to do it...

Create a `ModelStringProvider` implementation and pass it to the `TreePanel` instance using its `setLabelProvider()` method and you are done!

```
// set up the store and tree
  final TreeStore<FileModel> store = new TreeStore<FileModel>();

  final TreePanel<FileModel> tree = new TreePanel<FileModel>(store);
  tree.setSize(575, 250);
  tree.setBorders(true);
  tree.setLabelProvider(new ModelStringProvider<FileModel>() {

    @Override
    public String getStringValue(FileModel model, String property) {
      String label = model.getName().toUpperCase();
      if(model.isLeaf()){
        label = model.getPath();
      }
      return label;
    }
  });

  // Populate tree from RPC call
final FileServiceAsync fileService = (FileServiceAsync) GWT.create(FileService.class);
AsyncCallback<List<FileModel>> callback = new AsyncCallback<List<FileModel>>() {

  @Override
  public void onSuccess(final List<FileModel> result) {
    Scheduler.get().scheduleDeferred(new ScheduledCommand() {
      @Override
      public void execute() {
        store.add(result, true);
        tree.unmask();
      }
    });
  }

  @Override
  public void onFailure(Throwable caught) {
    Info.display("Error", "Cannot Fetch Data for Tree!");
  }
};
```

```
tree.mask("Busy ...");
fileService.getAll(null, callback);

/*
 * GxtCookbk is the application's entry point class.
 * We access its main content panel using the
 * static GxtCookBk.getAppCenterPanel() call.
 * We add our tree to the main content panel.
 */
GxtCookBk.getAppCenterPanel().add(tree);
```

How it works...

We create a `TreePanel` instance with a `TreeStore` instance, both parameterized with `FileModel` object, and then we use `tree.setLabelProvider()` to set a `ModelStringProvider<FileModel>` instance on the tree.

Within the `getStringValue()` method of the `ModelStringProvider` interface, we construct the label from the name property of the model parameter (`model.getName()`), formatted as uppercase, and if we are dealing with a leaf node (`model.isLeaf()`), we'll use its path property (`model.getPath()`) instead.

Therefore, the nodes in `TreePanel` will have different label formatting; leaf nodes will show the file path of the `FileModel` object, while parent nodes (directory) will be uppercase.

Finally the tree nodes are obtained from a RPC call on our clone of the GXT 2.2.3 `FileService/FileServiceAsync/FileServiceImpl` sample API, using `fileService.getAll(null, callback)` with the `onSuccess()` method of the `callback` instance adding the returned `FileModel` objects to the `TreeStore` instance.

Decorating trees with icons

The default `TreePanel` implementation only renders icons (arrow and folder) on parent nodes and can use a single icon on all child nodes, with a call to its `getStyle().setLeafIcon()` method, which takes icons as `AbstractImagePrototype` objects.

However, we can use a `ModelIconProvider` implementation to set any `AbstractImagePrototype` object (icon) on any node or type/group of nodes within a `TreePanel` instance, and we can do this with information around or within the model object of that particular node.

Consider a `TreePanel` instance of files, such that we have an icon for each mime-type the node represents, be it `.gif`, `.png`, `.jpg`, `.pdf`, `.txt`, `.class`, and so on.

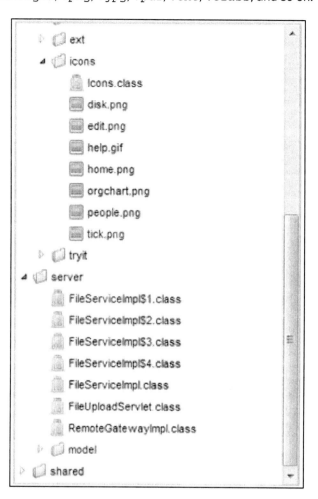

How to do it...

Create a `ModelIconProvider` implementation and pass it to the `TreePanel` instance by using its `setIconProvider()` method and you are done!

```
// set up the store and tree
  final TreeStore<FileModel> store = new TreeStore<FileModel>();

  final TreePanel<FileModel> tree = new TreePanel<FileModel>(store);
  tree.setSize(285, 450);
  tree.setBorders(true);
  tree.setDisplayProperty("name");
```

```java
// set icons
final Icons ICONS = GWT.create(Icons.class);
tree.setIconProvider(new ModelIconProvider<FileModel>() {

  @Override
  public AbstractImagePrototype getIcon(FileModel model) {
    if(model.isLeaf()){
      String fileName = model.getName();
    // get the file extension.
      String ext = fileName.substring(fileName.lastIndexOf(".") + 1);
    // set the icon type according to the
    // file extension.
      if ("class".equals(ext)){
        return ICONS.jar();
      } else if ("js".equals(ext)){
        return ICONS.json();
      } else if ("css".equals(ext)){
        return ICONS.css();
      } else if ("gif".equals(ext) || "png".equals(ext) || "jpg".equals(ext) || "jpeg".equals(ext)){
        return ICONS.image();
      }
    }
    return null;
  }
});

// Make RPC call
final FileServiceAsync fileService = (FileServiceAsync) GWT.create(FileService.class);
AsyncCallback<List<FileModel>> callback = new AsyncCallback<List<FileModel>>() {

  @Override
  public void onSuccess(List<FileModel> result) {
    store.add(result, true);
    tree.unmask();
  }

  @Override
  public void onFailure(Throwable caught) {
    Info.display("Error", "Cannot Fetch Data for Tree!");
  }
};

tree.mask("Busy ...");
fileService.getAll(null, callback);

GxtCookBk.getAppCenterPanel().add(tree);
```

Chapter 6

How it works...

First, we create a `TreeStore` instance and then use it to instantiate the `TreePanel` class, whose display property is set to `name`, with a call to `tree.setDisplayProperty("name")`.

Next, we give the tree an icon provider by passing a `ModelIconProvider<FileModel>` object to the tree by using `tree.setIconProvider()`. Our simple icon provider is implemented to get the extension of the file name of leaf nodes and then return an appropriate icon. We discuss the `Icons` class in *Appendix B*, when explaining how to integrate icons into GXT. The `TreeStore` instance bound to our `TreePanel` instance is then populated by adding the returned `FileModel` objects in the `onSuccess()` method of the `AsyncCallback` call given to the `getAll()` remote call on the `fileService` object that we instantiated from our clone of the GXT `FileService/FileServiceAsync/FileServiceImpl` sample by using the `GWT.create()` factory.

Augmenting trees with ContextMenu

Context menus are used to provide context-specific menu options on GXT `Component` objects, and since `TreePanel` is derived from `BoxComponent`, which is of course a descendant of `Component`, we can leverage the `Component` API to provide context menus for `TreePanel`, allowing users to right-click on a tree node to see what more they can do with that node, apart from just staring at it.

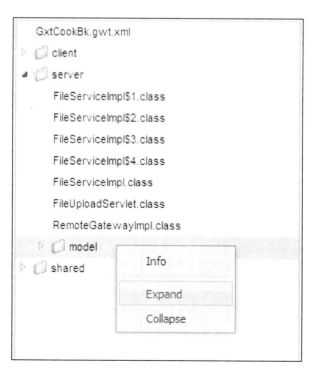

149

Data Hierarchy with Trees

How to do it...

Simply create a `Menu` object and add `MenuItem` objects to the `Menu` object; then, set the `Menu` object as a context menu on the `TreePanel` instance by using its `setContextMenu()` method.

```java
// set up the store and tree
  final TreeStore<FileModel> store = new TreeStore<FileModel>();

  // set up tree
final TreePanel<FileModel> tree = new TreePanel<FileModel>(store);
tree.setSize(285, 450);
tree.setBorders(true);
tree.setDisplayProperty("name");

// set up context menu
Menu ctxMenu = new Menu();
tree.setContextMenu(ctxMenu);

MenuItem info = new MenuItem("Info", new
SelectionListener<MenuEvent>() {
  @Override
  public void componentSelected(MenuEvent evt) {
    FileModel node = tree.getSelectionModel().getSelectedItem();
    if(node.isLeaf()){
      Info.display("Tree Node Info", "File is at " + node.getPath());
    } else {
      Info.display("Tree Node Info", "Node has " + node.
getChildCount() + " children");
    }
  }
});
ctxMenu.add(info);
ctxMenu.add(new SeparatorMenuItem());

// items in the menu
final MenuItem expand = new MenuItem("Expand", new
SelectionListener<MenuEvent>() {
  @Override
  public void componentSelected(MenuEvent evt) {
    FileModel node = tree.getSelectionModel().getSelectedItem();
    if(!node.isLeaf()){
      tree.setExpanded(node, true, true);
    }
  }
});
ctxMenu.add(expand);
```

```java
      final MenuItem collapse = new MenuItem("Collapse", new
SelectionListener<MenuEvent>() {
        @Override
        public void componentSelected(MenuEvent evt) {
          FileModel node = tree.getSelectionModel().getSelectedItem();
          if(!node.isLeaf()){
            tree.setExpanded(node, false, true);
          }
        }
      });
      ctxMenu.add(collapse);

      // let's be smart with the menu
      ctxMenu.addListener(Events.BeforeShow, new Listener<MenuEvent>() {
        @Override
        public void handleEvent(MenuEvent evt) {
          FileModel node = tree.getSelectionModel().getSelectedItem();
          expand.setEnabled(!node.isLeaf());
          collapse.setEnabled(!node.isLeaf());
        }
      });

      // Populate tree from RPC call
      final FileServiceAsync fileService = (FileServiceAsync) GWT.
      create(FileService.class);
      AsyncCallback<List<FileModel>> callback = new AsyncCallback<List<File
      Model>>() {

        @Override
        public void onSuccess(final List<FileModel> result) {
          Scheduler.get().scheduleDeferred(new ScheduledCommand() {
            @Override
            public void execute() {
              store.add(result, true);
              tree.unmask();
            }
          });
        }

        @Override
        public void onFailure(Throwable caught) {
          Info.display("Error", "Cannot Fetch Data for Tree!");
        }
      };
```

Data Hierarchy with Trees

```
tree.mask("Busy ...");
fileService.getAll(null, callback);

/*
 * GxtCookbk is the application's entry-point class.
 * We access its main content panel using the
 * static GxtCookBk.getAppCenterPanel() call.
 * We add our tree to the main content panel.
 */
GxtCookBk.getAppCenterPanel().add(tree);
```

How it works...

We begin by creating a `TreeStore` instance and then instantiating the `TreePanel` class with it, which we also configure to display the `name` property of its bound `FileModel` instance as the label of nodes, using `tree.setDisplayProperty("name")`.

Next, we create a GXT `Menu` object with `new Menu()` and set it as a context menu for the `TreePanel` instance by using `tree.setContextMenu(ctxMenu)`, and then we add three `MenuItem` objects to the context menu (`ctxMenu`) we've created.

The first `MenuItem` object (`info`) is used to display an info message when clicked. It will display the path of the `FileModel` instance if it is clicked for a leaf node, otherwise it will display the number of children the node has. The `expand MenuItem` item is used to expand the clicked node if it is not a leaf node, while the `collapse MenuItem` item is used to collapse the clicked node if it is also not a leaf node.

We can also make the `ctxMenu` instance a little smarter than a dummy `Menu` object by adding a `BeforeShow Listener` instance to it, from where we disable the `expand` and `collapse MenuItem` items from `Menu`, if the tree node at stake is a leaf node, because it won't have any children and therefore nothing to expand/collapse.

Finally, our `TreeStore` instance is populated from a call to the remote `getAll()` method introduced in our clone of the GXT `FileService/FileServiceAsync/FileServiceImpl` sample that returns the files under our `con/gxtcookbook/code` code base.

Building trees with checkbox selection

Sometimes you need more than to just be able to navigate a hierarchy of nodes in a tree, say maybe to select one or more nodes. By default, the `TreePanel` object allows selection of only a single node at a time; we can configure it to allow multiple node selection by passing `SelectionMode.MULTI` to `tree.getSelectionModel().SetSelectionMode()`.

Chapter 6

Here, we want to use the more flexible and more user-friendly checkbox selection that renders tree nodes with a checkbox, allowing the user to check/uncheck as many nodes as possible at any time, depending on the combination of the values given to `tree.setCheckNodes()` and `tree.setCheckStyle()`. The following screenshot displays a tree with a checkbox for each node:

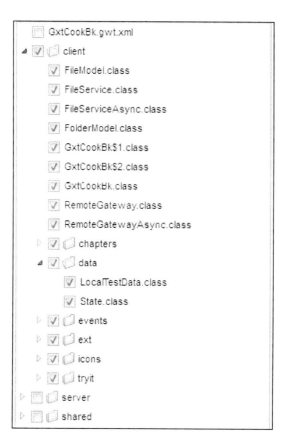

How to do it...

First, enable checkbox selection on the `TreePanel` object by passing `true` to its `setCheckable()` method, and then use its `setCheckNodes()` and `setCheckStyle()` methods to determine the behavior of node checking in the `TreePanel` object.

```
// set up the store and tree
   final TreeStore<FileModel> store = new TreeStore<FileModel>();

   final TreePanel<FileModel> tree = new TreePanel<FileModel>(store);
   tree.setSize(285, 450);
   tree.setBorders(true);
   tree.setDisplayProperty("name");
```

```
// enable checkbox selection
tree.setCheckable(true);
tree.setCheckNodes(CheckNodes.BOTH);
tree.setCheckStyle(CheckCascade.CHILDREN);

// Populate tree from RPC call
final FileServiceAsync fileService = (FileServiceAsync) GWT.
create(FileService.class);
AsyncCallback<List<FileModel>> callback = new AsyncCallback<List<File
Model>>() {

  @Override
  public void onSuccess(final List<FileModel> result) {
    Scheduler.get().scheduleDeferred(new ScheduledCommand() {
      @Override
      public void execute() {
        store.add(result, true);
        tree.unmask();
      }
    });
  }

  @Override
  public void onFailure(Throwable caught) {
    Info.display("Error", "Cannot Fetch Data for Tree!");
  }
};

tree.mask("Busy ...");
fileService.getAll(null, callback);

/*
 * GxtCookbk is the application's entry point class.
 * We access its main content panel using the
 * static GxtCookBk.getAppCenterPanel() call.
 * We add our tree to the main content panel.
 */
GxtCookBk.getAppCenterPanel().add(tree);
```

How it works...

As usual, we create a `TreeStore` instance with which we instantiate the `TreePanel` class. We also set the label of nodes in the tree to the name property of the `FileModel` objects bound to the `TreeStore` instance by using `tree.setDisplayProperty ("name")`.

The `enable checkbox selection` comment begins the tree's checkbox selection configuration section in the code. First, we make the `TreePanel` instance checkable with `tree.setCheckable(true)`, and then we allow both parent and leaf nodes to be checkable by passing `CheckNodes.BOTH` to `tree.setCheckNodes()`, which can also take `CheckNodes.LEAF` (checkboxes for only leaf nodes) and `CheckNodes.PARENT` (checkboxes for only parent nodes).

We also use `tree.setCheckStyle(CheckCascade.CHILDREN)` to configure checks on a tree node, to cascade to all its children instead of cascading only to parent nodes (`CheckCascade.PARENT`) or not cascading at all (`CheckCascade.NONE`).

All that is left now is to populate the instance of the `TreeStore` class by invoking the remote `getAll()` method on `fileService`, which is created with `GWT.create()` (from our clone of GXT 2.2.3 sample of `FileServiceAsync/FileServiceImpl` RPC API).

We can retrieve the list of selected `FileModel` objects by calling the `getCheckedSelection()` method of the `TreePanel` class. This method returns a `List<FileModel>` object that we can use to iterate through to process the selected `FileModel` objects.

Building asynchronous trees

If you are like me and have been following the recipes in this chapter (and probably the entire book) in sequence, you will have noticed that, in the previous recipes, we were loading the `TreeStore` instance bound to the `TreePanel` instance with a huge dataset, all at once. This is not always practical and may not be what you want. You may want to only load the nodes within a given parent first, and then load children of those nodes from the server on demand—usually when the node is clicked.

Data Hierarchy with Trees

It turns out that building this sort of asynchrony into `TreePanel` is so trivial that we don't have to do anything special besides:

- Loading data into the `TreeStore` instance from a `TreeLoader` instance that fetches the actual data using an `RpcProxy` instance
- Making sure we do not turn on automatic loading of child nodes on the `TreePanel` instance

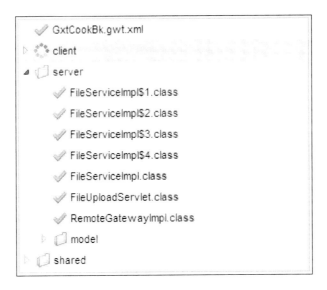

How to do it...

Simply create a `TreePanel` instance with a `TreeStore` instance that has a `TreeLoader` instance. The `TreeLoader` instance should do its data fetching with an `RpcProxy` instance, and make sure `tree.setAutoLoad()` is left untouched (as default) or called with `false`.

```
// Make RPC call via a proxy
final FileServiceAsync fileService = (FileServiceAsync) GWT.
create(FileService.class);
RpcProxy<List<FileModel>> rpcProxy = new RpcProxy<List<FileModel>>() {
  @Override
  public void load(Object cfg,
      AsyncCallback<List<FileModel>> callback) {
    fileService.getFolderChildren((FileModel) cfg, callback);
  }
};
```

```
// set up the store
TreeLoader<FileModel> loader = new BaseTreeLoader<FileModel>(
    rpcProxy) {
  @Override
  public boolean hasChildren(FileModel parent) {
    return parent instanceof FolderModel;
  }
};
TreeStore<FileModel> store = new TreeStore<FileModel>(loader);

final TreePanel<FileModel> tree = new TreePanel<FileModel>(
    store);
tree.setSize(300, 255);
tree.setBorders(true);
tree.setDisplayProperty("name");

// don't use this line
// it will automatically load all child nodes
// tree.setAutoLoad(true);

/*
 * GxtCookbk is the application's entry-point class.
 * We access its main content panel using the
 * static GxtCookBk.getAppCenterPanel() call.
 * We add our tree to the main content panel.
 */
GxtCookBk.getAppCenterPanel().add(tree);
```

How it works...

The code begins by creating a `fileService` instance from our clone of the GXT sample `FileService` class, using `GWT.create()`, and then invoking its remote `getFolderChildren()` method from the `load()` method of an `RpcProxy` object.

Next, we instantiate a `TreeLoader` object, giving it the `RpcProxy` object we created before and overriding its `hasChildren()` method to return `true` (yes, it has children), if the node in question is a `FolderModel` instance, which is the class our `FileService` implementation (`FileServicerImpl`) uses to represent folders.

We then create a `TreeStore` instance from the `TreeLoader` instance, and a `TreePanel` instance using the `TreeStore` instance. The `TreePanel` instance is also configured to display the `name` property of its store's bound models as the label for nodes.

The `TreePanel` instance will only display the first set of direct children when it gets attached to the DOM; the children of a node are only requested for and displayed when the node is clicked on, giving us an asynchronous load-demand feature on the `TreePanel` instance.

Data Hierarchy with Trees

Custom sorting within trees

The default lexicographic schemes employed when sorting strings (the `display` property) may not suffice in your `TreePanel` instance. Consider having a tree of nodes representing college students; you may want to sort based on other things besides the node's label—which would of course be the names of the students—such as sorting by their age, year of admission, number of extracurricular activities, and CGPA.

This sort of behavior, which is actually seen in the `TreeStore` instance, can be controlled by a custom `StoreSorter` implementation, set on the `TreeStore` instance with `store.setStoreSorter()`, and used to determine the ordinal index of a node (relative to its siblings) within a parent node.

```
▲ client
    ▷ chapters
    ▷ data
    ▷ events
    ▷ ext
    ▷ icons
    ▷ tryit
        FileModel.class
        FileService.class
        FileServiceAsync.class
        FolderModel.class
        GxtCookBk$1.class
        GxtCookBk$2.class
        GxtCookBk.class
        RemoteGateway.class
        RemoteGatewayAsync.class
    ▷ server
    ▲ shared
        FieldVerifier.class
    GxtCookBk.gwt.xml
```

How to do it...

Give the `TreeStore` instance a `StoreSorter` implementation whose `compare()` method should (like `compare()` from `Comparator`) compare its two node arguments for order and return a negative integer, zero, or a positive integer, if the first node argument is less than, equal to, or greater than the second.

```java
// set up the store and tree
final TreeStore<FileModel> store = new TreeStore<FileModel>();

// give store a sorter
store.setStoreSorter(new StoreSorter<FileModel>() {
  @Override
  public int compare(Store<FileModel> store, FileModel m1,
      FileModel m2, String property) {
    boolean m1Folder = m1 instanceof FolderModel;
    boolean m2Folder = m2 instanceof FolderModel;

    if (m1Folder && !m2Folder) {
      return -1;
    } else if (!m1Folder && m2Folder) {
      return 1;
    }

    return m1.getName().compareTo(m2.getName());
  }
});

final TreePanel<FileModel> tree = new TreePanel<FileModel>(
    store);
tree.setSize(285, 450);
tree.setBorders(true);
tree.setDisplayProperty("name");

// Populate tree from RPC call
final FileServiceAsync fileService = (FileServiceAsync) GWT
    .create(FileService.class);
AsyncCallback<List<FileModel>> callback = new AsyncCallback<List<File
Model>>() {

  @Override
  public void onSuccess(final List<FileModel> result) {
    Scheduler.get().scheduleDeferred(
        new ScheduledCommand() {
          @Override
          public void execute() {
            store.add(result, true);
```

```
                tree.unmask();
              }
            });
        }

        @Override
        public void onFailure(Throwable caught) {
          Info.display("Error", "Cannot Fetch Data for Tree!");
        }
      };

      tree.mask("Busy ...");
      fileService.getAll(null, callback);
      /*
       * GxtCookbk is the application's entry-point class.
       * We access its main content panel using the
       * static GxtCookBk.getAppCenterPanel() call.
       * We add our tree to the main content panel.
       */
      GxtCookBk.getAppCenterPanel().add(tree);
```

How it works...

The `TreeStore` class is instantiated and then given a `StoreSorter` implementation by passing it (the `StoreSorter` instance) to `store.setStoreSorter()`.

Within the `compare()` method of the `StoreSorter` interface, we return `-1` if the first node (among the two being compared at that time) is a parent (instance of `FolderModel`) and the second node is not; while `1` is returned if the first node is not a parent and the second is. This places parent nodes (folders) higher and leaf nodes (files) lower in the tree hierarchy, with the leaf nodes sorted with normal lexicographic ordering.

The `int` value returned by the `compare()` method of the `StoreSorter` interface conforms to the specs of the `compare()` method of the standard Java `Comparator` interface, therefore it compares its two node arguments for order and returns a negative integer, zero, or a positive integer, if the first node argument is less than, equal to, or greater than the second.

7
The Venerable Grid Component

In this chapter we will cover the following points:

- Basic grid: numbered rows, re-orderable columns
- Formatting cell data
- Grouping column headers
- Aggregating column data
- Easy record selection with checkboxes
- Entering validated data into a grid
- Automatic pagination in grids
- Data grouping in grids
- Custom rendering for grid groups
- Live data group summaries
- BeanModel grid
- Intuitive record filtering

Introduction

The grid is the most vivid manifestation of the will to order in graphic design. The main idea behind grid-based designs is the solid visual and structural balance you can create with them. Sophisticated layout structures offer more flexibility and enhance the visual experience of the user. In fact, users can easily follow the consistency of the layout/widget in a naturally consistent way.

The Venerable Grid Component

A grid is a two-dimensional structure made up of a series of intersecting vertical and horizontal axes used to structure content. The grid serves as an armature on which a designer can organize text and images in a rational, easy to absorb manner.

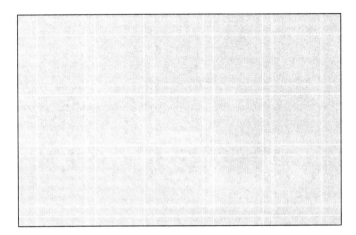

While grid systems have seen significant use in print media, interest from web developers has only recently seen a resurgence. Website design frameworks producing HTML and CSS had existed for a while before newer frameworks popularized the use of grid-based layouts.

The GXT `Grid` component features data sorting, paging, filtering, row selection, inline editing, column grouping as well as record grouping, custom cell formatting and rendering, column aggregation, and live data summaries. It is by far one of GXT's most advanced and desirable components. GXT also includes a rich collection of plugins. Plugins are components that implement the `ComponentPlugin` interface and can plugin into an existing component such as a `Grid`. They modify the behavior of the grid and add new features.

Basic grid: numbered rows, re-orderable columns

The GXT `Grid` component can be complex to new users, especially with its bells and whistles turned on. However, we can demonstrate a very basic and intuitive usage, one that can be grasped even by GXT beginners.

Chapter 7

It turns out that working with `Grids` basically boils down to working with a list of `ColumnConfig` objects (the columns) with which to make a `ColumnModel` which is in turn used alongside a `ListStore` (contains the data) to construct `Grid`.

	Company	Symbol	Last	Change	Last Updated
1	Apple Inc.	AAPL	123.43	-2.2099999999999!	Thu Jun 16 05:28:18 WAT 201
2	Cisco Systems, Inc.	CSCO	26.3	0.46000000000000	Thu May 26 05:28:18 WAT 20
3	Google Inc.	GOOG	512.6	-3.60000000000000	Tue May 31 05:28:18 WAT 20
4	Intel Corporation	INTC	21.53	0.17000000000000	Fri Jul 08 05:28:18 WAT 2011
5	Level 3 Communications, Inc.	LVLT	5.54	-0.00999999999999	Wed Jun 15 05:28:18 WAT 20
6	Microsoft Corporation	MSFT	29.72	0.16000000000000	Sun Aug 14 05:28:18 WAT 20
7	Nokia Corporation (ADR)	NOK	27.93	0.10000000000000	Wed Jul 13 05:28:18 WAT 201
8	Oracle Corporation	ORCL	18.98	0.25	Tue Aug 16 05:28:18 WAT 20
9	Starbucks Corporation	SBUX	27.36	0.03000000000000	Tue Aug 02 05:28:18 WAT 20
10	Yahoo! Inc.	YHOO	27.29	0.32000000000000	Fri Jul 15 05:28:18 WAT 2011
11	Applied Materials, Inc.	AMAT	18.66	0.26000000000000	Sun Jul 10 05:28:18 WAT 201
12	Comcast Corporation	CMCSA	26.4	0.5	Sun Jul 10 05:28:18 WAT 201
13	Sirius Satellite	SIRI	2.74	0.02000000000000	Sat Jul 02 05:28:18 WAT 2011

How to do it...

Create a `ColumnModel` object from a list of `ColumnConfig` objects and then create a `ListStore` to hold the data intended for the grid. The grid can now be constructed, configured, and then displayed on the screen.

```
@Override
public void onApply() {
  // A list for the column configurations
  List<ColumnConfig> configs = new ArrayList<ColumnConfig>();

  // This how you would make a normal column,
  // give it an id, label, and initial width
  // the id is a property in the bean you are trying to display
  ColumnConfig column = new ColumnConfig("name", "Company", 200);
  configs.add(column);

  column = new ColumnConfig("symbol", "Symbol", 75);
  configs.add(column);

  column = new ColumnConfig("last", "Last", 50);
  configs.add(column);
```

The Venerable Grid Component

```java
    column = new ColumnConfig("change", "Change", 100);
    configs.add(column);

    column = new ColumnConfig("date", "Last Updated", 150);
    configs.add(column);

    // An automatic serial number column,
    // RowNumberer is a special ColumnConfig
    RowNumberer serialNum = new RowNumberer();
    serialNum.setWidth(30);
    // make it the first column!
    configs.add(0, serialNum);

    // Populate the store with data
    ListStore<ModelData> store = new ListStore<ModelData>();
    store.add(LocalData.getStocks());

    // Create the grid with a ColumnModel instantiated
    // from our list of column configurations, and a store
    ColumnModel cm = new ColumnModel(configs);
    Grid<ModelData> grid = new Grid<ModelData>(store, cm);

    // RowNumberer is a special ColumnConfig,
    // actually a plugin !!
    grid.addPlugin(serialNum);

    // Some cosmetics on our beloved grid
    grid.setSize(600, 300);
    grid.setBorders(true);
    // show color strips for alternate rows
    grid.setStripeRows(true);
    // separate columns with vertical lines
    grid.setColumnLines(true);
    // allow re-ordering of columns
    grid.setColumnReordering(true);
    // expand the 'name' as much as possible
    grid.setAutoExpandColumn("name");

    // show it up, equivalent to
    // RootPanel.get().add(grid)

      GxtCookBk.getAppCenterPanel().add(grid);
}
```

How it works...

After creating an `ArrayList` to hold `ColumnConfig` objects, we create the `ColumnConfig` objects one after the other, giving each an `id`, a `header`, and an `initial width`. The columns will be displayed in the grid in their order in `ArrayList`. `id` given to a `ColumnConfig` via its constructor or `setId()` method maps to a field in the bean representing the data we want to be displayed on the grid. Although a basic grid can truly do without plugins, it often needs numbered rows to improve readability, so we add a special `ColumnConfig` called `RowNumberer` to help us with a serial number column which, we decide, will be more appropriate as the first column with `configs.add(0, serialNum)`.

Next we create a `ListStore` and populate it with stock records from our local repository of data using `LocalData.getStocks()`. Also, armed with a `ColumnModel` created with the list of `ColumnConfig` objects, we then instantiate a grid with `ListStore` and `ColumnModel`. Since `RowNumberer` doubles as a plugin (not just a column), we make our grid benefit by acknowledging it as such, hence the call to `grid.addPlugin(serialNum)`.

Some cosmetic configurations on the grid will not hurt or stop it from being basic so we indulge by setting a definite size and borders. `setStripeRows()` is used to enable an alternating color stripe on rows, while `setColumnLines(true)` gives the grid a vertical liner demarcating one column from another. `grid.setColumnRecordering(true)` allows us to drag a column from its original position and drop it elsewhere on the column's header thus reordering the columns. `setAutoExpandColumn()` is used to specify a column (by `id`) that will be expanded by the grid to fill up any extra horizontal space if the grid is wider than the columns can occupy.

Formatting cell data

Data formatting in cells is very critical to the success of the GXT grid. Imagine you have to render a date with a particular date format, or an age cell with *minor* or *adult* appended to the data depending on the age value, or even a numeric cell value displayed as standard decimal but with red if negative and green if positive, or even another color if above a certain value.

The Venerable Grid Component

No matter what your cell formatting needs will be, you are welcome to allow your imaginations to run wild because the various in-built data formatters, and those you can cook-up with the aid of a `GridCellRenderer`, will mostly suffice.

Company	Symbol	Last	Change	Last Updated
Apple Inc.	AAPL	US$123.43	-2.21	Jun 25, 2011
Cisco Systems, Inc.	CSCO	US$26.30	0.46	Jul 31, 2011
Google Inc.	GOOG	US$512.60	-3.60	Jun 22, 2011
Intel Corporation	INTC	US$21.53	0.17	Aug 23, 2011
Level 3 Communications, Inc.	LVLT	US$5.54	-0.01	Jun 08, 2011
Microsoft Corporation	MSFT	US$29.72	0.16	Aug 15, 2011
Nokia Corporation (ADR)	NOK	US$27.93	0.10	Jul 13, 2011
Oracle Corporation	ORCL	US$18.98	0.25	Aug 24, 2011
Starbucks Corporation	SBUX	US$27.36	0.03	May 24, 2011
Yahoo! Inc.	YHOO	US$27.29	0.32	Jul 02, 2011
Applied Materials, Inc.	AMAT	US$18.66	0.26	Jul 09, 2011
Comcast Corporation	CMCSA	US$26.40	0.50	Jun 18, 2011
Sirius Satellite	SIRI	US$2.74	0.03	Jun 25, 2011

How to do it...

Create a collection of `ColumnConfig` objects intended for use with a `Grid`. You can format a column by using a pre-built format object on its `ColumnConfig`, for example, `columnObject.setNumberFormat(NumberFormat.getDecimalFormat())` which will format cells in that column as a decimal number. However, a more flexible approach, especially with custom formatting, is passing in a `GridCellRenderer` to a call to `columnObject.setRenderer()`.

```
@Override
public void onApply () {
  // A list for the column configurations
  List<ColumnConfig> configs = new ArrayList<ColumnConfig>();

  // Create columns as ColumnConfig objects, add to the above list
  ColumnConfig column = new ColumnConfig("name", "Company", 200);
  configs.add(column);

  column = new ColumnConfig("symbol", "Symbol", 75);
  configs.add(column);

  column = new ColumnConfig("last", "Last", 75);
  // format value to show up right-aligned
  column.setAlignment(HorizontalAlignment.RIGHT);
```

```
    // format value to show 0.46 instead of 0.460000000000
    // and denote as a monetary value with a currency symbol
    column.setNumberFormat(NumberFormat.getCurrencyFormat());
    configs.add(column);

    column = new ColumnConfig("change", "Change", 85);
    column.setAlignment(HorizontalAlignment.RIGHT);
    // Hmmm.. a custom formatting solves all!
    // show a standard decimal value,
    // and green if positive else red.
    column.setRenderer(new GridCellRenderer<ModelData>() {
      @Override
      public Object render(ModelData model, String property,
          ColumnData config, int rowIndex, int colIndex,
          ListStore<ModelData> store, Grid<ModelData> grid) {

        double val = (Double) model.get(property);
        String style = val < 0 ? "red" : "green";
        String v = NumberFormat.getFormat("0.00").format(val);

        return "<span style='font-weight: bold;color:" + style
            + "'>" + v + "</span>";
      }
    });
    configs.add(column);

    column = new ColumnConfig("date", "Last Updated", 125);
    column.setAlignment(HorizontalAlignment.RIGHT);
    // format date value as Oct 1, 1960
    column.setDateTimeFormat(DateTimeFormat.getFormat("MMM dd, yyyy"));
    configs.add(column);

    // Populate store
    ListStore<ModelData> store = new ListStore<ModelData>();
    store.add(LocalData.getStocks());

    // Create and configure the grid.
    ColumnModel cm = new ColumnModel(configs);
    Grid<ModelData> grid = new Grid<ModelData>(store, cm);
    grid.setBorders(true);
    grid.setSize(600, 300);
    grid.setAutoExpandColumn("name");

    // show it up, equivalent to
    // RootPanel.get().add(grid)
      GxtCookBk.getAppCenterPanel().add(grid);
  }
```

The Venerable Grid Component

How it works...

Formatting cells in a `Grid` can be as simple as using an in-built formatter, or as involved as building one with a `GridCellRenderer`, but first we need the `ColumnConfig` objects which our code rightly begins with. The first two columns are given normal configurations but in the third we pass `NumberFormat.getCurrencyFormat()` to `column.setNumberFormat()`. Also, note the use of `HorizontalAlignment.RIGHT` with `column.setAlignment()` to make this currency value right-aligned instead of the default center alignment.

The `"change"` column (`ColumnConfig` with `id "change"`), however, gets a custom formatter with an adhoc and anonymous `GridCellRenderer` which takes the raw data from `model.get(property)` and returns a red or green colored `<Span>` HTML string containing the value formatted as a two-decimal-place number using `NumberFormat.getFormat("0.00").format(val)`.

The `"date"` column apart from also been right-aligned uses the `getFormat()` method of the `DateTimeFormat` class to render its data values such as Oct 1, 2011.

Grouping column headers

Column grouping is a very much desired feature in grids and is often used by many to ascertain the maturity of a grid widget in a UI toolkit. Thankfully, the GXT `Grid` component has a good implementation for grouped column headings that we can use right away. Grouped headers can be used to convey to the user a visual structure that otherwise would have been really difficult, unless we used long and funny names.

Imagine having to use something such as principal credit, principal debit, principal balance to express the transactions on the principal of a loan; and also interest credit, interest debit, and interest cumulative for transactions of the interest. Such column names are not only long and funny, they are monotonous too. We could simply have a *principal* column group containing credit, debit, and balance columns as well as an *Interest* column group containing credit, debit, and cumulative columns.

Stock Information		Stock Performance		Last Updated
Company	Symbol	Last	Change	
Apple Inc.	AAPL	US$123.43	-2.21	Jul 10, 2011
Cisco Systems, Inc.	CSCO	US$26.30	0.46	Jul 21, 2011
Google Inc.	GOOG	US$512.60	-3.6	Jun 28, 2011
Intel Corporation	INTC	US$21.53	0.17	May 28, 2011
Level 3 Communications, Inc.	LVLT	US$5.54	-0.01	Jul 19, 2011
Microsoft Corporation	MSFT	US$29.72	0.16	Aug 01, 2011
Nokia Corporation (ADR)	NOK	US$27.93	0.1	May 31, 2011
Oracle Corporation	ORCL	US$18.98	0.25	Jun 20, 2011
Starbucks Corporation	SBUX	US$27.36	0.03	Aug 06, 2011
Yahoo! Inc.	YHOO	US$27.29	0.32	Jul 12, 2011
Applied Materials, Inc.	AMAT	US$18.66	0.26	Jun 29, 2011
Comcast Corporation	CMCSA	US$26.40	0.5	Aug 24, 2011

How to do it...

Column header groups are configured on the `ColumnModel` used to instantiate the `Grid` component. A group can be added to `ColumnModel` by invoking its `addHeaderGroup()` method with three parameters, thus:

```
HeaderGroupConfig grpCfg;
grpCfg = new HeaderGroupConfig("Group Title", rowSpan, ColSpan);
colModel.addHeaderGroup(col, row, grpCfg);
```

Therefore, the following code means that in the first column in the first row (Column 0 in row 0), add a `"Stock Portfolio"` header group spanning 1 row and 2 columns:

```
HeaderGroupConfig grpCfg;
grpCfg = new HeaderGroupConfig("Stock Portfolio", 1, 2);
ColModel.addHeaderGroup (0, 0, grpCfg);
```

The Venerable Grid Component

Create a list of `ColumnConfig` object to be used by the `Grid`, just like we did in the previous recipe. Add a column header group labeled `"Stock Information"` to the first column, spanning 2 columns. Add a column header group labeled `"Stock Performance"` to the third column, spanning two columns.

```java
@Override
public void onApply() {
  // A list for the column configurations
  List<ColumnConfig> configs = new ArrayList<ColumnConfig>();

  // Create columns as ColumnConfig objects, add to the above list
  ColumnConfig column = new ColumnConfig("name", "Company", 200);
  configs.add(column);

  column = new ColumnConfig("symbol", "Symbol", 75);
  configs.add(column);

  column = new ColumnConfig("last", "Last", 75);
  // align value to right
  column.setAlignment(HorizontalAlignment.RIGHT);
  // format value as US currency
  column.setNumberFormat(NumberFormat.getCurrencyFormat());
  configs.add(column);

  column = new ColumnConfig("change", "Change", 85);
  // align value to right
  column.setAlignment(HorizontalAlignment.RIGHT);
  // format value as standard decimal
  column.setNumberFormat(NumberFormat.getDecimalFormat());
  configs.add(column);

  column = new ColumnConfig("date", "Last Updated", 125);
  column.setAlignment(HorizontalAlignment.RIGHT);
  column.setDateTimeFormat(DateTimeFormat
      .getFormat("MMM dd, yyyy"));
  configs.add(column);

  // Populate the store
  ListStore<ModelData> store = new ListStore<ModelData>();
  store.add(LocalData.getStocks());

  ColumnModel cm = new ColumnModel(configs);

  // To the first column in the first row (column 0 in row 0),
  // add a 'Stock Information' header group spanning 1 row & 2 columns
  cm.addHeaderGroup(0, 0, new HeaderGroupConfig("Stock Information",
  1, 2));
```

```
    // To the third column in the first row (column 2 in row 0),
    // add a 'Stock Performance' header group spanning 1 row & 2 columns
    cm.addHeaderGroup(0, 2, new HeaderGroupConfig("Stock Performance",
1, 2));

    // Create and configure the grid.
    Grid<ModelData> grid = new Grid<ModelData>(store, cm);
    grid.setBorders(true);
    grid.setSize(600, 300);
    grid.setAutoExpandColumn("name");

    // show it up, equivalent to
    // RootPanel.get().add(grid)

    GxtCookBk.getAppCenterPanel().add(grid);
}
```

How it works...

We define and populate an `ArrayList` of `ColumnConfig` objects which represent configurations for the columns in the `Grid`, we then create and populate a `ListStore` and also instantiate a `ColumnModel` with the list of column configurations.

However, before creating the grid with the `store` and `column` model, we invoke the `addHeaderGroup()` method of the `ColumnModel` class twice to set up two header groups on our `ColumnModel` object.

Using `cm.addHeaderGroup(0, 0, new HeaderGroupConfig("Stock Information" 1, 2))`, we add a "Stock Information" group spanning one row and two columns (will contain two child/nested columns) to the first column of the first row. The second `addHeaderGroup()` invocation adds a 'Stock Performance' group spanning one row and two columns just as the first group, but this one is added to the second column of the first row.

The summary of `addHeaderGroup()` is that it takes three parameters—a row index and a column index as the first two parameters indicating where to place the header group which is the third parameter and is an instance of `HeaderGroupConfig` specifying the group title, the number of rows it will span, and also the number of columns it will span. A column that is not spanned by the header group, like our fifth column, `"Last Updated"` will span all header rows.

Aggregating column data

Column aggregation allows us to do interesting things on the data of a grid's column, its implementation in the GXT `Grid` component places a section underneath the rows where the aggregates show up for each column it is configured for.

The Venerable Grid Component

With column aggregates, we can have an **Average** row (placed under/after the normal rows in the grid) that shows the average for a column with numeric data. Similarly, we can have a Sum aggregate that shows the total for the data in such a column.

Company	Symbol	Last	Change	Last Updated
Apple Inc.	AAPL	US$123.43	-2.21	Jul 23, 2011
Cisco Systems, Inc.	CSCO	US$26.30	0.46	Jul 13, 2011
Google Inc.	GOOG	US$512.60	-3.6	Jun 26, 2011
Intel Corporation	INTC	US$21.53	0.17	Jul 25, 2011
Level 3 Communications, Inc.	LVLT	US$5.54	-0.01	Jun 27, 2011
Microsoft Corporation	MSFT	US$29.72	0.16	Jun 12, 2011
Nokia Corporation (ADR)	NOK	US$27.93	0.1	Aug 29, 2011
Oracle Corporation	ORCL	US$18.98	0.25	Jul 28, 2011
Starbucks Corporation	SBUX	US$27.36	0.03	Jun 01, 2011
Average		US$43.17	-0.016	
Maximum		US$512.60	2.24	
Total		US$1,899.62	-0.72	

How to do it...

`ColumnModel` is where we add aggregates to a grid using the `addAggregationRow()` method of the `ColumnModel` class, which takes an `AggregationRowConfig` object.

`AggregationRowConfig` defines the configuration for an aggregation row; the values for each column can be calculated or configured with static HTML, a widget, or by using `SummaryType` which performs calculations based on data from the store and uses either a `NumberFormat` or an `AggretationRenderer` to format the display of the aggregation.

```
private String formatChangeCol(double val){
   String style = val < 0 ? "red" : "green";
   String v = NumberFormat.getDecimalFormat().format(val);
   return "<span style='font-weight: bold;color:" + style + "'>" + v +
"</span>";
}

@Override
public void onApply() {
   // A list for the column configurations
   List<ColumnConfig> configs = new ArrayList<ColumnConfig>();
```

```java
// Create columns as ColumnConfig objects, add to the above list
ColumnConfig column = new ColumnConfig("name", "Company", 200);
configs.add(column);

column = new ColumnConfig("symbol", "Symbol", 75);
configs.add(column);

column = new ColumnConfig("last", "Last", 75);
// align value to right
column.setAlignment(HorizontalAlignment.RIGHT);
// format value as US currency
column.setNumberFormat(NumberFormat.getCurrencyFormat());
configs.add(column);

column = new ColumnConfig("change", "Change", 85);
// align value to right
column.setAlignment(HorizontalAlignment.RIGHT);
// give me a richer formatting our formatChangeCol method
column.setRenderer(new GridCellRenderer<ModelData>() {
  @Override
  public Object render(ModelData model, String property,
      ColumnData config, int rowIndex, int colIndex,
      ListStore<ModelData> store, Grid<ModelData> grid) {
    return formatChangeCol((Double) model.get(property));
  }
});
configs.add(column);

column = new ColumnConfig("date", "Last Updated", 125);
// align value to right
column.setAlignment(HorizontalAlignment.RIGHT);
// format date value as Oct 1, 1960
column.setDateTimeFormat(DateTimeFormat
    .getFormat("MMM dd, yyyy"));
configs.add(column);

// Populate store
ListStore<ModelData> store = new ListStore<ModelData>();
store.add(LocalData.getStocks());

// Create a model from the list of column configurations
ColumnModel cm = new ColumnModel(configs);
```

```java
// Aggregation of averages
AggregationRowConfig<Stock> aggrgatn = new
   AggregationRowConfig<Stock>();
aggrgatn.setHtml("name", "Average");

// show average for data in the column with id of 'last'
// and format it as a standard decimal
aggrgatn.setSummaryType("last", SummaryType.AVG);
aggrgatn.setSummaryFormat("last",
    NumberFormat.getCurrencyFormat());

// show average for data in the column with id of 'change'
// and format it with a renderer that delegates to formatChangeCol
aggrgatn.setSummaryType("change", SummaryType.AVG);
aggrgatn.setRenderer("change",
    new AggregationRenderer<Stock>() {
      @Override
      public Object render(Number value, int colIndex,
         Grid<Stock> grid, ListStore<Stock> store) {
        return formatChangeCol(value.doubleValue());
      }
    });
cm.addAggregationRow(aggrgatn);

// Maximum aggregation, who's the highest ?
aggrgatn = new AggregationRowConfig<Stock>();
aggrgatn.setHtml("name", "Maximum");

// show max value in the column with id of 'last'
// and format as US currency
aggrgatn.setSummaryType("last", SummaryType.MAX);
aggrgatn.setSummaryFormat("last",
    NumberFormat.getCurrencyFormat());

// show max value in the column with id of 'change'
// and format it with a renderer that delegates to formatChangeCol
aggrgatn.setSummaryType("change", SummaryType.MAX);
aggrgatn.setRenderer("change",
    new AggregationRenderer<Stock>() {
      @Override
      public Object render(Number value, int colIndex,
         Grid<Stock> grid, ListStore<Stock> store) {
        return formatChangeCol(value.doubleValue());
      }
    });
cm.addAggregationRow(aggrgatn);
```

```
// Sum aggregation
aggrgatn = new AggregationRowConfig<Stock>();
aggrgatn.setHtml("name", "Total");

// show the total for values in the column with id of 'last'
// and format as US currency
aggrgatn.setSummaryType("last", SummaryType.SUM);
aggrgatn.setSummaryFormat("last",
    NumberFormat.getCurrencyFormat());

// show the total for values in the column with id of 'change'
// and format it with a renderer that delegates to formatChangeCol
aggrgatn.setSummaryType("change", SummaryType.SUM);
aggrgatn.setRenderer("change",
    new AggregationRenderer<Stock>() {
      @Override
      public Object render(Number value, int colIndex,
          Grid<Stock> grid, ListStore<Stock> store) {
        return formatChangeCol(value.doubleValue());
      }
    });
cm.addAggregationRow(aggrgatn);

// Create and configure the grid
Grid<ModelData> grid = new Grid<ModelData>(store, cm);
grid.setBorders(true);
grid.setSize(600, 300);
grid.setAutoExpandColumn("name");

// show it up, equivalent to
// RootPanel.get().add(grid)
    GxtCookBk.getAppCenterPanel().add(grid);
}
```

How it works...

The code follows the usual outline of working with grids that we have maintained in this chapter's recipes. We create a collection of the `ColumnConfig` objects and instantiate `ColumnModel` with it; this `ColumnModel` and `ListStore` is then used to create the grid. However, `ColumnModel` is augmented with column aggregation by invoking its `addAggregationRow()` method with a properly configured `AggregationRowConfig` object. The first aggregation row (as well as the others) is instantiated with new `AggregationRowConfig<Stock>()` and given a label of "Average". The label will show up in the column with an ID of "name" which according to our code happens to be the very first column (the "Company" column). Therefore, `aggregatn.setHtml("name", "Average")` means labeling this aggregation row as "Average" and show the said label in the "name" column.

The Venerable Grid Component

We have just defined an aggregation row, so now we must set up the aggregates to show on the row and on which columns. `aggrgatn.setSummaryType ("last", SummaryType.AVG)` indicates that we want to show averages on the column with an ID of `"last"` and we are formatting it as a currency with `setSummaryFormat ("last", NumberFormat.getCurrencyFormat())`.

Similarly, we display averages for the `"change"` column just as we did with the `"last"` column, but this time we use the `setRenderer()` method to configure a custom `AggregationRenderer` that will format the value using our private `formatChangeCol()` method. The `formatChangeCol()` method simply takes *double* and returns a red or green colored `<Span>` HTML element wrapping the *double* formatted as a decimal number.

The next aggregation row has a label of `"maximum"` and also shows up under the `"name"` column. It is equally given two aggregates with the `SummaryType.MAX` type that computes the maximum or highest value in each column, the first of which is the `"last"` column and the second being the `"change"` column. Both aggregates also adopt the formatting routines used by the previous ones.

The final aggregation row is labeled `"Total"` and positioned like the others before it. However, it uses `SummaryType.SUM` to display summation aggregates on the `"last"` and `"change"` columns.

We can only aggregate numeric columns, as an attempt to aggregate a non-numeric column will result in an exception.

Easy record selection with checkboxes

The default GXT `Grid` component allows record selection out of the box with its internal usage of `GridSelectionModel` which is configured with `SelectionMode.MULTI` to allow multiple record selections on the grid. This explains why GXT `Grid` (unless otherwise configured) allows you to select a row by clicking on it and also allows contiguous row selection by holding down the *Shift* key. You can equally select specific records if the *Ctrl* (control) key is down.

`CheckBoxSelectionModel` is a plugin that derives from the previously mentioned `GridSelectionModel` and then provides a column of checkboxes such that there is a checkbox for each record used to select, and more importantly, also deselect the record. It also places a checkbox in the column header that allows selection or de-selection of all records in the grid at once.

The `CheckBoxSelectionModel` plugin makes it super easy to select and de-select as many records as possible in a grid.

	Company	Symbol	Last	Change	Last Updated
☐	Apple Inc.	AAPL	US$123.43	-2.21	Jul 20, 2011
☐	Cisco Systems, Inc.	CSCO	US$26.30	0.46	Jul 09, 2011
☐	Google Inc.	GOOG	US$512.60	-3.6	Jul 01, 2011
☐	Intel Corporation	INTC	US$21.53	0.17	Jul 13, 2011
☐	Level 3 Communications, Inc.	LVLT	US$5.54	-0.01	Aug 08, 2011
☐	Microsoft Corporation	MSFT	US$29.72	0.16	Jul 12, 2011
☐	Nokia Corporation (ADR)	NOK	US$27.93	0.1	Jun 27, 2011
☐	Oracle Corporation	ORCL	US$18.98	0.25	Jun 19, 2011
☐	Starbucks Corporation	SBUX	US$27.36	0.03	Jul 28, 2011
☐	Yahoo! Inc.	YHOO	US$27.29	0.32	Aug 28, 2011
☐	Applied Materials, Inc.	AMAT	US$18.66	0.26	Jun 13, 2011
☐	Comcast Corporation	CMCSA	US$26.40	0.5	Jun 21, 2011
☐	Sirius Satellite	SIRI	US$2.74	0.03	Aug 14, 2011

How to do it...

Create a `CheckBoxSelectionModel` object and add its `getColumn()` return value to the collection of columns used to instantiate the grid's `ColumnModel`. Afterwards, configure the grid to use `CheckBoxSelectionModel` as its `SelectionModel` and as a plugin by passing in the `CheckBoxSelectionModel` object as the value to an invocation of `setSelectionModel()` and `addPlugin()` on the gird object.

```java
@Override
public void onApply () {
  // A list for the column configurations
  List<ColumnConfig> configs = new ArrayList<ColumnConfig>();

  // Create columns as ColumnConfig objects, add to the above list
  // CheckBoxSelectionModel becomes one of our columns, usually the first or the last
  CheckBoxSelectionModel<ModelData> selectionMdl = new CheckBoxSelectionModel<ModelData>();
  configs.add(selectionMdl.getColumn());

  ColumnConfig column = new ColumnConfig("name", "Company", 200);
  configs.add(column);
```

```
column = new ColumnConfig("symbol", "Symbol", 75);
configs.add(column);

column = new ColumnConfig("last", "Last", 75);
// align value to right & format value as US currency
column.setAlignment(HorizontalAlignment.RIGHT);
column.setNumberFormat(NumberFormat.getCurrencyFormat());
configs.add(column);

column = new ColumnConfig("change", "Change", 85);
// align value to right & format as decimal
column.setAlignment(HorizontalAlignment.RIGHT);
column.setNumberFormat(NumberFormat.getDecimalFormat());
configs.add(column);

column = new ColumnConfig("date", "Last Updated", 125);
// align value to right & format date as Oct 1, 1960
column.setAlignment(HorizontalAlignment.RIGHT);
column.setDateTimeFormat(DateTimeFormat
    .getFormat("MMM dd, yyyy"));
configs.add(column);

// Populate store
ListStore<ModelData> store = new ListStore<ModelData>();
store.add(LocalData.getStocks());

ColumnModel cm = new ColumnModel(configs);
Grid<ModelData> grid = new Grid<ModelData>(store, cm);

// Configure grid to use our CheckBoxSelectionModel
// for making record selections, and then add it as
// a plugin, that way U can select/de-select all
// records when U select/de-select the checkbox on
// header row of the grid.
grid.setSelectionModel(selectionMdl);
grid.addPlugin(selectionMdl);

grid.setBorders(true);
grid.setSize(600, 300);
grid.setAutoExpandColumn("name");

// show it up, equivalent to
// RootPanel.get().add(grid)
    GxtCookBk.getAppCenterPanel().add(grid);
}
```

How it works...

The code creates columns as `ColumnConfig` objects which get added to an `ArrayList` used to build the grid's `ColumnModel`. Next, we instantiate `CheckBoxSelectionModel` and add the return value of its `getColum()` call to our list of columns; this is how the column of checkboxes is created.

After the grid has been instantiated with `Store` and `ColumnModel`, we then use the `grid.setSelectionModel()` to set the grid's `SelectionModel` to our `CheckBoxSelelctionModel` object and also pass it to `grid.addPlugin()` so that it plugs into the grid to give us the much desired selection/deselection of one/some/all records in the grid.

Entering validated data into a grid

The `Grid` component displays data as records in rows and columns. Therefore, it can show a good number of records at a time, especially if it is configured with pagination. A natural consequence of this is the need to be able to edit the records being displayed. Although there will always be many ways of editing records in a grid, such as double-clicking to reveal a form, inline editing turns out to be the simplest and most intuitive approach from the user perspective.

Inline editing in a GXT grid entails a click (or double-click if configured) on a record to reveal input controls that allow entry of validated data just as in a GXT `FormPanel`.

The default inline editing in a GXT grid allows entry of data on a per-column basis in a particular row. However, we can use the `RowEditor` plugin which displays an overlay above the row being edited and presents input controls for every editable column in the row at once as well as a *cancel* and a *save* button, allowing data entry into several columns of the record and then either cancelling or persisting the entries.

In the previous screenshot, we saw that the date column **Last Updated** is edited using a date pop-up dialog.

The **Company** column is a text field and is edited with a `TextField` component.

How to do it...

Create an editable grid with the GXT `EditorGrid` component, instantiated with `ColumnModel` having `ColumnConfig` objects that have been configured with `CellEditor` that wraps a GXT `Field` descendant appropriate for the data expected on the column. If using the `RowEditor` plugin, not only do we not need `EditorGrid` (`Grid` will suffice) but we must use the `addPlugin()` method inherited by the `Grid` class to set it as a plugin on the grid.

```
private List<ColumnConfig> getColumnCfgs() {
  // A list for the column configurations
  List<ColumnConfig> configs = new ArrayList<ColumnConfig>();

  // Create columns as ColumnConfig objects, add to the above list
  ColumnConfig column = new ColumnConfig("name", "Company", 120);
  // Edit this column with a TextField that won't
  // accept an empty value
  TextField<String> txtField = new TextField<String>();
  txtField.setAllowBlank(false);
  column.setEditor(new CellEditor(txtField));
  configs.add(column);

  column = new ColumnConfig("last", "Last", 75);
  column.setAlignment(HorizontalAlignment.RIGHT);
  column.setNumberFormat(NumberFormat.getCurrencyFormat());
  // Edit this column with a NumberField that won't
  // accept empty or negative value
```

```
    NumberField numField = new NumberField();
    numField.setAllowBlank(false);
    numField.setAllowNegative(false);
    column.setEditor(new CellEditor(numField));
    configs.add(column);

    column = new ColumnConfig("date", "Last Updated", 100);
    DateTimeFormat frmt = DateTimeFormat.getFormat("MMM dd, yyyy");
    column.setDateTimeFormat(frmt);
    column.setAlignment(HorizontalAlignment.RIGHT);
    // Edit this column with a DateField, configured
    // with a specific date format.
    DateField dateField = new DateField();
    dateField.getPropertyEditor().setFormat(frmt);
    column.setEditor(new CellEditor(dateField));
    configs.add(column);

    return configs;
}

@Override
public void onApply () {
    // Populate the sore
    ListStore<ModelData> store = new ListStore<ModelData>();
    store.add(LocalData.getStocks());

    // Create and configure the editable grid
    List<ColumnConfig> configs = getColumnCfgs();
    ColumnModel cm = new ColumnModel(configs);
    EditorGrid<ModelData> grid = new EditorGrid<ModelData>(store, cm);
    grid.setBorders(true);
    grid.setSize(400, 200);
    grid.setStripeRows(true);
    grid.setAutoExpandColumn("name");
    grid.setStyleAttribute("marginBottom", "15px");

    // show it up, equivalent to
    // RootPanel.get().add(grid)
    centerPanel.add(grid);

    // We are making another grid, so give
    // us a fresh column list and store.
    configs = getColumnCfgs();
    store = new ListStore<ModelData>();
    store.add(LocalData.getStocks());
```

The Venerable Grid Component

```
        // This time we use a regular Grid object
        // watch this ...
        cm = new ColumnModel(configs);
        Grid<ModelData> rowEditorGrid = new Grid<ModelData>(store, cm);

        // Make this regular Grid editable with the
        // RowEditor plugin, allow edit on double-click event
        RowEditor<ModelData> rowEditor = new RowEditor<ModelData>();
        rowEditor.setClicksToEdit(ClicksToEdit.TWO);
        rowEditorGrid.addPlugin(rowEditor);

        // show it up, equivalent to
        // RootPanel.get().add(rowEditorGrid)
        GxtCookBk.getAppCenterPanel().add(rowEditorGrid);
    }
```

How it works...

Our code defines a private `getColumnCfgs()` method that returns a list of `ColumnConfig` objects that we will use for this two-grid recipe. The `ColumnConfig` object is first instantiated and then a GXT `Field` descendant (`TextField`, `DateField`, and so on) is created and configured with the necessary validation rules (for example, `setAllowBlank(false)`) and then wrapped with `CellEditor` which is eventually passed to the column's `setEditor()` method implying that the said column will be editable with the configured `Field`.

The `onApply()` method is where we actually build the grids; first we create and populate `ListStore` and then we create and configure two grids using `ListStore` and the columns from the `getColumnCfgs()` method. In building the first gird, we use the `EditorGrid` class which extends the normal `Grid` component with editing capabilities. Like its superclass, it is instantiated with `ListStore` and `ColumnModel`, after which we do some visual customizations and then display it using `centerPanel.add(grid)`.

After obtaining fresh instances of the columns, `Store` and `ColumnModel`, we instantiate a normal grid using `new Grid<ModelData>(store, cm)`, which we augment with *edit* behavior with the aid of `RowEditor` that is triggered after a double-click on a record (`ClicksToEdit.TWO`) and then added as a plugin to the grid using the `addPlugin()` method.

The `RowEditor` plugin grid finally gets displayed on the screen after we've turned on its borders, row-stripes, and also set a size, as well as a column that will expand to fill up extra horizontally space.

We can save or discard our editing changes by calling the appropriate methods on our `ListStore` object. In order to save our changes, we call the `commitChanges()` method on the `store` object, and in order to discard the changes we call the `rejectChanges()` method.

Automatic pagination in grids

Pagination in data-backed components such as `Grid` and `ComboBox` allows the user to access large datasets by presenting them in chunks (pages) and then retrieving more as the user requests, this is certainly better than presenting a huge list of 1000 customers all at once.

Pagination, especially when combined with sorting and filtering, can greatly improve the perusal of potentially large data. `PagingToolBar` is GXT's paging component and it really shines in the way it handles navigation of both in-memory and remote data.

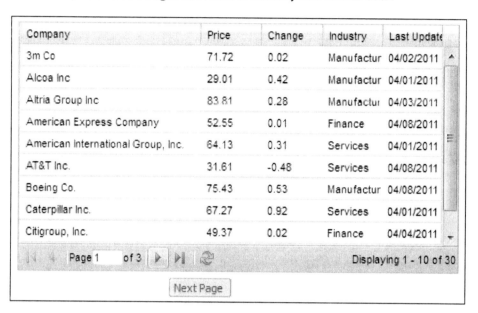

How to do it...

Build a grid with `ListStore`, using `PagingLoader` to load the data,, then create `PagingToolBar` with a page size and bind it to the loader. You can then wrap both the grid and the toolbar in `ContentPanel` such that the toolbar is set on the panel with the `setTopComponent()` or `setBottomComponent()` methods of the `ContentPanel` class.

```
@Override
public void onModuleLoad() {
    // Add paging support for a collection of local models.
    // To load remote models use RpcProxy instead for example
    // RpcProxy<PagingLoadResult<ModelData>>
    // then override the load() method and call your RPC service
    // method from it. Your RPC method should return the right type
    // for example, PagingLoadResult<Customer> instead of
ListLoadResult<Customer>
```

The Venerable Grid Component

```java
PagingModelMemoryProxy proxy = new PagingModelMemoryProxy(
    LocalData.getCompanies());

// configure it's loader
PagingLoader<PagingLoadResult<ModelData>> loader = new BasePagingLoader<PagingLoadResult<ModelData>>(
    proxy);
loader.setRemoteSort(true);

// create store from the loader
ListStore<ModelData> store = new ListStore<ModelData>(loader);

// setup columns
List<ColumnConfig> config = new ArrayList<ColumnConfig>();
ColumnConfig company = new ColumnConfig("name", "Company", 60);
config.add(company);

ColumnConfig price = new ColumnConfig("open", "Price", 20);
config.add(price);

ColumnConfig change = new ColumnConfig("change", "Change", 20);
config.add(change);

ColumnConfig industry = new ColumnConfig("industry",
    "Industry", 20);
config.add(industry);

ColumnConfig last = new ColumnConfig("date", "Last Updated", 20);
last.setDateTimeFormat(DateTimeFormat.getFormat("MM/dd/y"));
config.add(last);

// setup grid with store and columns
ColumnModel cm = new ColumnModel(config);
Grid<ModelData> pagedGrid = new Grid<ModelData>(store, cm);
pagedGrid.setStripeRows(true); // show colored strips on rows

// expand/contract columns to fit grid width
pagedGrid.getView().setForceFit(true);

// bind toolbar to loader
PagingToolBar tBar = new PagingToolBar(10);
tBar.bind(loader);

// Load first data-set, use pagedGrid.setLoadMask(true) to
// mask the grid if loading remote models with RpcProxy
loader.load(0, 10);
```

```
    // display the grid
    ContentPanel ctPanel = new ContentPanel();
    ctPanel.setHeaderVisible(false);
    ctPanel.setLayout(new FitLayout());
    ctPanel.add(pagedGrid);
    // display paging bar at the bottom
    ctPanel.setBottomComponent(tBar);
    ctPanel.setSize(455, 250);

    // show it up, equivalent to
    // RootPanel.get().add(ctPanel)
    centerPanel.add(ctPanel);
}
```

How it works...

`PagingModelMemoryProxy` is used here to proxy in-memory data which we get from our local `LocalData.getCompanies()`. The `PagingLoader` instance is then created with the proxy, and `ListStore` is eventually created with the loader. After creating a collection of `ColumnConfig` columns and a `ColumnModel` from them, we create a `Grid` object and later on a 10-paged `PagingToolBar` that is bound to our earlier `PagingLoader`.

Since we want the data to be sorted over all the pages we call `loader.setRemoteSort(true)`, so that the loader sorts the data before it is rendered by the grid. The loader sorts the data in ascending order by the first column. We can also specify a different column to sort by using the `setSortField()` method and specifying a custom `Comparator` for the sort using the `setComparator()` method.

The invocation of `loader.load(0, 10)` instructs `PagingLoader` to load 10 records from record 0, meaning it loads the first 10 records or page 1, such that `loader.load(30, 10)` would mean it loads page 4 or the 4th 10 records, or better still, 10 records from record 30.

The remainder of the code creates `ContentPanel`, adds the grid to it, adds `PagingToolBar` to it using the content-panel's `setBottomComponent()` method and eventually draws the output onscreen.

Note that we use the `pagedGrid.getView().setForceFit(true)` call on the grid to force the columns to fit the size of the grid so that we prevent a horizontal scroll bar from appearing.

There's more...

Although we have demonstrated paging of local in-memory data, to load and page remote data use `RpcProxy` instead of `PagingModelMemoryProxy` (for example, `RpcProxy<PagingLoadResult<ModelData>>`).

In order to load and page remote data we need to change our remote method so that it returns a different data page on each call. A `PagingLoadConfig` object will be passed to the call, which will specify the number of rows to return and the offset of the current page from the beginning of the full data list. We return a `PagingLoadResult` object from our remote call.

Our modified `getCompanies()` method might look something like the following:

```java
public PagingLoadResult<Stock> getCompanies(PagingLoadConfig config)
{
  List<Stock> companiesList = LocalData.getCompanies();
  int offset = config.getOffset();
  int limit = companiesList.size();
  if (config.getLimit() > 0) {
    limit = Math.min(offset + config.getLimit(), limit);
  }

  ArrayList<Stock> sublist = new ArrayList<Stock>();

  for(int i=offset; i < limit; ++i) {
    sublist.add(companiesList.get(i));
  }
  BasePagingLoadResult<Stock> result = new BasePagingLoadResult<Stock>(sublist,offset,companiesList.size());
  return(result);
}
/
```

We now need to use `RpcProxy`, override the `load()` method, and call our new RPC service method from it:

```java
RpcProxy<PagingLoadResult<Stock>> proxy = new RpcProxy<PagingLoadResult<Stock>>() {
    @Override
    public void load(Object loadConfig, AsyncCallback<PagingLoadResult<Post>> callback) {
        service.getCompanies((PagingLoadConfig) loadConfig, callback);
    }
};
```

So now we have our data loaded and paged remotely. However, we still need to have the grid trigger the RPC call when the user pages through the data. In order to do that, we need to make our grid stateful so it saves the offset and limit parameters. These parameters can then be retrieved from the grid's state and passed to the `PagingLoadConfig` object that will be passed to our remote method. We also need to listen to click events on the paging toolbar so that we can page remotely.

The following code snippet shows how we can do this:

```java
grid.setStateId("stockRpcGrid");
grid.setStateful(true);
EventType eventType = Events.OnClick;
tBar.addListener(eventType, new Listener<BaseEvent>() {
  @Override
  public void handleEvent(BaseEvent be) {
    PagingLoadConfig config = new BasePagingLoadConfig();
    config.setOffset(0);
    config.setLimit(50);

    Map<String, Object> state = grid.getState();
    if (state.containsKey("offset")) {
      int offset = (Integer)state.get("offset");
      int limit = (Integer)state.get("limit");
      config.setOffset(offset);
      config.setLimit(limit);
    }
    loader.load(config);
  }
});
```

Data grouping in grids

Grouping records in a grid provides a very simple yet powerful way to make meaningful deductions quickly from potentially large data. In a company stock data sheet grid, we could group the records by industry so that companies will be grouped together by their respective industries.

Company	Price	Change	Industry	Last Update
⊞ Automotive				
⊟ Computer				
Hewlett-Packard Co.	US$36.53	-0.03	Computer	04/03/2011
Intel Corporation	US$19.88	0.31	Computer	04/02/2011
International Business Machines	US$81.41	0.44	Computer	04/01/2011
Microsoft Corporation	US$25.84	0.14	Computer	04/02/2011
United Technologies Corporation	US$63.26	0.55	Computer	04/01/2011
⊟ Finance				
American Express Company	US$52.55	0.01	Finance	04/08/2011
Citigroup, Inc.	US$49.37	0.02	Finance	04/04/2011
JP Morgan & Chase & Co	US$45.73	0.07	Finance	04/02/2011

The Venerable Grid Component

How to do it...

Create a grid with `ColumnModel` from `ColumnConfig` objects, and `GroupingStore` instead of a regular `ListStore`, then set the column on which to perform the grouping operation using the `groupBy()` method of the `GroupingStore` class. Finally, set the grid's view to a `GroupingView` which extends the standard `GridView` class to provide specialized rendering for record grouping in a GXT `Grid`.

```java
@Override
public void onModuleLoad() {
  // A list for the column configurations
  // Create columns as ColumnConfig objects, then add to the list
  List<ColumnConfig> config = new ArrayList<ColumnConfig>();
  ColumnConfig company = new ColumnConfig("name", "Company", 60);
  config.add(company);

  ColumnConfig price = new ColumnConfig("open", "Price", 20);
  price.setNumberFormat(NumberFormat.getCurrencyFormat());
  config.add(price);

  ColumnConfig change = new ColumnConfig("change", "Change", 20);
  config.add(change);

  ColumnConfig industry = new ColumnConfig("industry",
      "Industry", 20);
  config.add(industry);

  ColumnConfig last = new ColumnConfig("date", "Last Updated", 20);
  last.setDateTimeFormat(DateTimeFormat.getFormat("MM/dd/y"));
  config.add(last);

  // Here is what really count.
  // Instead a ListStore, we use a
  // GroupingStore and call its
  // groupBy() method appropriately
  GroupingStore<Stock> store = new GroupingStore<Stock>();
  store.add(LocalData.getCompanies());
  store.groupBy("industry");
  ColumnModel cm = new ColumnModel(config);
  Grid<Stock> groupedGrid = new Grid<Stock>(store, cm);
```

```
    // Yeah, we've got to use a GroupingView too
    GroupingView view = new GroupingView();
    view.setForceFit(true);
    groupedGrid.setView(view);

    // Our standard cosmetology
    groupedGrid.setBorders(true);
    groupedGrid.setSize(455, 300);
    groupedGrid.setStripeRows(true);

    // show it up, equivalent to
    // RootPanel.get().add(groupedGrid)
    centerPanel.add(groupedGrid);
}
```

How it works...

For a GXT `Grid`, we always need a collection of `ColumnConfig` objects, so we create and populate an `ArrayList` with our choice columns after which `GroupingStore` is created and also populated. Grouping can only be done with `GroupingStore` (or its descendants) which allows us (among other things) to invoke its `groupBy()` method passing in the ID of the column we want the initial grouping to be done in.

A grid is created with the model of our column objects and our `GroupingStore` and then the grid is given `GroupingView`, suitable for displaying record groups. The view, which is set on the grid by invoking the grid's `setView()` method, not only displays record groups but also augments the column header menu with items allowing the user to change the grouping column or toggle on/off data grouping entirely.

With `GroupingStore` and `GroupingView` created and set on the grid, we can do some beautification on the grid but all that is really left is to display it on the screen.

Custom rendering for grid groups

Displaying grid records in groups can give the user powerful insight into their data especially when combined with sorting. However, the default rendering style of `GroupingView` may not meet the requirement of the user. Thankfully, GXT provides a mechanism that allows customization on the rendering and formatting of grouped data thereby giving the user better gratification.

The Venerable Grid Component

In a grid of company stocks grouped by an industry column, we could customize the groupings so that the number of items in each grouped will be displayed.

Company	Price	Change	Last Updated
⊞ Industry: Automotive (1 Item)			
⊟ Industry: Computer (5 Items)			
Hewlett-Packard Co.	US$36.53	-0.03	04/03/2011
Intel Corporation	US$19.88	0.31	04/02/2011
International Business Machines	US$81.41	0.44	04/01/2011
Microsoft Corporation	US$25.84	0.14	04/02/2011
United Technologies Corporation	US$63.26	0.55	04/01/2011
⊟ Industry: Finance (3 Items)			
American Express Company	US$52.55	0.01	04/08/2011

How to do it...

Create a grid with `GroupingStore` instead of the standard `ListStore` and invoke `groupBy()` on the store to set the initial column on which to perform the grouping. Afterwards, create `GroupingView` and optionally call its `setShowGroupedColumn()` method with false to hide the column the data is been grouped in. Implement the `GridGroupRenderer` interface and its `render()` method to customize the group formatting; pass this renderer to the view's `setGroupRenderer()` method and then pass the view to the grid's `setView()` method.

```
@Override
public void onModuleLoad() {
  // Populate the store and group the
  // data by on the 'industry' column, can
  // also use a RpcProxy via a ListLoader
  GroupingStore<Stock> store = new GroupingStore<Stock>();
  store.add(LocalData.getCompanies());
  store.groupBy("industry");

  List<ColumnConfig> config = new ArrayList<ColumnConfig>();
  ColumnConfig company = new ColumnConfig("name", "Company", 60);
  company.setGroupable(false); // don't allow grouping here
  config.add(company);
```

```java
ColumnConfig price = new ColumnConfig("open", "Price", 20);
price.setNumberFormat(NumberFormat.getCurrencyFormat());
price.setGroupable(false); // don't allow grouping here
config.add(price);

ColumnConfig change = new ColumnConfig("change", "Change", 20);
config.add(change);

ColumnConfig industry = new ColumnConfig("industry",
    "Industry", 20);
config.add(industry);

ColumnConfig last = new ColumnConfig("date", "Last Updated", 20);
last.setDateTimeFormat(DateTimeFormat.getFormat("MM/dd/y"));
config.add(last);

// Create and configure Grid
final ColumnModel cm = new ColumnModel(config);
Grid<Stock> groupedGrid = new Grid<Stock>(store, cm);
groupedGrid.setBorders(true);
groupedGrid.setSize(435, 250);
groupedGrid.setStripeRows(true);

// Must use a GroupingView for rendering
GroupingView view = new GroupingView();
view.setForceFit(true);
// don't show the grouped column.
view.setShowGroupedColumn(false);
// Customize how the groups show up
view.setGroupRenderer(new GridGroupRenderer() {
  @Override
  public String render(GroupColumnData data) {
    String header = cm.getColumnById(data.field)
        .getHeader();
    String sizeStr = data.models.size() == 1 ? "Item"
        : "Items";
    return header + ": " + data.group + " ("
        + data.models.size() + " " + sizeStr + ")";
  }
});
groupedGrid.setView(view);

// show it up, equivalent to
// RootPanel.get().add(groupedGrid)
    GxtCookBk.getAppCenterPanel().add(grid);

}
```

The Venerable Grid Component

How it works...

We create `GroupingStore` (not `ListStore`), populate it, and use its `groupBy()` method to configure which column to begin the grouping in. Next, we create some columns which get added to an `ArrayList` that is eventually used to make a `ColumnModel`. However, note the use of the `setGroupable()` method to disable grouping on select columns; this should be done when using a `GroupingView` since the default value for the columns is groupable. After creating the grid, we set its view to a `GroupingView` whose `setGroupRenderer()` method is called to set a `GridGroupRenderer` that will be responsible for formatting the title of the groups in the grid.

Live data group summaries

Grouping data in GXT grids is simple and powerful, allowing users to easily make insightful deductions from the data. The `Grid` component can also be configured to aggregate the data in columns such that we can see a summation or average computation of a column having numeric data.

However, whether grouped or aggregated, we have no way of reflecting changes to the data without having to re-group the records or programmatically redraw the grid.

This is what live group summaries can achieve in a GXT grid. Similar to data aggregates, we can summarize a column's data, say as summation (total) or a count (now many), but more importantly, additions or changes to existing records are automatically reflected in whichever summaries have been configured.

Therefore, we can build a grid for soles of products, grouped by the product categories and having a *summation* summary in a **Price** column, such that as we enter new sales or edit existing ones we would be given the price summation instantly.

Company	Price	Change	Last Updated
⊟ Industry: Automotive (1 Company)			
General Motors Corporation	US$30.27	1.09	Apr 3, 2011
	Total : US$30.27	Avg : 1.09	Within 24 Hours
⊟ Industry: Computer (5 Companies)			
Hewlett-Packard Co.	US$36.53	-0.03	Apr 3, 2011
Intel Corporation	US$19.88	0.31	Apr 2, 2011
International Business Mach	US$81.41	0.44	Apr 1, 2011
Microsoft Corporation	US$25.84	0.14	Apr 2, 2011
United Technologies Corpor	US$63.26	0.55	Apr 1, 2011
	Total : US$226.92	Avg : 0.282	Within 2 Days
⊟ Industry: Finance (3 Companies)			
American Express Compan	US$52.55	0.01	Apr 8, 2011

How to do it...

Create a list of columns but use `SummaryColumnConfig` instead of `ColumnConfig` and then in the columns that you want live summaries use an appropriate, or even custom `SummaryType` (for example, `SummaryType.SUM`), on a call to `column.setSummaryType()`. If need be, you can also configure the rendering of the summary with the use of a `SummaryRenderer` in `column.setSummaryRenderer()` much as you would do with a `GridCellRenderer`.

```
@Override
public void onApply() {
  List<ColumnConfig> config = new ArrayList<ColumnConfig>();

  // Got to use SummaryColumnConfig instead
  // of just ColumnConfig even on columns we
  // are not summarizing, else we get a ClassCastException
  SummaryColumnConfig<Integer> company = new
SummaryColumnConfig<Integer>(
      "name", "Company", 100);
  config.add(company);
```

The Venerable Grid Component

```java
// Show the Sum of the 'price'
// column for each group in the grid.
// We allow edit on this column to show
// how changes are instantly reflected.
SummaryColumnConfig<Double> price = new SummaryColumnConfig<Double>(
    "open", "Price", 75);
price.setSummaryType(SummaryType.SUM);
price.setEditor(new CellEditor(new NumberField()));
price.setNumberFormat(NumberFormat.getCurrencyFormat());
// Use a renderer to customize its look,
// render it as -> Total : USD$ 30.27
price.setSummaryRenderer(new SummaryRenderer() {
  @Override
  public String render(Number value, Map<String, Number> data) {
    String val = NumberFormat.getFormat("0.00").format(
        value.doubleValue());
    return "Total : "
        + NumberFormat.getCurrencyFormat().format(
            new Double(val));
  }
});
config.add(price);

// Show the Average of the 'change'
// column for each group in the grid.
SummaryColumnConfig<Double> change = new SummaryColumnConfig<Double>(
    "change", "Change", 75);
change.setSummaryType(SummaryType.AVG);
// Use a renderer to customize its look,
// render it as -> Avg : 1.09
change.setSummaryRenderer(new SummaryRenderer() {
  @Override
  public String render(Number value, Map<String, Number> data) {
    return "Avg : "
        + NumberFormat.getDecimalFormat().format(
            value.doubleValue());
  }
});
config.add(change);
```

```java
    // Must use SummaryColumnConfig even
    // when not summarizing
    SummaryColumnConfig<Double> industry = new
SummaryColumnConfig<Double>(
         "industry", "Industry", 85);
    config.add(industry);

    // We also allow edit on
    // this column to show how changes are
    // instantly reflected in the summaries.
    SummaryColumnConfig<Double> last = new SummaryColumnConfig<Double>(
         "date", "Last Updated", 85);
    last.setEditor(new CellEditor(new DateField()));

    // Use a custom SummaryType, here we
    // obtain the number of elapsed days
    // between the lowest and highest dates
    // from a group.
    last.setSummaryType(new SummaryType<Double>() {
      @Override
      public Double render(Object v, final ModelData m, final String field,
            Map<String, Object> data) {

        Date now = (Date) m.get(field);
        Date min = now;
        Date max = now;

        String minFieldKey = field + "_min";
        String maxFieldKey = field + "_max";

        if(data.containsKey(minFieldKey)){
          min = (Date) data.get(minFieldKey);
          if(now.before(min)){
            min = now;
          }
        }
        data.put(minFieldKey, min);

        if(data.containsKey(maxFieldKey)){
          max = (Date) data.get(maxFieldKey);
          if(now.after(max)){
            max = now;
          }
```

```
        }
        data.put(maxFieldKey, max);

        long diff = Math.abs(max.getTime() - min.getTime());
        long daysDiff = diff / 1000 / 60 / 60 / 24;
        return new Double(daysDiff);
      }

    });

    // Use a renderer to customize its look,
    // render it as -> Within 2 days
  last.setDateTimeFormat(DateTimeFormat.getFormat("MMM d, yyy"));
    last.setSummaryRenderer(new SummaryRenderer() {
      @Override
      public String render(Number value, Map<String, Number> data) {
        int intVal = value.intValue();
        return "Within " + (intVal == 0 ? "24 Hours" : intVal + " Days");
      }
    });
    config.add(last);

    // Populate the store and group the
    // data on the 'industry' column, can
    // also use a RpcProxy via a ListLoader
    GroupingStore<ModelData> store = new GroupingStore<ModelData>();
    store.add(LocalData.getCompanies());
    store.groupBy("industry");

    final ColumnModel cm = new ColumnModel(config);
    EditorGrid<ModelData> smryGrid = new EditorGrid<ModelData>(store, cm);

    // Got to use a GroupSummaryView view
    GroupSummaryView view = new GroupSummaryView();
    view.setForceFit(true);

    // hide the grouped column
    view.setShowGroupedColumn(false);

    // Use a renderer for the groups,
    // render as -> Industry : Computer (5 Companies)
    view.setGroupRenderer(new GridGroupRenderer() {
      @Override
      public String render(GroupColumnData data) {
        String header = cm.getColumnById(data.field)
```

```
                    .getHeader();
            String sizeStr = data.models.size() == 1 ? "Company"
                    : "Companies";
            return header + ": " + data.group + " ("
                    + data.models.size() + " " + sizeStr + ")";
        }
    });
    smryGrid.setView(view);

    // Some cosmetics on the Grid
    smryGrid.setBorders(true);
    smryGrid.setSize(485, 300);
    smryGrid.setStripeRows(true);

    // show it up, equivalent to
    // RootPanel.get().add(smryGrid)

      GxtCookBk.getAppCenterPanel().add(smryGrid);
    }
```

How it works...

We create an `ArrayList` of `ColumnConfig` objects although we populate it with objects of `SummaryColumnConfig`, worthy descendants of `ColumnConfig`. Our `SummaryColumnConfig` objects are constructed with the same parameters as with `ColumnConfig`, and given a `SummaryType` which will determine the summary computation it will get.

The price column (with ID `"open"`) will be summarized as a summation (`SummaryType.SUM`), editable with `NumberField` and rendered as a monetary value using `NumberFormat.getCurrencyFormat()` on the column. The rendering of the summation computation is, however, customized by passing a `SummaryRenderer` to `price.setSummaryRenderer()` wherein we first format the value as a decimal and later as a currency, which is then appended to a string literal producing something like **Total: $285.00**.

The **Change** column (with the ID `"change"`) also gets summarized, but as an average, thus we will be showing the average of the figures in this column. Closely following is the `"date"` column, editable with a `DateField` but given a custom `SummaryType`. Our aim here is to display the number of days (or hours) that have elapsed between the earliest and latest date values for this column in any given group. After obtaining the date value from `m.get(field)`, we assign it to `now` and temporarily to `min` and `max`, and we also define two matching strings used to inspect the data collection for a pre-existing `date` value, which is then assigned to `min` or `max` if it is before or after the date represented by `now`. The custom `SummaryType` finally returns the difference between the `min` and `max` dates in days as a `Double` value.

The same `date` column, after being given a `date` format for its column formatting, also gets a `SummaryRenderer` that displays `"Within 24 Hours"` if the computed value from its custom `SummaryType` is `0` (zero) otherwise it displays something like `"Within 2 Days"`.

What follows in the outline of the code is some what customary for working with grids, since we are grouping data we set()up and populate a `GroupingStore` which is used together with a `ColumnModel` made from our column collection to create an `EditorGrid`. Also required for data grouping, we give the grid a `GroupingView` configured to hide the column on which the grouping is done using `view.setShowGroupedColumn(false)`, and also give a `GroupRenderer` that displays a singular or plural label.

BeanModel grid

For brevity and simplicity, the recipes in this chapter relied on local (client-side) data, in real life. However, you will certainly be exposed to the challenge of working with models (objects) on/from the server, requiring a slightly different approach to the set up of at least the store on which the grid is built.

`BeanModel` is a `ModelData` instance that wraps a bean, which is usually a server-side model object, that implements `BeanModelTag` interface. They cannot be instantiated directly, rather they are returned by a `BeanModelFactory`.

The following screenshot shows the simple three-column grid that we will be using for this recipe:

How to do it...

Set()up a `ListStore` using a `ListLoader` that in turn uses a `RpcProxy` to get the remote beans. Create a `ColumnModel` from a collection of columns and then use it in conjunction with the `ListStore` to instantiate the grid which can be configured to your taste. Make sure the grid, store, and loader are parameterized with `BeanModel` or `ModelData`.

```
@Override
public void onApply() {
   // Make RPC call via a proxy, see appendixes for info.
   // here we want to fetch a bunch of Customer beans
   final RemoteGatewayAsync rpcService = (RemoteGatewayAsync) GWT
       .create(RemoteGateway.class);
   RpcProxy<ListLoadResult<Customer>> rpcProxy = new RpcProxy<ListLoadResult<Customer>>() {
      @Override
      public void load(Object cfg,
          AsyncCallback<ListLoadResult<Customer>> callback) {
        rpcService
            .getCustomers((ListLoadConfig) cfg, callback);
      }
   };

   // set up the store for beans
   ListLoader<ListLoadResult<BeanModel>> loader = new BaseListLoader<ListLoadResult<BeanModel>>(
       rpcProxy, new BeanModelReader());
   ListStore<BeanModel> store = new ListStore<BeanModel>(loader);

   // set up column model
   List<ColumnConfig> columns = new ArrayList<ColumnConfig>();

   // Show the 'name' property in the bean
   ColumnConfig col = new ColumnConfig("name", "Name", 200);
   columns.add(col);

   // Show the 'email' property in the bean
   col = new ColumnConfig("email", "Email", 150);
   columns.add(col);

   // Show the 'age' property in the bean
   col = new ColumnConfig("age", "Age", 50);
   col.setAlignment(HorizontalAlignment.RIGHT);
   columns.add(col);
```

The Venerable Grid Component

```
    // Create and configure the Grid
    ColumnModel cm = new ColumnModel(columns);
    Grid<BeanModel> beanGrid = new Grid<BeanModel>(store, cm);
    beanGrid.setAutoExpandColumn("name");    // expand "name" column as much as possible
    beanGrid.setBorders(true);       // give us borders
    beanGrid.setLoadMask(true);      // mask while loading
    beanGrid.setSize(400, 200);
    beanGrid.setStripeRows(true);        // show colored strips on rows

    // Go fetch the data
    loader.load();

    // show it up, equivalent to
    // RootPanel.get().add(beanGrid)

    GxtCookBk.getAppCenterPanel().add(beanGrid);
}
```

How it works...

We want to work with server-side beans so we invoke the remote `getCustomers()` method on our RPC service object within the overridden `load()` method of a `RpcProxy` object, which is in turn used with a `BeanModelReader` to instantiate a `ListLoader` since the remote `getCustomers()` call returns a `ListLoadResult`.

`ListStore` is then created with the loader and used together with `ColumnModel` to create a grid that is parameterized with `BeanModel` just as it is with `ListStore` and `ListLoader`.

Once the `load()` method of `ListLoader` is invoked, an RPC request is made to the server resulting in a response containing a list of `Customer`beans which is then displayed in the grid for all to see.

Intuitive record filtering

A common use case with grids is the need for record filtering, allowing users to easily locate records that match the given filter while temporarily eliminating the others. Filtering a GXT grid is done with the use of `GridFilter`, a plugin that provides a more robust filtering than the implementation found in a GXT store.

`GridFilter` provides a programmatic and graphical interface, an event model, and adds a new menu to the header menu on a grid with which users can enable, disable, and configure the filter on a given column.

Chapter 7

Using a `GridFilter` one can filter the records on a grid from a "price" column such that only records with price values between a range and having a specific value will show up.

How to do it...

Create a `GridFilters` object to house and manage the individual filters needed then invoke its `setLocal()` method with a Boolean indicating whether you desire local (within the grid store) or remote (from the server) filtering. Next, create the filter objects (for example, `StringFilter`, `NumericFilter`, and `DateFilter`), mapping each to a column by the column's ID and ensuring that you are using the right filter type (indicated by its name) in a column based on the type of data (for example, `string` or `date`) handled by said column.

Add the filter objects to the `GridFilters` object we first created; this should in turn be added to the grid as a plugin using the `addPlugin()` method on the `grid` object.

```
@Override
public void onApply() {
  // A list for the column configurations
  List<ColumnConfig> configs = new ArrayList<ColumnConfig>();

  ColumnConfig column = new ColumnConfig("name", "Company", 200);
  configs.add(column);

  column = new ColumnConfig("symbol", "Symbol", 75);
  configs.add(column);

  column = new ColumnConfig("last", "Last", 75);
  // align value to right & format value as US currency
  column.setAlignment(HorizontalAlignment.RIGHT);
  column.setNumberFormat(NumberFormat.getCurrencyFormat());
  configs.add(column);

  column = new ColumnConfig("date", "Last Updated", 125);
  // align value to right & format date as Oct 1, 1960
  column.setAlignment(HorizontalAlignment.RIGHT);
  column.setDateTimeFormat(DateTimeFormat
      .getFormat("MMM dd, yyyy"));
  configs.add(column);
```

```java
// Populate store
ListStore<ModelData> store = new ListStore<ModelData>();
store.add(LocalData.getStocks());

ColumnModel cm = new ColumnModel(configs);
Grid<ModelData> grid = new Grid<ModelData>(store, cm);

// Our collection of filters
GridFilters filters = new GridFilters();
filters.setLocal(true);

// A string filter for the
// column with id of "name"
StringFilter nameFilter = new StringFilter("name");
filters.addFilter(nameFilter);

// Another string filter, but for
// the column with id of "symbol"
StringFilter symbolFilter = new StringFilter("symbol");
filters.addFilter(symbolFilter);

// A numeric filter for the column
// with id of "last"
NumericFilter numericFilter = new NumericFilter("last");
filters.addFilter(numericFilter);

// A date filter for the column
// with id of "date"
DateFilter dateFilter = new DateFilter("date");
filters.addFilter(dateFilter);

// Add them to the grid as a
// plugin an you are done
// with basic record filtering
grid.addPlugin(filters);

grid.setBorders(true);
grid.setSize(600, 300);
grid.setAutoExpandColumn("name");

// show it up, equivalent to
// RootPanel.get().add(grid)
centerPanel.add(grid);
}
```

How it works...

We are attempting to filter records on a grid, therefore we have to set up the grid as usual and then add the `"filtering"` plugin. After creating a collection of columns (`ColumnConfig`) which is in turn used to instantiate a `ColumnModel`, we create and populate `ListStore` which is then used together with the `ColumnModel` object to create the grid.

The filtering functionality is added with a `GridFilters` object to which we add individual filters mapped to columns by the column ID. Therefore, `StringFilter` (we have called `nameFilter`) will act on string values from the column whose ID is `"name"`.

Once we are done configuring filters for our columns of interest and adding them to the `GridFilters` object, we then invoke `grid.addPlugin(filters)` to finally seal the deal as far as record filtering on the grid is concerned.

There's more...

In this recipe we demonstrated local filtering. Just like paging, filtering can also be done remotely. In order to support remote filtering we need to pass a `FilterPagingLoadConfig` to our remote call so we can get the list of `FilterConfig` objects. We can then filter the data in our server-side method by using the values in the `FilterConfig` objects.

The following code snippet shows how to create the `FilterPagingLoadConfig` object and pass it to our RPC call:

```
RpcProxy<PagingLoadResult<Stock>> proxy = new RpcProxy<PagingLoadResult<Stock>>() {
  @Override
  public void load(Object loadConfig, AsyncCallback<PagingLoadResult<Stock>> callback) {
    service.getStocks((FilterPagingLoadConfig) loadConfig, callback);
  }
};
final PagingLoader<PagingLoadResult<ModelData>> loader = new BasePagingLoader<PagingLoadResult<ModelData>>(proxy) {
  @Override
  protected Object newLoadConfig() {
    BasePagingLoadConfig config = new BaseFilterPagingLoadConfig();
    return config;
  }
};
loader.setRemoteSort(true);
```

8
Templates and Views

In this chapter we will cover the following points:

- Formatting data with a basic template
- Doing logic in templates
- Doing math in templates
- Custom ComboBox displays
- Giving details with RowExpander

Introduction

A **template processor** (or **template parser**) is a component that is designed to combine one or more templates with a data model to produce one or more result documents or document fragments.

Template and XTemplate are very useful classes in GXT for overriding and defining how certain components handle the presentation of their data. Template supports simple formatting of the data using text or HTML markup and inserts the data into the formatted template using place holders wrapped in curly braces. XTemplate supports, in addition to Template's features, auto-filling arrays, conditional processing with basic comparison operators, sub-templates, basic math function support, special built-in template variables, inline code execution, and more. These make it possible to easily take control over how data is formatted and presented in widgets.

Templates and Views

In GXT, we can use templates to display a collection of beans representing files in several ways like it's done in a file explorer. We can use one template to display them as a list and another to display them as icons, and yet another to display them with details of their file properties. In the same vein, we could use templates to customize the rows of a grid and the drop-down list of a combo, showing meaningful aspects of the data beyond the columns' definition of the grid or display field of the combo.

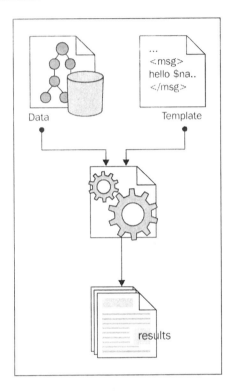

Templates allow us to easily work with data presentation on a collection of beans. The template itself is a string of HTML fragments containing properties of the bean wrapped between curly braces ({ }). Personally, I am considering building a reporting component allowing the user to put together ad-hoc layouts with templates that can now be saved and used for displaying or even printing the data; yes, it's possible with templates in GXT.

Formatting data with a basic template

The `template` class in the GXT toolkit provides a very simple mechanism for generating formatted HTML fragments from data objects which can be instances of `ModelData` or `Params`.

Once we apply the data to the `Template` object, the result is the formatted HTML interpolated with values from the provided data.

> Age: 31
> Sex: Male
> Name: Odili Charles Opute
> Email: chalu@lol.com
> Purchases: 9350.00

> Age: 6
> Sex: Female
> Name: Jessica Ogbebor
> Email: jj@live.com
> Purchases: 565.00

How to do it...

Instantiate a `Template` object with a string representing the desired HTML formatting and the placeholders. We will replace the `Template` placeholders with values using a `Params` object.

```java
//Local convenience method
private String getTemplate(){
    StringBuilder sb = new StringBuilder();
    sb.append("<p>Age: {age}</p>");
    sb.append("<p>Sex: {gender}</p>");
    sb.append("<p>Name: {name}</p>");
    sb.append("<p>Email: {email}</p>");
    sb.append("<p>Purchases: {purchases:number(\"00.00\")}</p>");
    return sb.toString();
};

@Override
public void onApply() {
    // Create a Template with the HTML from getTemplate
    final Template tpl = new Template(getTemplate());

    // Forge some local data for demonstration
    // we use a Params object and set some
    // properties like age and gender for it.
    Params localData = new Params();
```

Templates and Views

```java
        localData.set("age", 31);
        localData.set("gender", "Male");
        localData.set("email", "chalu@lol.com");
        localData.set("name", "Odili Charles Opute");
        localData.set("purchases", 9350);

        // We will display the Template in this panel
        ContentPanel panel = new ContentPanel();
        panel.setWidth(325);
        panel.setAutoHeight(true);
        panel.setHeaderVisible(false);
        panel.setBodyStyle("padding:7px");

        // Apply the Template on the data,
        // then use return HTML as body for
        // the panel above.
        String htmlStr = tpl.applyTemplate(localData);
        panel.addText(htmlStr);

        // put it on screen, equivalent to
        // RootPanel.get().add(panel)
           GxtCookBk.getAppCenterPanel().add(panel);
        // Let's deal with data across the wire this time
        // so we need another panel, just so our code is clean
        final ContentPanel panel_2 = new ContentPanel();
        panel_2.setWidth(325);
        panel_2.setAutoHeight(true);
        panel_2.setHeaderVisible(false);
        panel_2.setBodyStyle("padding:7px");
        panel_2.setStyleAttribute("marginTop", "10px");

        // put it on screen, equivalent to
        // RootPanel.get().add(panel_2)
           GxtCookBk.getAppCenterPanel().add(panel_2);
        // Make RPC call, see appendixes for more info
        final RemoteGatewayAsync rpcService = (RemoteGatewayAsync) GWT.
    create(RemoteGateway.class);
        AsyncCallback<Customer> callback = new AsyncCallback<Customer>() {
          @Override
          public void onFailure(Throwable caught) {
            Info.display("Error", "RPC Error");
          }
```

```
      @Override
      public void onSuccess(Customer result) {
        if(result != null){
          // Just give us the data in a way
          // we can use it with Templates.
          // We will be using the Util.getJsObject()
          // method for that, it expects a ModelData
          // object which our remote Customer is
          // exactly not, but can be made to comply
          // with since it implements BeanModelTag.
          BeanModel data = BeanModelLookup.get().getFactory(Customer.
  class).createModel(result);

          // Apply the Template to the Customer data
          // and overwrite the body of panel_2 with
          // the returned HTML.
          tpl.overwrite(panel_2.getBody().dom, Util.getJsObject(data));
        }
      }
    };

    // Give me the Customer with 'id' 3!
    rpcService.getCustomer(3, callback);
}
```

How it works...

First, we define a private `getTemplate()` method that returns the HTML string we intend to format our data with. The HTML string is built with `StringBuilder` and our code shows that we want to render the data as paragraphs enclosing the `age`, `gender`, `name`, `email`, and `purchases` properties of our intended data. Notice how the "Purchases" paragraph differs from the others; it uses the in-built value formatting in `Template` to format the `purchases` property as a decimal number and it also uses slashes to properly escape the two seemingly unwieldy quotes.

The `onApply()` method begins with the instantiation of `Template` constructed with the return string from a call to `getTemplate()`. We then use a `Params` object to simulate some data which is then formatted by our `Template` object by calling `tpl.applyTemplate(localData)`, resulting in HTML that is eventually set on the `ContentPanel` with `panel.addText(htmlStr)`.

We wrap up the demo by showing a second `ContentPanel` whose contents is set with an RPC call to the remote `getCustomer()` method.

In the `AsyncCallback` success handler we convert the returned `Customer` object to a `BeanModel`. We then convert the `BeanModel` to a GXT `JavaScriptObject` using GXT's `Util` class and pass it to the template's `overwrite()` method which applies the template.

Templates and Views

Doing logic in templates

I personally would not be so thrilled if all that GXT templates offer red was basic string interpolation. Luckily, we can also benefit from some level of conditional processing in the `XTemplate` class making it possible to vary the rendering or formatting of the intended data depending on the state of things in the data itself.

A simple example of this would be to only show data for customers over a certain age; we can also modify this to use a different formatting style for customers of the requisite age.

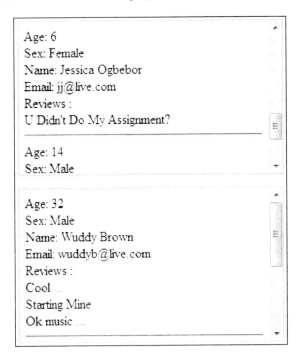

How to do it...

Instantiate an `XTemplate` object with a string representing the desired HTML formatting, and in it use the `if` keyword enclosed in a `<tpl>` tag to express the condition which will likely need to be escaped with slashes and HTML entities.

```
private String getTemplate(boolean all){
    StringBuilder sb = new StringBuilder();
    if(!all){
      sb.append("<tpl if=\"age &gt; 30\">");
    }else{
      sb.append("<tpl>");
    }
```

```java
    sb.append("<p>Age: {age}</p>");
  sb.append("<p>Sex: {gender}</p>");
  sb.append("<p>Name: {name}</p>");
  sb.append("<p>Email: {email}</p>");
  sb.append("<p>Reviews : </p>");
  sb.append("<ul>");
  sb.append("<tpl for=\"reviews\">");
  sb.append("<li>{title}</li>");
  sb.append("</tpl>");
  sb.append("</ul>");
  sb.append("<hr />");
  sb.append("</tpl>");
    return sb.toString();
};

// We will reuse this code block severally
// so a convenience function is handy!
private void configurePanel(ContentPanel panel){
  panel.setSize(325, 185);
  panel.setHeaderVisible(false);
  panel.setBodyStyle("padding:7px");
  panel.setScrollMode(Scroll.AUTOY);
  panel.setStyleAttribute("marginTop", "15px");
}

@Override
public void onApply() {
  // allPanel is where we display
  // the templated data without
  // applying the if condition in
  // the Template.
  final ContentPanel allPanel = new ContentPanel();
  configurePanel(allPanel);

  // abv30Panel renders the results
  // of applying the if condition in
  // the Template, displaying only
  // customers who are above 30
  final ContentPanel abv30Panel = new ContentPanel();
  configurePanel(abv30Panel);

  // put them on screen, equivalent
  // to RootPanel.get().add(...)
```

Templates and Views

```java
      GxtCookBk.getAppCenterPanel().add(allPanel);
      GxtCookBk.getAppCenterPanel().add(abv30Panel);

   // Make RPC call, see appendixes for more info
   final RemoteGatewayAsync rpcService = (RemoteGatewayAsync) GWT.
create(RemoteGateway.class);
   AsyncCallback<List<Customer>> callback = new
AsyncCallback<List<Customer>>() {
      @Override
      public void onFailure(Throwable caught) {
         // We are back, with errors anyway,
         // so turn off the 'loading' signal
         // on both panels
         allPanel.unmask();
         abv30Panel.unmask();

         Info.display("Error", "RPC Error");
      }

      @Override
      public void onSuccess(List<Customer> result) {
         if(result != null){
            // Create the templates as XTemplate objects
            // instead of Template objects,
            // else we can't utilize the 'if' and 'for' logic.
            // We have one for all customers and another for
            // those above 30, note the boolean flags passed
            // into the call to our getTemplate() private method.
            XTemplate allTpl = XTemplate.create(getTemplate(true));
            XTemplate abv30Tpl = XTemplate.create(getTemplate(false));

            // Just give us the customer data
            // in a way that is usable with Templates.
            // The Util.getJsObject() method expects a
            // ModelData which our remote Customer is
            // exactly not, but can be made to comply
            // with since it implements BeanModelTag.
            List<BeanModel> beans = BeanModelLookup.get().
getFactory(Customer.class).createModel(result);

            // Apply the templates to each Customer bean,
            // remember that we are using the 'for' keyword
            // in <tpl> to display the title of a Review as we
            // iterate over the 'reviews' of a Customer, so
```

```
                // we use Util.getJsObject(bean, 2) to say give us
                // this bean as a JsObject that has a child ('reviews')
                // which itself needs processing as a JsObject.
                for (BeanModel bean : beans) {
                    allPanel.addText( allTpl.applyTemplate(Util.
getJsObject(bean, 2)) );
                    abv30Panel.addText( abv30Tpl.applyTemplate(Util.
getJsObject(bean, 2)) );
                }

                // turn off the 'loading' signal
                // on both panels, and render
                // their contents again properly.
                allPanel.unmask();
                allPanel.layout();

                abv30Panel.unmask();
                abv30Panel.layout();
            }
        }
    };

    // show a 'loading' signal
    // to give the user a visual cue
    // that we are 'busy'
    allPanel.mask();
    abv30Panel.mask();

    // Now go 'over-board' and
    // fetch some real customers
    rpcService.listCustomers(null, callback);
}
```

How it works...

Our intention is to demonstrate conditional logic in GXT templates by showing a panel containing all customers and then another panel containing only customers above 30 years of age. However, we will also show the use of the `for` keyword of a `<tpl>` tag to format and render properties of the intended data that are collections of objects.

We start by defining a `getTemplate()` method that accepts a Boolean flag which uses an empty `<tpl>` tag if it is `true` (that is, display all customers), but uses an `if` condition if it is `false` (that is, display customers above 30 years of age).

The `if` conditional logic is placed as an attribute of the `<tpl>` tag and is given a value wrapped with escaped quotes. The condition itself is written as `age > 30`, but the greater than operator is escaped as `&gt;` using the HTML entity format. The rest of the `StringBuilder` appendages are simple HTML paragraphs enclosing the properties we want to display from our intended data until it gets to another `<tpl>` tag usage (nested in the first one) which I must explain right!

The second `<tpl>` tag within the string being built is intended to display customer reviews. It uses the `for` keyword, attribute of the `<tpl>` tag, to iterate over the property called `reviews` in the intended data, and then displays the `title` property of each item in the `reviews` list.

As we will be rendering the data over two panels, we also create a `configurePanel()` method used to localize the common cosmetics applied to the panels, which we create and configure in the beginning of `onApply()`.

After adding the panels to the screen, we mask them and then invoke the remote `listCustomers()` method to return the list of customers for formatting and display.

The success handler for our RPC invocation is where we do the heavy lifting. We first create two matching `XTemplate` objects by calling its `create()` method with `getTempalte(true)` and `getTemplate(false)`, implying that `allTpl` will be used on `allPanel` to display all customers, while `abv30Tpl` will be used on `abv30Panel` to display only customers above 30 years.

Since we need the `ModelData` objects to work with GXT templates, we use the `BeanModelLookup` mechanism to obtain a list of `BeanModel` objects from the returned list of `Customer` objects, and then from a loop of the beans, we apply the templates to the data obtained from using `Util.getJsObject(bean, 2)` which is eventually rendered on the respective panels.

Our use of `Util.geJsObject(bean, 2)` is worthy of note especially with the second parameter (2) which is used to indicate the depth of processing done on the bean, needed for rendering the reviews of each customer bean.

Doing math in templates

It is my sincere hope that our talk of math doesn't give you goose bumps, dispelling such fears this early is necessary for some to be able to complete this recipe especially since we are not attempting such things as used in RSA cryptography.

We basically want to be able to count stuff and do simple arithmetic operations which in my humble opinion is quite safe.

```
Name: Wuddy Brown
Email: wuddyb@live.com
Purchase: 2000
Est. Avg. Annual Purchase: 240
Reviews :
(1) Cool ...
(2) Starting Mine
(3) Ok music ...
```

How to do it...

Make an `XTemplate` object with the HTML format string which should contain property names from the intended data wrapped in curly brackets. Arithmetic operations can be done on a property value by applying an arithmetic operator to the property and a numeric literal.

Counting items in a list or showing the ordinal value of an item within a list being processed within a `<tpl for="...">` block is done with the use of a special `{#}` expression.

```java
    private String getTemplate(){
        StringBuilder sb = new StringBuilder();
    sb.append("<p>Name: {name}</p>");
    sb.append("<p>Email: {email}</p>");
    sb.append("<p>Purchase: {purchases}</p>");
    sb.append("<p>Est. Avg. Annual Purchase: {purchases*0.12}</p>");
    sb.append("<p>Reviews :</p>");
    sb.append("<ul>");
    sb.append("<tpl for=\"reviews\">");
    sb.append("<li>({#}) {title}</li>");
    sb.append("</tpl>");
    sb.append("</ul>");
        return sb.toString();
    };

    @Override
    public void onApply() {
      // We will display the template
      // data on this content panel
      final ContentPanel panel = new ContentPanel();
      panel.setSize(325, 185);
      panel.setHeaderVisible(false);
      panel.setBodyStyle("padding:7px");
      panel.setScrollMode(Scroll.AUTOY);
```

Templates and Views

```java
    // put it on screen, equivalent
    // to RootPanel.get().add(panel)
       GxtCookBk.getAppCenterPanel().add(panel);

    // Create the template as XTemplate object
    // instead of Template, else we
    // can't do any real math logic.
    final XTemplate tpl = XTemplate.create(getTemplate());

    // Make RPC call, see appendixes for info
    final RemoteGatewayAsync rpcService = (RemoteGatewayAsync) GWT.
create(RemoteGateway.class);
      AsyncCallback<Customer> callback = new AsyncCallback<Customer>() {
        @Override
        public void onFailure(Throwable caught) {
          panel.unmask();
          Info.display("Error", "RPC Error");
        }

        @Override
        public void onSuccess(Customer result) {
          if(result != null){
            // Just give us the customer data
            // in a way that is usable with Templates.
            // The Util.getJsObject() method expects a
            // ModelData which our remote Customer is
            // exactly not, but can be made to comply
            // with since it implements BeanModelTag.
            BeanModel bean = BeanModelLookup.get().getFactory(Customer.
class).createModel(result);

            // Apply the templates to each Customer bean,
            // remember that we are using the 'for' keyword
            // in <tpl> to display the title of a Review as we
            // iterate over the 'reviews' of a Customer, so
            // we use Util.getJsObject(bean, 2) to say give us
            // this bean as a JsObject that has a child ('reviews')
            // which itself needs processing as a JsObject.
            tpl.overwrite(panel.getBody().dom, Util.getJsObject(bean, 2));
          }
          panel.unmask();
        }
      };

    // show 'busy' signal on the
    // panel while we fetch data
    panel.mask();
    rpcService.getCustomer(0, callback);
  }
```

How it works...

Our remote `Customer` object has a `purchases` property, presumably indicative of a total annual purchase for a particular customer. Given a total purchase for all customers we can determine what percentage of this overall total is a particular customer's purchase, and that is what `{purchases*0.0038}` calculates for each customer formatted with the HTML string from `getTemplate()`. Note that `purchases*0.0038` is the mathematical equivalent of `(purchases/26375) * 100` where `26375` is the total purchases by all customers.

Also, the `<tpl>` block within the template string in the `getTemplate()` method uses the special `{#}` expression to display a count number for the reviews of a customer as it displays the title of each review in the list.

After setting up a `ContentPanel` to display the formatted data, we use `XTemplate.create()` to obtain an instance with the string gotten from our `getTemplate()` method, which we discussed in the chapter's first recipe, *Formatting data with a basic template*. We then invoke the remote `getCustomer()` method to fetch the customer with the ID of `3`.

Custom ComboBox displays

The GXT `ComboBox` widget uses a `ListView` object which in turn uses a `Template` to render the drop-down list presented by the combo. Perhaps you've thought of a combo that displays a list formatted a certain way, such as a list of customers with all parts of their names or only last names bold and italicized for emphasis. What about a combo of countries with an icon of their flag shown on the left-hand side, the country name in the middle, and a computed value (for example, GDP) showing on the far right.

These and more can be achieved in `ComboBox` as well as other data-bound GXT widgets that render items directly or indirectly with templates, like the case of a `ListView`. Combining such flexible data formatting with the power of a `ModelProcessor` used to compute values into data objects means the possibilities are endless.

Templates and Views

How to do it...

Build and configure a `ComboBox`, setting its `display` and `value` fields appropriately, as well as its store. Then use the `setTemplate()` method of the `ComboBox` class to set the template string that its internal `ListView` will use to format and display items from its bound store.

```java
private String getTemplate(){
    StringBuilder sb = new StringBuilder();
    sb.append("<tpl for=\".\">");
    sb.append("<div class=\"x-combo-list-item\" >");
    sb.append("<span><b>{name}</b></span>");
    sb.append("</div>");
    sb.append("</tpl>");
    return sb.toString();
}

private String getAdvTemplate(){
    StringBuilder sb = new StringBuilder();
    sb.append("<tpl for=\".\">");
    sb.append("<div class=\"x-combo-list-item\" >");
    sb.append("<span class=\"tpl-lft {gender}\"></span>");
    sb.append("<span class=\"tpl-lft\">{name}</span>");
    sb.append("<span class=\"tpl-rgt\">{age} Yrs</span>");
    sb.append("</div>");
    sb.append("</tpl>");
    return sb.toString();
}

private void configureCombo(ComboBox<BeanModel> combo, String label){
    combo.setValueField("id");
    combo.setDisplayField("name");
    combo.setFieldLabel(label);
    combo.setTriggerAction(TriggerAction.ALL);
    combo.setEmptyText("choose a customer ...");
    combo.setLoadingText("loading please wait ...");
}

public void onApply() {
    // A form to render the combo's
    FormPanel panel = new FormPanel();
    panel.setWidth(350);
    panel.setLabelSeparator("");
    panel.setHeaderVisible(false);
    panel.setLabelAlign(LabelAlign.TOP);
```

```
    // Make RPC call via a proxy, see appendixes for info
    final RemoteGatewayAsync rpcService = (RemoteGatewayAsync) GWT.
create(RemoteGateway.class);
    RpcProxy<ListLoadResult<Customer>> rpcProxy = new RpcProxy<ListLoadR
esult<Customer>>() {
        @Override
        public void load(Object cfg, AsyncCallback<ListLoadResult<Custom
er>> callback) {
            rpcService.getCustomers((ListLoadConfig) cfg, callback);
        }
    };

    // set up the store used by the combo's
    ListLoader<ListLoadResult<ModelData>> loader = new BaseListLoader<Li
stLoadResult<ModelData>>(rpcProxy, new BeanModelReader());
    ListStore<BeanModel> customerStore = new
ListStore<BeanModel>(loader);

    // The first combo
    // this one uses the simple
    // template to show bold names,
    // we'll call them 'Bold Customers'
    ComboBox<BeanModel> combo1 = new ComboBox<BeanModel>();
    combo1.setStore(customerStore);
    combo1.setTemplate(getTemplate());
    configureCombo(combo1, "Bold Customers");
    panel.add(combo1);

    // The second combo
    // this one uses the advance
    // template to show customer name
    // with their gender on the left
    // and their age on the right,
    // we'll call them 'Gender Sensitive Customers'
    ComboBox<BeanModel> combo2 = new ComboBox<BeanModel>();
    combo2.setStore(customerStore);
    combo2.setTemplate(getAdvTemplate());
    configureCombo(combo2, "Gender Sensitive Customers");
    panel.add(combo2);

    // put the form on screen, equivalent
    // to RootPanel.get().add(panel)
       GxtCookBk.getAppCenterPanel().add(panel);
}
```

Templates and Views

How it works...

First, we define two private methods `getTemplate()` and `getAdvTemplate()`, both of which return format strings intended for the construction of the `XTemplate` objects. The `getTemplate()` method features a `bold name` property wrapped by a `<span>` tag inside a `<div>` tag which has the `x-combo-list-item` CSS class used by GXT for proper rendering of items in a combo's drop-down list. The `getAdvTemplate()` method however wraps three empty `<span>` elements having custom CSS class names, in a `<div>` tag similar to that used by `getTemplate()`. Although they differ in the returned format strings, note the escaped umbrella `<tpl for=".">` which is used internally to iterate over all items in the combo's bound store.

There is also a handy `configureCombo()` method used to set up the combos we will be using for this recipe. The main recipe code begins in the `onApply()` method with the setting up of a `FormPanel` to hold the combos; we then set up a `ListStore` represented as `customerStore`, using a `RpcProxy` that invokes the remote `getCustomers()` method as our RPC service object. Our combos are then built, giving each the `customerStore` `ListStore`, then we use the `setTemplate()` method of the `ComboBox` class to set the template strings from `getTemplate()` and `getAdvTemplate()` on combo1 and combo2 respectively, before configuring and eventually adding them to `FormPanel` which is also displayed on the screen with `centerPanel.add(panel)`.

When the combo's trigger is clicked, we can see the difference that our custom templates (and some CSS) make as far as the formatting of the drop-down items is concerned.

Giving details with RowExpander

`RowExpander` is one of the many plugins used to tweak the default behavior of a GXT `Grid` component. It adds an additional column to the said grid (it actually extends `ColumnConfig`) with a tiny button used to toggle an extra area placed underneath each row so that more data or content about each row in the grid can be placed in this extra area. The GXT `Grid` component was discussed in *Chapter 7, The Venerable Grid Component*.

The `RowExpander` plugin employs the use of templates in the formatting of the data it renders, and while not a `RowExpander` requisite, we could use a `ModelProcessor` to prepare the data that will eventually be handed to the template.

How to do it...

Instantiate a `RowExpander` and then invoke its `setTemplate()` method passing in an `XTemplate` object created with the template string representing the format you want/prefer. As with most grids, set up a collection of `ColumnConfig` objects (the `Grid` columns) and add the `RowExpander` object to it (yes add it to the column list), and finally add the `RowExpander` object to the grid as a plugin using its `addPlugin()` method derived from the top-level `Component` class.

```
@Override
public void onApply() {
  // A list for the column configurations
  List<ColumnConfig> configs = new ArrayList<ColumnConfig>();

  // Create columns as ColumnConfig objects, add to the above list
  ColumnConfig column = new ColumnConfig("name", "Company", 200);
  configs.add(column);

  column = new ColumnConfig("last", "Last", 75);
  //format value as US currency
  column.setNumberFormat(NumberFormat.getCurrencyFormat());
  configs.add(column);
```

Templates and Views

```java
column = new ColumnConfig("date", "Last Updated", 125);
// format date as Oct 1, 1960
column.setDateTimeFormat(DateTimeFormat
    .getFormat("MMM dd, yyyy"));
configs.add(column);

// Create the expander with a Template,
// it's just HTML with mapped place-holders
// (properties in the intended bean model)
// wrapped in curly brackets for example, {name} or {about}
// RowExpander is a special ColumnConfig
XTemplate tpl = XTemplate.create("<p><b>Company:</b> {name}</p><br><p><b>Summary:</b> {about}</p><br />");
RowExpander expander = new RowExpander();
expander.setTemplate(tpl);

// make the expander the first column!
configs.add(0, expander);

ListStore<ModelData> store = new ListStore<ModelData>();
store.add(LocalData.getStocks());

ColumnModel cm = new ColumnModel(configs);
Grid<ModelData> grid = new Grid<ModelData>(store, cm);

// Our RowExpander template uses a {about} place-holder
// meaning it expects an 'about' property in the bean model.
// We'll quickly set()up one with a ModelProcessor since there's
// no 'about' property in our beans.
grid.setModelProcessor(new ModelProcessor<ModelData>() {
  @Override
  public ModelData prepareData(ModelData model) {
    Stock stk = (Stock) model;
    double last = stk.getLast();
    Date date = stk.getLastTrans();
    double change = stk.getChange();

    StringBuilder sb = new StringBuilder(stk.getName());
    sb.append(" identified as ").append(stk.getSymbol());
    sb.append(change < 0 ? ", lost " : ", gained ");
    sb.append(NumberFormat.getDecimalFormat().format(
      Math.abs(change)));
    sb.append(" over it's ").append(
        NumberFormat.getCurrencyFormat().format(last));
    sb.append(" share value on ");
    sb.append(DateTimeFormat.getFormat("MMMM dd, yyyy")
        .format(date));
```

```
            // Put the 'about' property in this model
            stk.set("about", sb.toString());
            return stk;
         }
      });

      // RowExpander is a special
      // ColumnConfig, actually a plugin!
      grid.addPlugin(expander);

      grid.setBorders(true);
      grid.setSize(400, 300);
      grid.setAutoExpandColumn("name");

      // show it up, equivalent to
      // RootPanel.get().add(grid)
         GxtCookBk.getAppCenterPanel().add(grid);
   }
```

How it works...

First, we define a private native `getTemplate()` method which returns a string. Unlike the other recipes of this chapter, we use the JSNI syntax in coding the template string that is returned. We use JSNI syntax here just to demonstrate the use of JavaScript native code. Of course we could simply use a `StringBuilder` to build the template string as we did in previous recipes.

The `onApply()` method starts out with a list for `ColumnConfig` objects which after been created and configured, are added to the list. Just after the `date` column, we instantiate a `RowExpander` and use its `setTemplate()` method to pass in the `XTemplate` made with our return from `getTempalate()`, the expander is then added to the column list as the first `ColumnConfig` object.

After some regular configurations, a `ModelProcessor` is then set on the grid and used to prepare data, especially the `about` property that is used by the template format string.

Once the `RowExpander` object is added to the grid with its `addPlugin()` method, and shown on the screen, we can then toggle the expand/collapse tool it provides for each row on the grid to show or hide detailed information for the row.

9
Data Makeovers with Charts and Visualizations

In this chapter, we will cover the following points:

- Using a bar chart
- Using a pie chart
- Using a line chart
- Using an area chart
- Visualizing data from a component
- Visualizing remote data
- Drawing on a canvas

Introduction

A chart is a graphical representation of structured data using symbols such as bars (in a bar chart), lines (in a line chart) and slices (in a pie chart). Charts, as visualization tools, are used to ease comprehension of large structured data and effectively communicate the intrinsic connections and relationships between parts of the data.

Visualizations through still or animated imagery are a compelling way to communicate both abstract and concrete data in ways beyond the provisions of mere charts. Several examples abound in the wild that we can sight; however, a worthy mention is *tweets* for the Twitter notification service.

Data Makeovers with Charts and Visualizations

Twitter is a bustling place of tweets, retweets, and replies, allowing news to spread organically (people-to-people). Kunel Anard of the BBC played on this idea of Twitter as an organic ecosystem and created tweets, a visualization wherein Twitter users float around like organisms, having shapes, color and size depending on the user's score on reputation (trust, friendliness, interestingness, and so on) thus making it easy to communicate a perspective of Twitter, never thought of before.

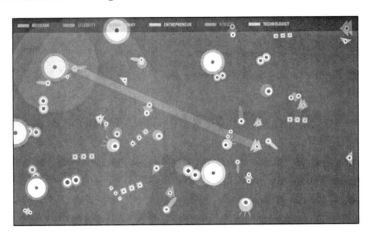

Using a bar chart

A bar chart is a visualization with rectangular bars having lengths proportional to the values represented. These rectangular bars can be drawn or plotted vertically (by tradition) or horizontally (if supported by the API).

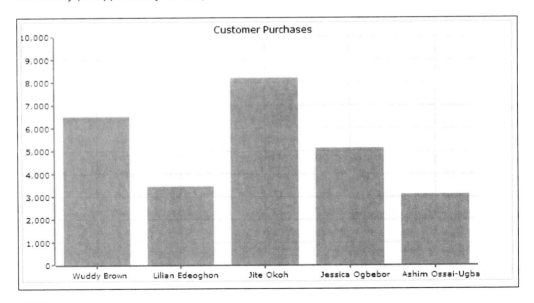

Getting ready

The charts API is not core to GXT, instead it's a plugin based on the Open Flash Charts 2 library and this requires some extra plumbing to get it up and running. The required steps are as follows:

1. Include the `charts` module in your `.gwt.xml` file by adding the line `<inherits name="com.extjs gxt.charts.chart" />` to the `.gwt.xml` file.
2. If you have not already done so, copy the `chart` and `flash` folders from the `resources` folder in GXT into your `projects` war folder, such that the `flash` and `chart` folders are now siblings with the `css` folder from where the `gxt-all.css` file must have been included to the host page; that is, `<GWT project path>/war/resources/flash` and `war/resources/chart`.
3. Include the JavaScript file from within the `flash` folder (from step 2) into the host page inside the `<head>` tag with a `script` tag, that is, `<script type="text/javascript" src="resources/flash/swfobject.js"></script>`.

After adding the `chart` module (step 1), copying the necessary files (step 2), and loading the chart's JavaScript file (step 3), all that is left to make use of the chart API is to instantiate a `Chart` instance using the `swf` file from the `chart` folder we copied in step 2.

```
new Chart("resources/chart/open-flash-chart.swf");
```

Working with GXT charts boils down to instantiating `Chart` (using the `open-flash-chart.swf` file), using `ChartModel` (derived from `BaseModel` to provide a proper data model for the chart API) and `ChartConfig` (an abstract `BaseModel` with concrete descendants such as `BarChart` and `LineChart` for creating specific charts).

How to do it...

Create a `Chart` instance and a `ChartModel` instance as well, configure `XAxis` and `YAxis` on `ChartModel`, and then set the model on the `Chart` object with `chart.setChartModel()`. Create a `BarChart` `ChartConfig` object and add values to it with its `addValues()` method, and finally add the `BarChart` configuration object to `ChartModel` and draw (or re-draw if needed) it on the screen.

```
@Override
public void onApply() {
   Chart chart = new Chart("resources/chart/open-flash-chart.swf");

   final ChartModel model = new ChartModel("Customer Purchases");
   final BarChart chartCfg = new BarChart();

   final XAxis xAxis = new XAxis();
   model.setXAxis(xAxis);
```

Data Makeovers with Charts and Visualizations

```java
    YAxis yAxis = new YAxis();
    yAxis.setRange(0, 10000, 1000);
    model.setYAxis(yAxis);

    chart.setChartModel(model);
    chart.setBorders(true);

    final LayoutContainer chartPanel = new LayoutContainer(new
FitLayout());
    chartPanel.setSize(650, 335);
    chartPanel.add(chart);

    // put it on screen, equivalent
    // to RootPanel.get().add(chartPanel)

     GxtCookBk.getAppCenterPanel().add(chartPanel);

    // Make RPC call, see appendix C for more info
     // on GWT RPC
    final RemoteGatewayAsync rpcService = (RemoteGatewayAsync) GWT.
create(RemoteGateway.class);
    AsyncCallback<List<Customer>> callback = new
AsyncCallback<List<Customer>>(){
       @Override
       public void onFailure(Throwable caught) {
         chartPanel.unmask();
         Info.display("Error", "RPC Error");
       }

       @Override
       public void onSuccess(List<Customer> result) {
         chartPanel.unmask();
         if(result != null){
            List<Label> labels = new ArrayList<Label>();
            List<Number> values = new ArrayList<Number>();

for(Customer cust : result) {
            labels.add(new Label(cust.getName()));
            values.add(new Double(cust.getPurchases()));
}
         xAxis.addLabels(labels);
         chartCfg.addValues(values);

         model.addChartConfig(chartCfg);
         chartPanel.layout();
        }
      }
    };

    // fetch some real customers
    chartPanel.mask();
    rpcService.listCustomers(null, callback);
 }
```

How it works...

First we instantiate `Chart` with the path to the chart API's `open-flash-chart.swf` file and then we create a `ChartModel` labeled `"Customer Purchases"` and a `BarChart` configuration object as well. Next, we add `XAxis` and `YAxis` objects to the model; the `YAxis` is configured to have values between 0 and 10,000 calibrated in 1000 steps.

After adding `ChartModel` to `Chart` with `chart.setChartModel(model)` and then adding the chart to a `LayoutContainer`, which is eventually placed onscreen with `GxtCookBk.getAppCenterPanel().add(chartPanel);`, we make an RPC call to fetch customer objects. We do this by invoking `rpcService.listCustomers()`. We then iterate over the list of returned customer objects and populate a list of `Label` and `Number` objects with the name `cust.getName()` and purchases `cust.getPurchases()` of each customer respectively. Afterwards, we configure the labels on our `XAxis` to show customer names and also add their purchase values to the `BarChart` configuration.

`model.addChartConfig(chartCfg)` is then invoked to pass in the values to the `ChartModel` model object which gives us a beautiful bar chart after `chartPanel.layout()` is called to refresh the panel.

Note that we use the `mask()` method on our `chartPanel` in order to display a "Busy" message on `chartPanel` as it is loading. We remove this message by calling `unmask()` as the data is returned from the RPC call.

There's more...

`BarChart` is further extended by `CylinderBarChart` and `FilledBarchart` which is in turn extended by `SketchBarChart`. All of these provide different styles for a bar chart visualization and all it takes to charge one style to the other is to use the appropriate descendant.

```
BarChart sketchCfg = new SketchBarChart();
```

You can also choose between a normal, 3D, or glass style during instantiation of the `BarChart` by passing a `BarStyle` to the constructor.

```
new SketchBarChart(BarStyle.GLASS);
```

Data Makeovers with Charts and Visualizations

Using a pie chart

A pie chart is a visualization with colored arcs or sectors called **slices**, within a circle, each representing the value of a distinct fragment of the data as a percentage that is reflected by its size relative to that of other sectors. Most pie chart implementations have labeled slices that are animated during mouse gestures on them. However, a good label and appropriate colors for each slice usually suffice.

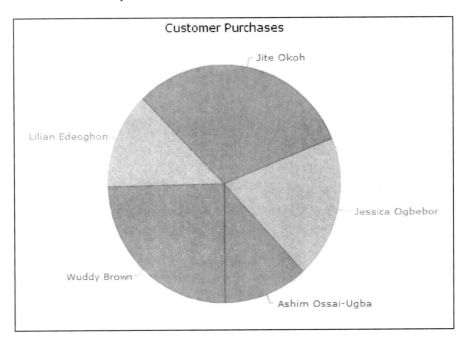

How to do it...

Create a `Chart` instance, a `ChartModel`, and then a `PieChart` object, set the model on the chart with `chart.setChartModel()` and then place the chart on the screen with a `LayoutContainer`. When the data is ready, use `pieChart.addSlice()` to add the slices to the chart, afterwards invoke `addChartConfig()` on `ChartModel` to pass in the `PieChart` to it and then refresh the screen if needs be.

```
@Override
public void onModuleLoad() {
   Chart chart = new Chart("resources/chart/open-flash-chart.swf");

   final ChartModel model = new ChartModel("Customer Purchases");
   final PieChart chartCfg = new PieChart();
```

```
    chart.setBorders(true);
    chart.setSize(650, 335);
    chart.setChartModel(model);

    final LayoutContainer chartPanel = new LayoutContainer(new
FitLayout());
    chartPanel.setSize(650, 335);
    chartPanel.add(chart);

    // put it on screen, equivalent
    // to RootPanel.get().add(chartPanel)
     GxtCookBk.getAppCenterPanel().add(chartPanel);

    // Make RPC call, see appendixes for more info
    final RemoteGatewayAsync rpcService = (RemoteGatewayAsync) GWT.
create(RemoteGateway.class);
    AsyncCallback<List<Customer>> callback = new
AsyncCallback<List<Customer>>(){
      @Override
      public void onFailure(Throwable caught) {
        chartPanel.unmask();
        Info.display("Error", "RPC Error");
      }

      @Override
      public void onSuccess(List<Customer> result) {
        chartPanel.unmask();
        if(result != null){

  }
        for(Customer cust : result) {
chartCfg.addSlice(cust.getPurchases(), cust.getName());
}
        model.addChartConfig(chartCfg);
            // refresh the center panel.
            GxtCookBk.getAppCenterPanel().layout();
       }
      }
    };

    // fetch some real customers
    chartPanel.mask();
    rpcService.listCustomers(null, callback);
}
```

How it works...

A `Chart` object is instantiated with the path to the chart API's `open-flash-chart.swf` file and then we create a `ChartModel` labeled `Customers Purchases`. After creating a `PieChart` (a subclass of `ChartConfig`) we pass the model to the `chart` object using `chart.setChartModel(model)` before placing the chart on the screen from within a `LayoutContainer` with `GxtCookBk.getAppCenterPanel().add(chartPanel);`. The `chartPanel.mask()` is used to hint the user of a potentially long process as we call the remote `listCustomers()` method on a RPC object so as to fetch customer objects from the server. The callback success handler first unmasks `chartPanel` and then obtains a list of customer beans which is iterated upon to add slices to `PieChart` using `chartCfg.addSlice()`, with each customer's purchase and name representing a slice.

After setting the slices on the pie chart `ChartConfig` object, we proceed by adding it to the model with `model.addChartConfig(chartcfg)` and refreshing the panel with `GxtCookBk.getAppCenterPanel().layout()`.

Using a line chart

The line chart is a simple yet very useful visualization that draws a line across the calibrated points of intersection on both axes such that it becomes easier for one to see a sequence or path flow for the data. It is mostly used to show the occurrence of data over time but it can be well suited for other purposes.

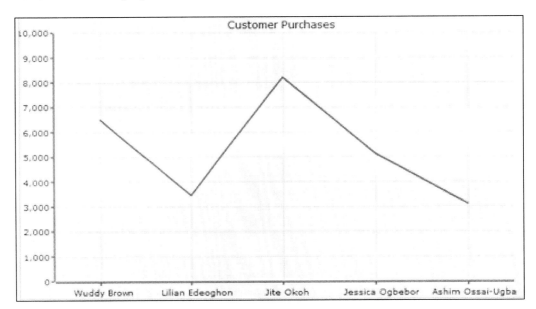

How to do it...

Create a `Chart` object with the correct path to the `open-flash-chart.swf` file, then create a `ChartModel` and a `LineChart` configuration object. A `XAxis` and then a `YAxis` object configured with an appropriate range need to be set on `ChartModel` using the `setXAxis()` and `setYAxis()` method respectively. Once the model is set on the chart with the chart's `setChartModel()` and the chart rendered onscreen with a `LayoutContainer`, we can then add a line when the data is ready by invoking `lineChart.addValues()` while not forgetting to set up reasonable labels on the x axis using `xAxis.addLabels()`.

```java
    @Override
    public void onApply() {
      // create the Chart object
      Chart chart = new Chart("resources/chart/open-flash-chart.swf");

      // create the model and the
      // line-chart config object
      final ChartModel model = new ChartModel("Customer Purchases");
      final LineChart chartCfg = new LineChart();

      // set up x and y axis
      final XAxis xAxis = new XAxis();
      model.setXAxis(xAxis);

      YAxis yAxis = new YAxis();
      // calibrate y axis from
      // 0 to 10000 in 1000 steps
      yAxis.setRange(0, 10000, 1000);
      model.setYAxis(yAxis);

      chart.setChartModel(model);
      chart.setBorders(true);

      // place chart on the screen
      final LayoutContainer chartPanel = new LayoutContainer(new
    FitLayout());
      chartPanel.setSize(650, 335);
      chartPanel.add(chart);

      // put it onscreen, equivalent
      // to RootPanel.get().add(chartPanel)
        GxtCookBk.getAppCenterPanel().add(chartPanel);

      // Make RPC call, see appendixes for more info
      final RemoteGatewayAsync rpcService = (RemoteGatewayAsync) GWT.
    create(RemoteGateway.class);
        AsyncCallback<List<Customer>> callback = new
    AsyncCallback<List<Customer>>(){
          @Override
```

```java
      public void onFailure(Throwable caught) {
        chartPanel.unmask();
        Info.display("Error", "RPC Error");
      }
      @Override
      public void onSuccess(List<Customer> result) {
        chartPanel.unmask();
        if(result != null){
          List<Label> labels = new ArrayList<Label>();
          List<Number> values = new ArrayList<Number>();

          List<BeanModel> beans = BeanModelLookup.get().
    getFactory(Customer.class).createModel(result);
          for (BeanModel bean : beans) {
            Customer cust = (Customer) bean.getBean();

            labels.add(new Label(cust.getName()));
            values.add(new Double(cust.getPurchases()));
          }
          xAxis.addLabels(labels);
          chartCfg.addValues(values);

          model.addChartConfig(chartCfg);

              // refresh the center panel.
              GxtCookBk.getAppCenterPanel().layout();
          }
        }
    };
    // fetch some real customers
    chartPanel.mask();
    rpcService.listCustomers(null, callback);
}
```

How it works...

A `Chart` object is created with a correct path to the `open-flash-chart.swf` file, and then we create a `ChartModel` and a `LineChart` object. Next, we create `XAxis` and a `YAxis` object configured to calibrate values between 0 and 10,000 in 1,000 steps. Both axis objects are then given to the model which is in turn given to the chart using `chart.setChartModel(model)`.

After rendering the chart onscreen from within a `LayoutContainer` and masking it to indicate we are about to get really busy, we invoke the remote `listCustomers()` method on an RPC service object to fetch a list of customer objects. The list of customer objects in the success handler of the RPC callback is iterated over to populate a list of `Label` objects and another for `Number` objects. These lists of `Label` objects and `Number` objects are respectively used to configure the `XAxis` labels and `LineChart` values so that once we invoke `model.addChartConfig()` with the `LineChart` configuration object, our line chart is ready to be drawn.

Chapter 9

There's more...

You can add more lines to a single line chart by simply configuring another `LineChart` instance, setting up values on it and adding it to the model using the `addChartConfig()` method of the `ChartModel` class. This is how most `AreaChart` visualizations are built except that they are colored to show the area under each line and also appropriately labeled to identify what each area stands for.

Using an area chart

The area chart is actually a line chart, but with added ability to communicate the scope of its coverage with a solid fill color under its line. It is basically a colored line chart with two or more line plots.

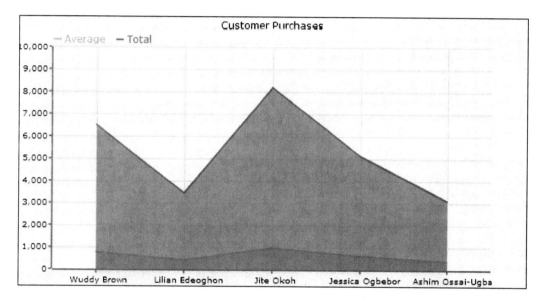

How to do it...

Create a `Chart` and `ChartModel` object and then an `AreaChart` object for each area you want to plot, each having an appropriate label/legend and color with its `setText()` and `setColour()` methods respectively. The `ChartModel` can then be set on the chart object after giving the model a `XAxis` and `YAxis` object.

Data Makeovers with Charts and Visualizations

Once the data is ready, we build a list of `Label` objects for `XAxis` and then a list of `Number` values for each area in the chart. The values built are then given to their respective `AreaChart` object with `areaChart.addValues()` and then they are in turn added to `ChartModel` using `model.addChartConfig()` for each.

```java
@Override
public void onModuleLoad() {
  // create the Chart object
  Chart chart = new Chart("resources/chart/open-flash-chart.swf");

  // create the model and the
  // area-chart config objects
  final ChartModel model = new ChartModel("Customer Purchases");

   // create an AreaChart for the Average
  final AreaChart avgCfg = new AreaChart();
  avgCfg.setText("Average");
  avgCfg.setColour("#ff8800");

   // create an AreaChart for the total
  final AreaChart totalCfg = new AreaChart();
  totalCfg.setText("Total");

  // set up x and y axis
  final XAxis xAxis = new XAxis();
  model.setXAxis(xAxis);

  YAxis yAxis = new YAxis();
  // calibrate from 0 to 10000 in 1000 steps
  yAxis.setRange(0, 10000, 1000);
  model.setYAxis(yAxis);

  chart.setChartModel(model);
  chart.setBorders(true);

  // wrap chart with a panel
  // for easy refresh
  final LayoutContainer chartPanel = new LayoutContainer(new
 FitLayout());
  chartPanel.setSize(650, 335);
  chartPanel.add(chart);

  // put it on screen, equivalent
  // to RootPanel.get().add(chartPanel)
   GxtCookBk.getAppCenterPanel().add(chartPanel);
```

```java
   // Make RPC call, see appendixes for more info
   final RemoteGatewayAsync rpcService = (RemoteGatewayAsync) GWT.
create(RemoteGateway.class);
   AsyncCallback<List<Customer>> callback = new
AsyncCallback<List<Customer>>(){
      @Override
      public void onFailure(Throwable caught) {
        chartPanel.unmask();
        Info.display("Error", "RPC Error");
      }

      @Override
      public void onSuccess(List<Customer> result) {
        chartPanel.unmask();
        if(result != null){
          List<Label> labels = new ArrayList<Label>();
          List<Number> values = new ArrayList<Number>();
          List<Number> avgValues = new ArrayList<Number>();

          List<BeanModel> beans = BeanModelLookup.get().
getFactory(Customer.class).createModel(result);
          for (BeanModel bean : beans) {
            Customer cust = (Customer) bean.getBean();

            labels.add(new Label(cust.getName()));
            values.add(new Double(cust.getPurchases()));
            avgValues.add(new Double(cust.getPurchases()*0.12));
          }
          xAxis.addLabels(labels);
          // add values to the average chart.
          avgCfg.addValues(avgValues);
              // add the average chart to the model.
          model.addChartConfig(avgCfg);
          // add values to the total chart.
          totalCfg.addValues(values);   // add the total chart to the
model.
          model.addChartConfig(totalCfg);
          chartPanel.layout();
        }
      }
   };

   // fetch some real customers
   chartPanel.mask();
   rpcService.listCustomers(null, callback);
}
```

How it works...

A `Chart` instance is created with an accurate path to the chart API's `open-flash-chart.swf` file and then a `ChartModel` labeled `Customer Purchases` is also created. Next, we create two `AreaChart` configuration objects. The first one is intended to show an average plot and as such is given a legend value of `Average` with `avgCfg.setText()` and a color with `avgCfg.setColour()`. The second `AreaChart` gets the default color but is given a legend label of `Total` because we want to plot the total customer purchases with this one. After setting on the model, `XAxis` and a `YAxis` calibrated from 0 to 10,000 in 1,000 steps the model is eventually configured for the chart using `chart.setChartModel(model)` and the chart gets placed on the screen (with a wrapper `LayoutContainer`) ready for data. The data is received via RPC by calling the remote `listCustomers()` method with an `AsyncCallback` having a success handler, wherein we populate a list of `Label` objects for the x axis as the customer names and two lists of `Number` objects as values for the "total" and "average" `AreaChart` configuration objects. These configuration objects finally get passed to `ChartModel` by `model.addChartConfig(avgCfg)` and `model.addChartConfig(totalCfg)` before the screen is refreshed with `chartPanel.layout()`.

Visualizing data from a component

It is often required to display a chart alongside a data-bound component so that the chart provides a graphical representation of the same data that is presented by the other component. This can be instantly gratifying and serve as a real-time feedback system if data changes in the component are immediately reflected in the chart.

Consider having a pie chart that shows the stock performance of an industry. A sort of binding can be set()up between the chart and the grid so that as stock prices change, the grid's data is updated thereby triggering an update to the chart as well.

Chapter 9

We will simulate this with a grouped grid that allows changes to a **Price** column and see how we can benefit by instantly translating the updates to the pie chart.

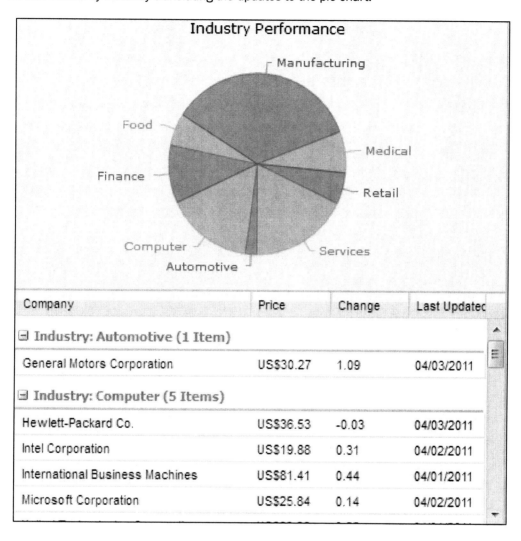

Data Makeovers with Charts and Visualizations

How to do it...

Configure and render a pie chart with a grouped editable grid and calculate the value of each slice of the chart from the total of the price column in each group of the grid this can be done within `GroupRenderer`, since we are already using `GroupRenderer` in order to generate a custom header for each group. `GroupingStore` can then override `afterCommit()` (or listen for `Events.Update`) to reconfigure or refresh the chart after changes to the price column have been saved.

```
@Override
public void onApply() {
  // create the Chart object
  final Chart chart = new Chart("resources/chart/open-flash-chart.swf");

  // create the model and the
  // pie-chart config object
  final String chartLbl = "Industry Performance";
  final ChartModel chartModel = new ChartModel(chartLbl);
  final PieChart chartCfg = new PieChart();

  chart.setBorders(true);
  chart.setChartModel(chartModel);

  // wrap chart in a
  // refresh-able panel
  final LayoutContainer chartPanel = new LayoutContainer(new FitLayout());
  chartPanel.setSize(435, 235);
  chartPanel.add(chart);

  // put chart onscreen, equivalent
  // to RootPanel.get().add(chartPanel)

   GxtCookBk.getAppCenterPanel().add(chartPanel);

  // Populate the store and group the
  // data on the 'industry' column, can
  // also use a RpcProxy via a ListLoader.
  // Refresh chart after changes are saved
  final GroupingStore<Stock> store = new GroupingStore<Stock>(){
    @Override
    protected void afterCommit(Record record) {
      super.afterCommit(record);
      chartCfg.getValues().clear();
      this.groupBy("industry", true);
```

```
            ChartModel model = new ChartModel(chartLbl);
            model.addChartConfig(chartCfg);
            chart.setChartModel(model);
            chartPanel.layout();
        }
    };
    store.add(LocalData.getCompanies());
    store.groupBy("industry");

    List<ColumnConfig> config = new ArrayList<ColumnConfig>();
    ColumnConfig company = new ColumnConfig("name", "Company", 60);
    company.setGroupable(false); // don't allow grouping here
    config.add(company);

    ColumnConfig price = new ColumnConfig("open", "Price", 20);
    price.setNumberFormat(NumberFormat.getCurrencyFormat());
    price.setGroupable(false); // don't allow grouping here

    // We want to enter values here
    NumberField numField = new NumberField();
    numField.setAllowBlank(false);
    numField.setAllowNegative(false);
    price.setEditor(new CellEditor(numField));
    config.add(price);

    ColumnConfig change = new ColumnConfig("change", "Change", 20);
    change.setGroupable(false); // don't allow grouping here
    config.add(change);

    ColumnConfig industry = new ColumnConfig("industry",
        "Industry", 20);
    config.add(industry);

    ColumnConfig last = new ColumnConfig("date", "Last Updated", 20);
    last.setDateTimeFormat(DateTimeFormat.getFormat("MM/dd/y"));
    last.setGroupable(false); // don't allow grouping here
    config.add(last);

    // Create and configure Grid
    final ColumnModel cm = new ColumnModel(config);
    EditorGrid<Stock> groupedGrid = new EditorGrid<Stock>(store, cm);
    groupedGrid.setBorders(true);
    groupedGrid.setSize(435, 200);
    groupedGrid.setStripeRows(true);
```

```java
    // Must use a GroupingView for rendering
    GroupingView view = new GroupingView();
    view.setForceFit(true);
    // don't show the grouped column.
    view.setShowGroupedColumn(false);
    // Customize how the groups show up
    view.setGroupRenderer(new GridGroupRenderer() {
      @Override
      public String render(GroupColumnData data) {
        String header = cm.getColumnById(data.field)
            .getHeader();
        String sizeStr = data.models.size() == 1 ? "Item"
            : "Items";

        double value = 0.0;
        for(ModelData model : data.models){
          value += new Double(model.get("open").toString()).
doubleValue();
        }
           // add a slice to the pie chart.
        chartCfg.addSlice(value, data.gvalue.toString());
        return header + ": " + data.group + " ("
            + data.models.size() + " " + sizeStr + ")";
      }
    });
    groupedGrid.setView(view);
    groupedGrid.addListener(Events.ViewReady, new Listener<GridEvent<Mo
delData>>() {
      @Override
      public void handleEvent(GridEvent<ModelData> be) {
        chartModel.addChartConfig(chartCfg);
      }
    });

    // show grid up, equivalent to
    // RootPanel.get().add(groupedGrid)

      GxtCookBk.getAppCenterPanel().add(groupedGrid);


    final Button saveBtn = new Button("Save Changes");
    saveBtn.addSelectionListener(new SelectionListener<ButtonEvent>() {
      @Override
```

```
      public void componentSelected(ButtonEvent evt) {
        store.commitChanges();
        saveBtn.disable();
      }
    });
    // put button on screen, equivalent
    // to RootPanel.get().add(saveBtn)
    GxtCookBk.getAppCenterPanel().add(saveBtn);

    // enable the button if we made changes to the grid.
    groupedGrid.addListener(Events.AfterEdit,new Listener<BaseEvent>() {
      @Override
      public void handleEvent(BaseEvent be) {
        // TODO Auto-generated method stub
        saveBtn.setEnabled(store.getModifiedRecords().size() > 0);
      }
    });
  }
```

How it works...

We instantiate `Chart`, a labeled `ChartModel`, and then a `PieChart` configuration object; the model is then set on the chart with `chart.setChartModel(model)` and the chart is eventually rendered with a `LayoutContainer` for easy refreshing.

Next, we create a `GroupingStore`, which is a specialized store that provides grouping of the data model by one of the fields. We group our data by the industry field. In the `GroupingStore` we override the `afterCommit()` method so that we can refresh the pie chart after changes have been made to the grid. The refresh is done by first clearing previous values from the chart and performing a grouping of stock prices by industry on the store in order to calculate new values for the chart.

After that we add the new values (`chartCfg`) to a new model which is then given to the `chart` object, and then `chartPanel.layout()` is finally used to redraw the chart.

A set of columns only editable on the price column are built and used to eventually instantiate an `EditorGrid`, whose `GroupingView` is given a `GridGroupRenderer` that adds slices to the pie chart based on the total price data for each group.

Finally, for intuitive use, we added a save button that is only enabled when there are changes to the grid. Try altering some price data and hit *save changes* to see the effect on the pie chart.

Data Makeovers with Charts and Visualizations

Visualizing remote Data

With over six billion people on earth and about two billion internet users, the world is getting overwhelmed by data which has really been on the rise since we began the social and participation era in computing. Therefore, there's a high chance that the data for the chart you want to present is out there behind one RSS feed, RESTful service, or some sort of API call that will produce either XML or most likely JSON formatted data.

You may want to know how much your country owes the World Bank or what the emission/pollution ratings of your country have been for the past five years. I decided a good example will be to plot how many Nigerian primary school children are out of school over a certain period of time with a line chart having two line plots, one for male and the other for female children, so that at a glance we can tell who is worst hit.

Getting ready

Fetching data from an external/another server will most likely be blocked by the browser's same origin policy security model, requiring us to use a `RequestBuilder` which brings the GWT HTTP module dependency into the mix. Since we intend to work with JSON data, we are also required to inherit the GWT JSON module.

Therefore, add the following lines to your `.gwt.xml` file:

```
<inherits name= "com.google.gwt.json.JSON" />
<inherits name= "com.google.gwt.http.HTTP"/>
```

How to do it...

Create and configure a `Chart` and `ChartModel` with two `AreaChart` configurations, an `XAxis` with labels for `"2003"` to `"2007"` and also a `YAxis` having a range of 50,000 to 6000000 in 50,000 steps. Fetch the data from the World Bank's open data API in JSON format using a `RequestBuilder`, put the values into the `AreaChart` configuration objects then refresh the chart.

```
private void fetchData(String url, final AreaChart chartCfg,final
LayoutContainer panel){
   RequestBuilder builder = new RequestBuilder(RequestBuilder.GET, URL.
encode(url));
   try {
     builder.sendRequest(null, new RequestCallback(){
       @Override
       public void onError(Request request, Throwable ex) {
         Info.display("Connection Error", ex.getMessage());
       }
```

```java
        @Override
        public void onResponseReceived(Request request,
            Response response) {
          // check for an ok html response code (200).
          if (200 == response.getStatusCode()){
            JSONValue jsonVal = JSONParser.parseStrict(response.
getText());
            drawChart(jsonVal, chartCfg,panel);
          } else {
            GWT.log("response:" + response.getText());
            Info.display("Error Status", response.getStatusText());
          }
        }
      });
    } catch (RequestException ex) {
      Info.display("Connection Error", ex.getMessage());
    }
}

private void drawChart(JSONValue json, AreaChart chartCfg,
LayoutContainer panel){
    JSONArray data = (JSONArray) json;
    JSONArray values = (JSONArray) data.get(1);

    List<Number> chartValues = new ArrayList<Number>();

    for(int i = 0; i < values.size(); i++){
      JSONObject dataValue = (JSONObject) values.get(i);
      String strVal = dataValue.get("value").toString();
      strVal = strVal.replaceAll("\"", "");
      chartValues.add(0, new Double(strVal));
    }
    chartCfg.addValues(chartValues);
    // refresh to reveal data
    panel.layout();
}

@Override
public void onApply() {

    // create chart object
    Chart chart = new Chart("resources/chart/open-flash-chart.swf");

    // create model and
    // as well as labeled
    // and colored area-chart
    // config objects
```

```
ChartModel model = new ChartModel("Nigerian Children out of primary
school: courtesy World Bank");
  final AreaChart maleCfg = new AreaChart();
  maleCfg.setText("Male");
  maleCfg.setColour("#ff8800");

  final AreaChart femaleCfg = new AreaChart();
  femaleCfg.setText("Female");
  femaleCfg.setColour("#808080");

  // set up x and y axis
  XAxis xAxis = new XAxis();
  xAxis.addLabels(new Label("2003"), new Label("2004"), new
Label("2005"), new Label("2006"), new Label("2007"));
  model.setXAxis(xAxis);

  YAxis yAxis = new YAxis();
  yAxis.setTickLength(5);
  yAxis.setRange(500000, 6000000, 500000);
  model.setYAxis(yAxis);

  model.addChartConfig(maleCfg);
  model.addChartConfig(femaleCfg);

  chart.setChartModel(model);
  chart.setBorders(true);
  // prepare for easy refresh
  final LayoutContainer chartPanel = new LayoutContainer(new
FitLayout());
  chartPanel.setSize(685, 335);
  chartPanel.add(chart);

  // put it on screen, equivalent
  // to RootPanel.get().add(chartPanel)
  GxtCookBk.getAppCenterPanel().add(chartPanel);

  // add <inherits name="com.google.gwt.json.JSON" /> and
  // <inherits name="com.google.gwt.http.HTTP" /> to module XML file
  // http://127.0.0.1:8888/files/maledata.json
  // http://127.0.0.1:8888/files/femaledata.json
  // http://api.worldbank.org/countries/NGA/indicators/SE.PRM.UNER.
MA?date=2004:2007&format=json
  // http://api.worldbank.org/countries/NGA/indicators/SE.PRM.UNER.
FE?date=2004:2007&format=json
```

```
    String mUrl = "http://api.worldbank.org/countries/NGA/indicators/
SE.PRM.UNER.MA?date=2004:2007&format=json";
    String fUrl = "http://api.worldbank.org/countries/NGA/indicators/
SE.PRM.UNER.FE?date=2004:2007&format=json";
    fetchData(mUrl, maleCfg,chartPanel);
    fetchData(fUrl, femaleCfg,chartPanel);

}
```

How it works...

We have a private `fetchData()` method that uses a `RequestBuilder` to get JSON from a given URL. When the data arrives, the `onResponseReceived()` method parses the JSON data which is then fed with the given `AreaChart` configuration object to a second private `drawChart()` method that iterates over the JSON data to put values into the `AreaChart` object.

The aforementioned private methods simplify our `onModuleLoad()` method; we create and configure a `Chart`, `ChartModel`, and two `AreaChart` configurations. Next, we set up the x axis and y axis for the model, add the `maleCfg` and `femaleCfg` `AreaChart` objects to the model and then give the model to the `chart` object with the `setChartModel()` method of the `Chart` class.

After rendering the chart with a `LayoutContainer` we call our private `fetchData()` twice with the URL to make a REST API call to the World Bank open datasets and the matching (male or female) `AreaChart` object. These calls fetch the data and populate the `AreaChart` with parsed and formatted values so that `chartPanel.layout()` can now repaint the screen showing the chart and of course a startling revelation, as shown in the following screenshot:

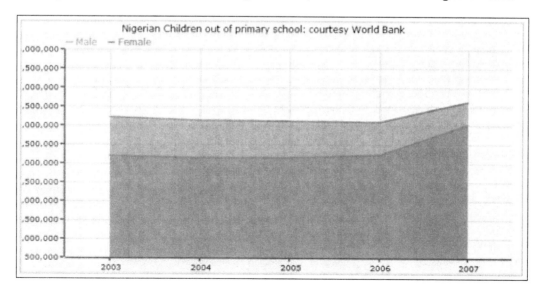

Drawing on a canvas

HTML 5 is the buzz of the web now; it is here and ready to be used. Although not fully baked into GWT, especially with varying levels of support even from A grade browsers, we can draw custom and fun visualizations on the HTML 5 `canvas` element if the underlying browser supports it. The web page at http://gwtcanvasdemo.appspot.com has a good collection GWT-based `canvas` demos.

Although HTML 5 is not integrated into GXT components, in the future HTML 5 will become the standard and will be integrated into the major web frameworks. This recipe, although not using GXT components, will give you a taste of HTML 5 capabilities.

The GXT Chart API supports horizontal bar charts, but I'll show off the `canvas` element drawing capabilities by trying to draw a horizontal bar chart and some random shapes.

How to do it...

The `Canvas` class has a static `createIfSupported()` method which will return null if the underlying implementation (the browser in use) does not (or is yet to) support it, therefore this check should be performed first before proceeding.

Once we have a `Canvas` object, obtain its 2D context (3D can wait) with the `getContext2d()` method and then fill, stroke, or draw with the appropriate methods. Really, it's that simple!

```
private void configureCanvas(Canvas canvas, int size){
    canvas.setStyleName("chartcanvas");
    canvas.setWidth(size + "px");
    canvas.setCoordinateSpaceWidth(size);
    canvas.setHeight(size + "px");
    canvas.setCoordinateSpaceHeight(size);
}
```

```
@Override
public void onApply() {
  // online demo : http://gwtcanvasdemo.appspot.com/

  // is there support ??
  Canvas canvas = Canvas.createIfSupported();
    if (canvas == null) {
      Info.display("Notice", "Sorry, your browser doesn't support the
HTML5 Canvas");
        return;
    }

    // ok, configure and
    // place it on screen
    configureCanvas(canvas, 350);
    centerPanel.add(canvas);

    // draw several filled
    // rectangles to simulate
    // a horizontal bar-chart
    Context2d ctx = canvas.getContext2d();
    ctx.setFillStyle("#ff8800");
    ctx.fillRect(20,20,100,50);

    ctx.setFillStyle("#808080");
    ctx.fillRect(20,80,155,50);

    ctx.setFillStyle("#f6f6f6");
    ctx.fillRect(20,140,190,50);

    ctx.setFillStyle("#aa7290");
    ctx.fillRect(20,200,285,50);

    ctx.setFillStyle("#141414");
    ctx.fillRect(20,260,80,50);

    // another canvas to draw
    // something obscure
    canvas = Canvas.createIfSupported();
    configureCanvas(canvas, 200);

    GxtCookBk.getAppCenterPanel().add(canvas);
```

Data Makeovers with Charts and Visualizations

```
            // give me some shapes
            ctx = canvas.getContext2d();
            ctx.beginPath();
            ctx.moveTo(110,75);
        for(int i=0;i<4;i++){
          for(int j=0;j<3;j++){
            ctx.beginPath();
               int x                 = 25+j*50;
               int y                 = 25+i*50;
               int radius            = 20;
               int startAngle        = 0;
               double endAngle       = Math.PI+(Math.PI*j)/2;
               boolean anticlockwise = i%2==0 ? false : true;
               ctx.arc(x, y, radius, startAngle, endAngle, anticlockwise);
               if (i>1){
                   ctx.fill();
               } else {
                   ctx.stroke();
               }
          }
        }
      }
```

How it works...

The `onApply()` method begins with a check for `Canvas` support using `Canvas.createIfSupported()` and only proceeds if there is support. The private `configureCanvas()` is then invoked to set the dimension (width and height) for the `Canvas` element which is also given a style name that is used to give it some margin, a border, and a background image.

After adding it to the screen, with `GxtCookBk.getAppCenterPanel().add(chartPanel);`, we then draw various colored horizontal bars by invoking the `setFillStyle()` and `fillRect()` methods of the `Context2d` class. The `fillRect()` methods draws a filled (with solid color specified by the last `setFillStyle()` invocation) rectangle with the specified dimension (width and height) on a point (x and y).

The second `Canvas` draws random and arbitrary shapes which is perhaps not very useful to anyone except to demonstrate that `Canvas` can draw just about anything!

10
Drag-and-drop

In this chapter we will cover:

- Dragging any component
- Simple DnD within components
- DnD across components
- DnD from desktop, with HTML5
- Implementing custom DnD on tabs

Introduction

Drag-and-drop (**DnD**) is one of the most widely underestimated and underused features in web applications. Although there are several libraries that enhance the browser's native support and handling of DnD, we are yet to see widespread adoption of this UI interaction magic maker. Using drag-and-drop with a web application can make it a lot easier, user friendly, and more fun, giving users flexibility to easily move, sort, or swap objects that can be very difficult and sometimes ugly to accomplish with buttons or links.

Drag-and-drop operations must have a starting point (such as where the mouse button was clicked, or the start of the selection or element that was selected for the drag), may have any number of intermediate steps (elements that the mouse moves over during a drag or elements that the user picks as possible drop points as he cycles through possibilities) and must either have an end point (the element over which the mouse button was released, or the element that was finally selected) or be cancelled. The end point must be the last element selected as a possible drop point before the drop occurs (so if the operation is not cancelled, there must be at least one element in the middle step).

Drag-and-drop

Some good online DnD implementations include Mockingbird (https://gomockingbird.com/), an HTML5 canvas-based tool that makes it easy to create mockups of your website or application. Its ease of use and simplicity comes from being able to drag-and-drop elements into your mockup.

HTML 5 drag-and-drop is supported on Chrome version 17 and above, Firefox version 8.0 and above, and is partially supported on IE 9.

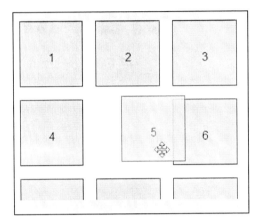

Dragging any component

Many GXT components have specialized classes for handling DnD in ways that are best suited for them. However, any GXT component can be dragged with just a single line of code. Of course, there are several other bells and whistles we can turn on for such a drag operation, but still with very minimal configuration. The following screenshot shows the draggable buttons in this recipe:

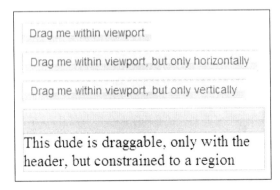

How to do it...

Simply wrap the widget or component with `Draggable`, a GXT class, and it becomes draggable! Optionally, you can constrain the orientation (horizontal or vertical) and region/dimension of the drag operation by invoking the appropriate `setConstrain()` method and `setContainer()` method of the `Draggable` class.

```
private Button makeBtn(String label) {
  Button btn = new Button(label);
  btn.setStyleAttribute("margin", "8px");
  return btn;
}

@Override
public void onApply() {
  Draggable canDrag = null;

  // Drag within the browser's
  // viewable region (viewport)
  Button btn1 = makeBtn("Drag me within viewport");
  canDrag = new Draggable(btn1);
  // centerPanel is the main content panel of the application.
  // it is initialized statically in the recipe class.
  centerPanel.add(btn1);

  // Constrained vertically,
  // thus we can only drag
  // horizontally
  Button btn2 = makeBtn("Drag me within viewport, but only horizontally");
  canDrag = new Draggable(btn2);
  canDrag.setConstrainVertical(true);
  centerPanel.add(btn2);

  // Constrained horizontally,
  // thus we can only drag
  // vertically
  Button btn3 = makeBtn("Drag me within viewport, but only vertically");
  canDrag = new Draggable(btn3);
  canDrag.setConstrainHorizontal(true);
  // centerPanel is the main content panel of the application.
  // it is initialized statically in the recipe class.
  centerPanel.add(btn3);
```

Drag-and-drop

```
    ContentPanel textPanel = new ContentPanel();
    textPanel.setWidth(250);
    textPanel.setStyleAttribute("margin", "8px");
    textPanel.addText("<p>This dude is draggable, only with the header,
but constrained to a region</p>");

    // drag with the header,
    // and only within the region
    // defined by centerPanel
    canDrag = new Draggable(textPanel, textPanel.getHeader());
    canDrag.setContainer(centerPanel);
    // centerPanel is the main content panel of the application.
    // it is initialized statically in the recipe class.
    centerPanel.add(textPanel);
}
```

How it works...

The `onApply()` method generally creates a set of components, wraps them with an instance of `Draggable` and optionally sets some configurations to control the drag operation. The first component—a standard GXT button—is wrapped and placed onscreen, allowing it to become draggable with the default settings. It can be dragged arbitrarily but within the browser's viewable space—often called **viewport**.

The second button, `btn2`, though draggable, is vertically constrained with `canDrag.setConstrainVertical(true)`. Thus, we can only move it in a horizontal direction. Conversely, the third button, `btn3`, can only move vertically, having been constrained horizontally.

The last component we made draggable is a regular GXT `ContentPanel` object displaying some text, however it can only be dragged from its header, because we instantiated its wrapper—`Draggable`—using the overloaded constructor that expects a second component that will serve as the handle from which drags will be initiated. We also use the `setContainer()` method of the `Draggable` class to make our panel only draggable within the region/dimension of the component that `centerPanel` refers to, preventing it from being dragged everywhere in the browser's viewport.

Simple DnD within components

As seen in the previous recipe, *Dragging any component*, any GXT component can be dragged after wrapping it with an instance of `Draggable`. However, certain GXT components have specialized DnD class implementation, which handles the specifics of DnD for them. These GXT components are generally implemented as a pair of classes for each component. The pair is made up of a `DragSource` implementation and a `DropTarget` implementation, responsible for drags and drops, respectively. The `Grid` implementation, therefore, has a `GridDragSource` instance and a `GridDropTarget` instance with others listed, as in the following table:

Component	DragSource	DropTarget
`ListView`	`ListViewDragSource`	`ListViewDropTarget`
`TreePanel`	`TreePanelDragSource`	`TreePanelDropTarget`
`TreeGrid`	`TreeGridDragSource`	`TreeGridDropTarget`

With a few additional lines of code, we can augment some recipes from previous chapters to allow drag-and-drop within them, such as reordering of columns and records in a `Grid` object or nodes in a `TreePanel` instance.

The following screenshot shows columns moved within a `Grid` component:

Drag-and-drop

The following screenshot shows nodes moved within a `TreePanel` instance:

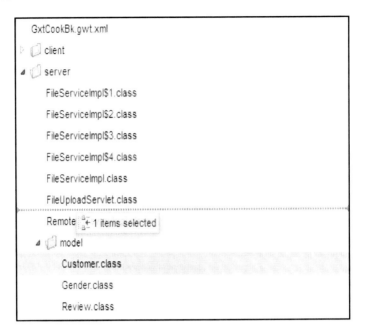

How to do it...

1. Create and configure a `Grid` component with the needed store and columns, and then instantiate the `GridDragSource` class and the `GridDropTarget` class with the configured `Grid` instance.
2. On the target object for the drop operation, call the `setFeedBack()` and `setAllowSelfAsSource()` methods appropriately.
3. Create and configure a `TreePanel` instance with which to instantiate the `TreeDragSource` and `TreeDropTarget` classes.
4. Set `FeedBack` as well as calling `setAllowSelfAsSource(true)` on the tree's drop-target object.

    ```
    @Override
    public void onApply() {
      centerPanel.setLayout(new ColumnLayout());

      // 1. Simple DnD in Grid
      // A list for the column configurations
      List<ColumnConfig> configs = new ArrayList<ColumnConfig>();
    ```

```
// This is how you would make a normal column,
// give it an id, label, and initial width
// the id is a property in the bean you are trying to display
ColumnConfig column = new ColumnConfig("name", "Company", 200);
configs.add(column);

// additional columns
.....

// Populate the store with data
ListStore<ModelData> gridStore = new ListStore<ModelData>();
gridStore.add(LocalData.getStocks());

// Create the grid with a ColumnModel instantiated
// from our list of column configurations, and a store
ColumnModel cm = new ColumnModel(configs);
Grid<ModelData> grid = new Grid<ModelData>(gridStore, cm);

// Some cosmetics on our beloved grid
....

// DnD Setup
// allow DnD re-ordering of columns
grid.setColumnReordering(true);

// allow DnD re-ordering of rows
new GridDragSource(grid);
GridDropTarget gridTarget = new GridDropTarget(grid);
gridTarget.setAllowSelfAsSource(true);
gridTarget.setFeedback(Feedback.INSERT);

// show it up, equivalent to
// RootPanel.get().add(grid)
centerPanel.add(grid, new ColumnData(.35));

// 2. Simple DnD in Tree
// Make RPC call via a proxy
// setup the TreeStore
// code omitted.
;
  TreeStore<FileModel> treeStore = new TreeStore<FileModel>(
      loader);
```

Drag-and-drop

```
        TreePanel<FileModel> tree = new TreePanel<FileModel>(treeStore);
        tree.setHeight(300);
        tree.setBorders(true);
        tree.setDisplayProperty("name");
        // load nodes automatically
        tree.setAutoLoad(true);

        // Move nodes around
        // within the tree.
        new TreePanelDragSource(tree);
        TreePanelDropTarget treeTarget = new TreePanelDropTarget(tree);
        treeTarget.setAllowSelfAsSource(true);
        treeTarget.setFeedback(Feedback.BOTH);

        // Place tree on screen like
        // RootPanel.get().add(tree)
        centerPanel.add(tree, new ColumnData(.40));
    }
```

How it works...

The first part of the code from `onApply()` creates and configures a `Grid` component. The `setColumnReordering(true)` method is used to enable ad hoc rearrangement of columns for DnD on the `Grid` component.

This DnD capability on the `Grid` component does not require wrapping the `Grid` component in a `GridDragSource` or `GridDropTarget` instance.

We then create a `GridDragSource` instance and a `GridDropTarget` instance with the `Grid` object and then invoke the `setAllowSelfAsSource()` method on the `gridTarget` instance with `true`; this allows us to drag rows to different positions within the grid.

Closely following is a `TreePanel` instance configured as in *Chapter 6, Data Hierarchy with Trees*, with which we also create a `TreePanelDragSource` instance and an accompanying `TreePanelDropTarget` instance that allows dragging and dropping of nodes within it after we've called the `treeTarget.setAllowSelfAsSource(true)` method. We determine the visual indicator that will be displayed when we drag an item by calling the `treeTarget.setFeedback()` method and passing a `DND.Feedback` object.

We can now drag nodes to different positions within the tree.

See also

- Chapter 7, The Venerable Grid Component

DnD across components

Drag-and-drop operations, especially as seen in the first recipe of this chapter, can be carried out with any widget and from any part of the screen to another. Therefore, nothing stops us from dragging a node from a tree of tasks, a record from a grid of tickets, or an item from a list of orders, into a form for processing. Better still, we could drag a collection of these items (tasks, tickets, or orders) into a visualization region and get a pie chart plot of some sort.

This kind of functionality is not only desirable but can improve the user experience and provide instant gratification. We will demonstrate it by creating an instance of `ListView` that lists customers from which we are expected to drag items into the **Male** or **Female** groups within a `TreePanel` instance, depending on the gender of the customer items being dragged.

The following screenshot shows the items being dragged from a `ListView` object into a `TreePanel` object:

How to do it...

1. Create and configure a `TreePanel` object, set its display property (`setDisplayProperty()`) and give it two (male and female) root nodes (`ModelData` objects with `name` and `gender` properties set to `male` or `female`).

2. Create a `TreePanelDropTarget` instance and override its `handleAppend()` method to cancel the drop event, if the item (customer) being dropped does not have the same gender as the target tree node.

Drag-and-drop

3. Set an appropriate group, `Operation`, and `FeedBack` values for `TreePanelDropTarget`.
4. Create a `ListView` instance of customer objects and its corresponding `ListViewDropTarget`, on which the appropriate `FeedBack` and `Operation` should be set.
5. You can now create a `ListViewDragSource` instance that has the same group as the earlier `TreePanelDropTarget` instance, and an overridden `onDragStart()` method that will set the current selection of the `ListView` object as data for the `DNDEvent` object.

```java
private ModelData createRoot(String name, String gender) {
  ModelData m = new BaseModelData();
  m.set("name", name);
  m.set("gender", gender);
  return m;
}

// generate a template for the list
private String getTemplate(){
  StringBuilder sb = new StringBuilder("<tpl for=\".\">");
  sb.append("<div class=\"x-customer-item\">");
  sb.append("<div class=\"name\">{name}</div>");
  sb.append("<div class=\"email\">E-mail:{email}</div>");
  sb.append("<div class=\"purchases\">Purchases:{purchases}</div>");
  sb.append("</div></tpl>");
  return sb.toString();
}

@Override
public void onApply() {

  // some layout structure
  centerPanel.setLayout(new ColumnLayout());
  LayoutContainer treeCt = new LayoutContainer();
  centerPanel.add(treeCt, new ColumnData(.35));

  // Set up Tree from TreeStore
  TreeStore<ModelData> treeStore = new TreeStore<ModelData>();
  TreePanel<ModelData> tree = new TreePanel<ModelData>(treeStore);
  tree.setDisplayProperty("name");

  // some eye-candy
  tree.getStyle().setNodeCloseIcon(IconSet.misc.people());
  tree.getStyle().setNodeOpenIcon(IconSet.misc.people());
  treeCt.add(tree);
```

```java
// add some root nodes
// we will be dropping stuff
// here later
treeStore.add(createRoot("Male", "male"), false);
treeStore.add(createRoot("Female", "female"), false);
tree.setLeaf(treeStore.getRootItems().get(0), false);
tree.setLeaf(treeStore.getRootItems().get(1), false);

TreePanelDropTarget treeTarget = new TreePanelDropTarget(tree){
  // This won't let you drop
  // just about anything here!
  // If U dragged "males" from the
  // list then you can only drop it
  // under the "Male" tree-node
  @Override
  protected void handleAppend(DNDEvent evt, TreeNode item) {
    if(item != null){
      ModelData treeNodeModel = item.getModel();
      String nodeGrp = treeNodeModel.get("gender").toString();

      List<BeanModel> sel = evt.getData();
      BeanModel bm = sel.get(0);
      String modelGrp = bm.get("gender").toString();
      if(!nodeGrp.equalsIgnoreCase(modelGrp)){
        evt.setCancelled(true);
        return;
      }
      super.handleAppend(evt, item);
    }
  }
};

// only components with this
// same group can participate
// in this DnD operation
treeTarget.setGroup("GenderBiased");

// Items dragged here are
// "moved" from their source
// and appended to any existing
// nodes within where they are dropped.
treeTarget.setOperation(Operation.MOVE);
treeTarget.setFeedback(Feedback.APPEND);

// Set up ListView, will act as our drag source
// Make RPC call via a proxy, see appendixes for info.
// here we want to fetch a bunch of Customer beans
// code omitted
```

```java
// Create the list-view,
// giving it the store of beans
// and the template from a call
// to our private getTemplate().
// We also configure setItemSelector()
// and setSelectStyle() responsible for
// how items in the list behave when
// they are selected.
final ListView<BeanModel> listView = new ListView<BeanModel>();
listView.setStore(store);
listView.setItemSelector("div.x-customer-item");
listView.setSelectStyle("x-customer-item-sel");
listView.setTemplate(getTemplate());

// select only males or females,
// not both! don't need it for DnD,
// but you'll like it.
listView.setSelectionModel(new ListViewSelectionModel<BeanModel>
() {
   @Override
   protected void doSelect(List<BeanModel> models,
       boolean keepExisting, boolean supressEvent) {
     if(locked){
       return;
     }

     if(selectionMode == SelectionMode.SINGLE) {
       BeanModel m = models.size() > 0 ? models.get(0) : null;
       if(m != null) {
         doSingleSelect(m, supressEvent);
       }
     } else {
       if(lastSelected != null) {
         String selectionGrp = lastSelected.get("gender").
toString();
         for(int i = (models.size() - 1); i >= 0; i--) {
           BeanModel m = models.get(i);
           String currGender = m.get("gender").toString();
           if(!selectionGrp.equalsIgnoreCase(currGender)) {
              // phew - often throws UnsupportedOperationException
              models.remove(m);
           }
         }
       }
       doMultiSelect(models, keepExisting, supressEvent);
     }
   }
});
```

```java
    // set some state info
    // are we dragging "males" or "females"
    ListViewDragSource listViewSrc = new
ListViewDragSource(listView) {
       @Override
       protected void onDragStart(DNDEvent evt) {
          super.onDragStart(evt);
          evt.setData(listView.getSelectionModel().getSelection());
       }
    };

    // only components with this
    // same group can participate
    // in this DnD operation
    listViewSrc.setGroup("GenderBiased");

    // allow DnD re-ordering of items within the list
    ListViewDropTarget listViewTarget = new
ListViewDropTarget(listView);
    listViewTarget.setAllowSelfAsSource(true);
    listViewTarget.setOperation(Operation.MOVE);
    listViewTarget.setFeedback(Feedback.INSERT);

    // only components with this
    // same group can participate
    // in this DnD operation
    listViewTarget.setGroup("GenderBiased");

    // Display the list from within a panel
    ContentPanel ctPanel = new ContentPanel();
    tPanel.setBodyBorder(false);
    ctPanel.setHeaderVisible(false);
    ctPanel.setButtonAlign(HorizontalAlignment.CENTER);
    ctPanel.setLayout(new FitLayout());
    ctPanel.setHeight(244);
    ctPanel.add(listView);

    // show it up, equivalent to
    // RootPanel.get().add(ctPanel)
    centerPanel.add(ctPanel, new ColumnData(.47));

    // All is now set,
    // for the ListView.
    // Go fetch the data!
    loader.load();
```

Drag-and-drop

```
        // A second "control" tree
        // configured much the same
        // as the earlier one but
        // given a different group
        // It has a conspicuous border,
        // try dragging into it ...
        treeStore = new TreeStore<ModelData>();
        tree = new TreePanel<ModelData>(treeStore);
        tree.setBorders(true);
        tree.setDisplayProperty("name");

        treeStore.add(createRoot("Male", "male"), false);
        treeStore.add(createRoot("Female", "female"), false);
        tree.setLeaf(treeStore.getRootItems().get(0), false);
        tree.setLeaf(treeStore.getRootItems().get(1), false);
        treeCt.add(tree);

        treeTarget = new TreePanelDropTarget(tree);

        // only components with this
        // same group can participate
        // in this DnD operation
        treeTarget.setGroup("ControlTree");
    }
```

How it works...

First, we set up the tree that will be the drop target for the customers that will be dragged from the list of customers. We set up a `TreePanel` instance backed by a `TreeStore` instance that has two `ModelData` root nodes containing a gender property that is either `male` or `female`. These gender-based root nodes form the groups into which customer items from a `ListView` will be dragged into. Consequently, a `TreePanelDropTarget` instance is created using an overridden `handleAppend()` method that will cancel (reject) the drop operation if the item (customer) being dropped has a different `gender` value from the drop target. Thus, only male customer items can be dropped under the **Male** tree node!

We also give the drop target the gender-based group and use the `Operation.MOVE` value on its `setOperation()` method, to move the customer items into the tree. `FeedBack.APPEND` is then used on the drop target's `setFeedBack()` method to add the dropped customer to the end of the items under the target tree node (actually root) instead of inserting it at the drop point.

Next, we set up our customer list, which will be our DnD source. We create a `ListView` instance backed by a remotely loaded `ListStore` instance, configured with the methods `setItemSelector()` and `setSelectedStyle()`, and given the template from the private `getTemplate()` method. Although not a necessity, but as a visual aid, `ListView` is given a custom `SelectionModel` method that allows only male or female customer items to be selected at a time, not both.

A `ListViewDragSource` instance is created with a custom `onDragStart()` method from where we obtain the current selection from the `ListView` object and set it as the data for the drag operation. The drag-source is also given the same gender-based group as was set on the tree's drop target, otherwise we'll be wasting our time. This is demonstrated with the second control tree that is identical in form and function with the first, except that it is given a `ControlTree` instance as its group instead.

> The changes to the tree will be reflected in the `TreeStore` object, however if we want these changes to persist, we need to make the changes to the backend by implementing an RPC call that will save the updated tree `ModelData`.

DnD from desktop, with HTML5

Dragging and dropping files from your desktop to a browser is one of the ultimate goals for web application integration. HTML5 truly rocks. Though still in the works, it aims to provide standardized APIs for the many propriety hacks we have come to accept in building tomorrow's engaging apps. GWT's implementation of the HTML5 file and DnD API makes it a tad easier to build into your app the ability to drag a file from your computer desktop into the browser and have a specific behavior as a result. Sharing bragging rights with pioneers such as Gmail, we can now drag files into a browser and have them uploaded; however, we will attempt to demonstrate dragging media files (audio, video, and images) into the browser and have them display or play back accordingly.

The following screenshot shows the process of displaying an image dragged from the desktop:

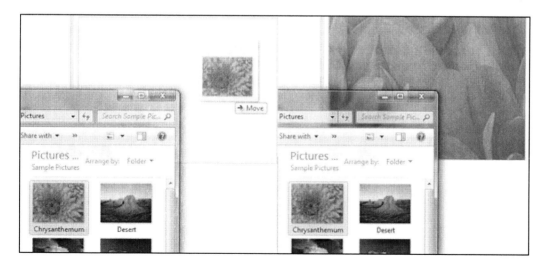

Drag-and-drop

The following screenshot shows the process of playing a movie dragged from the desktop:

Getting ready

Although GWT supports HTML5, the file API is not fully backed as of this writing, so we would augment its native support with a third-party GWT module called `lib-gwt-file` (see the *Preface* of the book for the download link of the book's source code), thus requiring that we add the module's JAR file to our build path and `<inherits name="org.vectomatic.libgwtfile" />` to the `.gwt.xml` file in our project.

How to do it...

Create a `DropPanel` instance (from the `lib-gwt-file` API) and add a `DragOverHandler` instance to it, from where the default browser behavior can be prevented. Then add a `DropHandler` instance to it, which will be responsible for determining the file's MIME type and whether to display it (if image) or play it (audio/video).

```
private MediaBase handleMedia(MediaBase media, String path){
  media.setSrc(path);
  media.setControls(true);
  // pre-load it right away
  media.load();
  return media;
}

@Override
public void onApply() {
  // A wrapper container
```

```
final LayoutContainer arena = new LayoutContainer(new FitLayout());
arena.setBorders(true);
arena.setSize(350, 250);

// The panel where we'll
// drag stuff into
final DropPanel dropPanel = new DropPanel();

// add drag-over handler and
// prevent default behavior
// else browser's in-built
// DnD handling will kick-in
dropPanel.addDragOverHandler(new DragOverHandler() {
  @Override
  public void onDragOver(DragOverEvent evt) {
    evt.preventDefault();
  }
});

// When items are dragged here
// inspect their file type,
// display images and playback
// audio/video files
dropPanel.addDropHandler(new DropHandler() {
  @Override
  public void onDrop(DropEvent evt ) {
    // Hey browser we got this
    // we know what we're doing
    evt.preventDefault();

    // Obtain the dragged file
    // and some meta about it.
    DataTransfer dtTrnsfr = evt.getDataTransfer();
    Iterator<File> fIterator = dtTrnsfr.getFiles().iterator();
    File file = fIterator.next();
    String fType = file.getType();
    String fPath = file.createObjectURL();

    if(fType.startsWith("image")){ // display images
      dropPanel.clear();
      Image img = new Image(fPath);
      img.setWidth(String.valueOf(arena.getWidth()));
      img.setHeight(String.valueOf(arena.getHeight()));
      dropPanel.add(img);
```

```
      } else if(fType.startsWith("audio")){ // play audio
        Audio audio = Audio.createIfSupported();
        if(audio == null){
          Info.display("DnD Info", "Unsupported Operation Or
Format!");
          return;
        }

        dropPanel.clear();
        audio = (Audio) handleMedia(audio, fPath);
        dropPanel.add(audio);
      } else if(fType.startsWith("video")){ // play video
        Video video = Video.createIfSupported();
        if(video == null){
          Info.display("DnD Info", "Unsupported Operation Or
Format!");
          return;
        }

        dropPanel.clear();
        video = (Video) handleMedia(video, fPath);
        video.setSize(String.valueOf(arena.getWidth()), String.
valueOf(arena.getHeight()));
        dropPanel.add(video);
      } else {
        Info.display("Hey C'mon", "Are U dragging a Mule in here?
Gimme image or audio/video files");
      }

      // refresh the screen
      arena.layout(true);
    }
  });

  // add DnD target panel
  // to our wrapper panel
  arena.add(dropPanel);

  // show it up, equivalent to
  // RootPanel.get().add(arena)
  centerPanel.add(arena);
}
```

How it works...

We first create a wrapper `LayoutContainer` and then a `DropPanel` instance that will serve as the special area into which files from the desktop will be dragged. To prevent the browser's default handling of dragging files into it (such as clearing its contents and displaying the image that was dragged into it), we add a `DragOverHandler` instance to the `DropPanel` instance. As it is aptly called, the handler is triggered when the drag cursor enters the drop panel's region. Therefore, the `evt.preventDefault()` function in its overridden `onDragOver()` method ensures that the browser's native behavior is prevented.

The real heavy lifting is done inside the `Drophandler` instance added to the `DropPanel` instance. First, we cancel the browser's default DnD behavior (again) with the `evt.preventDefault()` function and then obtain the file, its MIME, and its path, from the `DataTransfer` object in the `DropEvent` object. With the help of a conditional block, the metadata from the `file.getType()` method is queried and used to create an `Image`, `Audio`, or `Video` element, which is then attached to the `DropPanel` instance to be displayed or played back accordingly.

Implementing custom DnD on tabs

It is quite worthy to note that most drag-and-drop samples or tutorials illustrate features with UI components that are already rendered and visible on screen. However, we may sometimes need to drop something on a target that may not currently be visible on the screen. A good example would be dragging a component from the currently selected tab item in a tabbed view, to another tab item. The contents of the target tab item are not visible on the screen because it is not selected, and yet we want to drop our component in it. Such a DnD implementation may be useful when implementing a task board application, where we want to drag tasks from a "tasks in progress" tab to the "tasks done" tab.

The following screenshot shows the process of dragging a tab by its header:

Drag-and-drop

The following screenshot shows the Tab 5 dragged by its header and inserted over Tab 3:

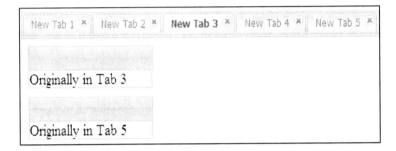

The following screenshot shows the process of dragging an item from Tab 3 into Tab 5. The dragged component from Tab 5 is now in Tab 3.

How to do it...

Create a `TabPanel` instance and add a number of `TabItem` objects (containing the UI components to be dragged) to it. Next, enable dragging of the tab headers and the components within the tabs by implementing a `DragSource` instance and setting the appropriate data on the `DNDEvent` object. Conversely, configure dropping of the tab headers and the UI components within the tabs by implementing a `DropTarget` instance for them that swaps the tab headers and appends the UI components respectively.

```
private int index = 0;
private TabPanel tabPanel;

@Override
public void onApply() {
  tabPanel = new TabPanel();
  tabPanel.setSize(550, 400);
  tabPanel.setCloseContextMenu(true);

  while(index < 5) {
    addTab();
  }
```

```java
    // display it, equivalent to
    // RootPanel.get().add(tabPanel)
    centerPanel.add(tabPanel);
    tabPanel.setSelection( tabPanel.getItem(index-1) );
  }

  /*
   * Add a tab to the TabPanel
   */
  private void addTab() {
    // make tab,
    final TabItem item = new TabItem();
    item.setClosable(true);
    item.setText("New Tab " + ++index);

    // Place a panel in
    // the Tab
    ContentPanel textPanel = new ContentPanel();
    textPanel.setWidth(150);
    textPanel.setStyleAttribute("margin", "8px");
    textPanel.setTitle("In Tab : " + index);
    textPanel.addText("<p>Originally in Tab " + index + "</p>");
    item.add(textPanel);

    // add tab to tabpanel
    tabPanel.add(item);

    // Configure DnD
    // support on the tab
    supportDrag(item);
    supportDrop(item);

  }

  // Swap or re-order tab with
  // DnD and allow contained
  // panel to be dragged
  private void supportDrag(final TabItem tabItem) {

    // Make header item draggable
    // and set it as the data
    final HeaderItem headerItem = tabItem.getHeader();
    DragSource source = new DragSource(headerItem) {
      @Override
      protected void onDragStart(DNDEvent event) {
```

Drag-and-drop

```java
        event.setData(headerItem);
        event.getStatus().update(headerItem.getText());
      }
    };
    source.setGroup("DDtabs");


    // Make the panel inside
    // the tab draggable and
    // set it as the data
    // been dragged.
    final ContentPanel textPanel = (ContentPanel) tabItem.getItem(0);
    source = new DragSource(textPanel){
      @Override
      protected void onDragStart(DNDEvent event) {
        event.setData(textPanel);
        event.getStatus().update(textPanel.getTitle());
      }
    };
    source.setGroup("DDtabs");
  }


  private void supportDrop(final TabItem tabItem) {

    // When dropping stuff
    // on a HeaderItem
    final HeaderItem headerItem = tabItem.getHeader();
    DropTarget target = new DropTarget(headerItem) {

        // If what is been dragged
        // is not a HeaderItem, then
        // select the tab, perhaps we
        // want to drop the item inside
        // the tab itself!
      @Override
      protected void onDragEnter(DNDEvent evt) {
        super.onDragEnter(evt);
        if(evt.getData() instanceof HeaderItem){
          return;
        }
        tabPanel.setSelection(tabItem);
      }

        // When a tab's header is moved
        // to a new position, swap the tab
        // and make it the active one
```

```java
    @Override
    protected void onDragDrop(DNDEvent event) {
      super.onDragDrop(event);

        // Insert the dragged tab at
        // the position of the target tab
      if(event.getData() instanceof HeaderItem){
        TabItem tabOfDraggedHeader = (TabItem) ((HeaderItem) event.getData()).getParent();
        int indexTarget = tabPanel.indexOf(tabItem);
        tabPanel.insert(tabOfDraggedHeader, indexTarget);
        tabPanel.setSelection(tabOfDraggedHeader);
      }

    }
  };
  target.setGroup("DDtabs");

  target = new DropTarget(tabItem){
      // Don't allow tab headers to be
      // dragged into tabs!
    @Override
    protected void onDragEnter(DNDEvent evt) {
      super.onDragEnter(evt);
      if(evt.getData() instanceof HeaderItem){
        evt.setCancelled(true);
        StatusProxy status = StatusProxy.get();
        status.setStatus(false);
        evt.setStatus(status);
      }
    };

      // U are dropping a Component
      // here, so we'll just add it.
    @Override
    protected void onDragDrop(DNDEvent evt) {
      super.onDragDrop(evt);
      tabItem.add((Component) evt.getData());
      tabItem.layout();
    };
  };
  target.setGroup("DDtabs");
  target.setOperation(Operation.MOVE);
  target.setFeedback(Feedback.APPEND);
}
```

Drag-and-drop

How it works...

The recipe starts out by creating, configuring, and then adding a `TabPanel` object to the screen, with the last tab selected. The tabs are added within a loop by using the private `addTab()` method that creates a titled and closable `TabItem` object containing a `ContentPanel` instance. The `TabItem` object is added to the `TabPanel` using the `add()` method of `TabPanel`. We wrap up the method by configuring our custom drag and drop behavior on each tab with the invocation of the `supportDrag()` and `supportDrop()` methods.

The `supportDrag()` method makes a tab header draggable by wrapping it in a `DragSource` instance whose `onDragStart()` method set the header item as the data on the `DNDEvent` instance. Similarly, the `ContentPanel` instance within the tab is made draggable with the wrapper—`DragSource`—which also passes the panel to the `DNDEvent` instance as data. Both `DragSource` implementations show a proper visual cue during the drag operation, using the `event.getStatus().update()` function inside the `onDragStart()` method. They also belong to the same DnD group as the `source.setGroup()` method.

The `supportDrop()` method configures dropping items on a tab or its header. A wrapper `DropTarget` is created for the tab's header, and the control `onDragEnter()` method is simply saying, "if what is been dragged is not a HeaderItem, select the tab; perhaps the user wants to drop the item inside the tab itself". The `onDragDrop()` handler then obtains the tab of the dragged header, inserts it at the position of the target tab, and makes it active, thus giving the effect of swapping the tabs.

A second `DropTarget` instance is also in place to handle dropping items on a tab. But we make sure the user is not allowed to drop a tab header inside a tab—by overriding the `onDragEnter()` method and cancelling the drop operation—if determined to have begun. Otherwise, it is considered a valid drop operation and the `onDragDrop()` override simply appends the component to the tab.

11
Advanced Tips

In this chapter we will cover the following points:

- Client/server persistence setup
- Client/server persistence
- A novel UI with MVP, actions, and a bus
- History and view transitions
- Real-time server push

Introduction

The recipes in this chapter will deal with several advanced topics, which are not directly related to GXT, but are worth presenting.

The *Client/server persistence setup* recipe deals with integrating GWT with **Java Persistence Architecture** (**JPA**), by using JPA for our server-side persistence. The *A novel UI with MVP, actions, and a bus* recipe demonstrates the use of the **Model-View-Presenter** (**MVP**) pattern in a GWT application. In the *History and view transitions* recipe, we add history support to our MVP-based application. Since GWT is not a page-centric architecture, the browser's built-in history mechanism cannot be used out of the box.

Finally in the *Real-time server push* recipe, we introduce server-side push using the comet programming model.

Advanced Tips

Client/server persistence setup

Persistence is a critical ingredient for realizing the value proposition in many applications. Fortunately the Java platform has tremendous support in terms of APIs and tooling necessary for doing persistence. Using the Java Persistence Architecture (JPA) and any of its several providers (notably Hibernate) one can easily annotate a server-side POJO, map it to a database table, and have a GWT application load, edit, or insert data to the database by transparent interaction with the POJO.

Whereas the client side of a persistent GWT app remains the same for the most part (just a bunch of regular RPC requests), a lot of configuration is usually done on the server side to correctly set it up the GWT way and this is where most developers have challenges.

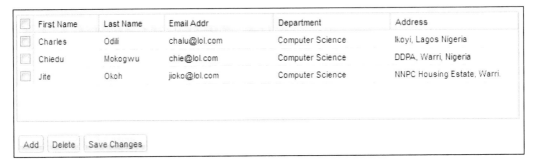

How to do it...

Putting together the many puzzle pieces for persistence on a GWT app can be daunting for beginners. However, these steps will highlight the important points to take home; ready?

1. You've got to have a database system in place, if not already installed grab and install a copy of **MySQL** from `http://dev.mysql.com/downloads/`.

2. Download Hibernate (using 3.6.4), Hibernate Validator (using 4.1.0), Log4J, GILEAD (using 1.3.2), and BeanLib (using 5.0.2). Add their jars to the projects build path by right-clicking the project, selecting **Properties** at the bottom, and then selecting **Java Build Path**. Once there, click the **Libraries** tab at the top and then the **Add Library** or **Add External Jars** to include the downloaded APIs resources to the project.

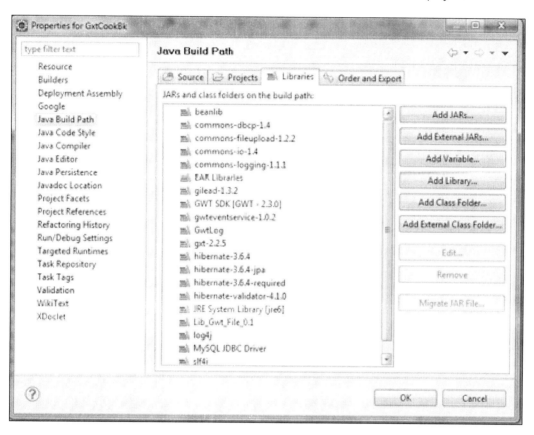

Advanced Tips

3. We need to configure a persistence unit, so right-click the project, select **JPA Tools** (or **Configure**), then select **Convert to JPA Project**. This opens up the configuration wizard shown as follows:

4. After selecting **Minimal JPA 2.0 configuration** for the **Configuration** field, click **Next** to go to the JPA facet screen where **Generic 2.0** is selected for **Platform** and the required **hibernate/hibernate-validator** libraries are selected for use with persistence unit. Click **Add connection** on the bottom-right of the **Connection** field to reveal the **Connection Profile** screen used to configure a named database connection which I have called **GxtCookBKDB**.

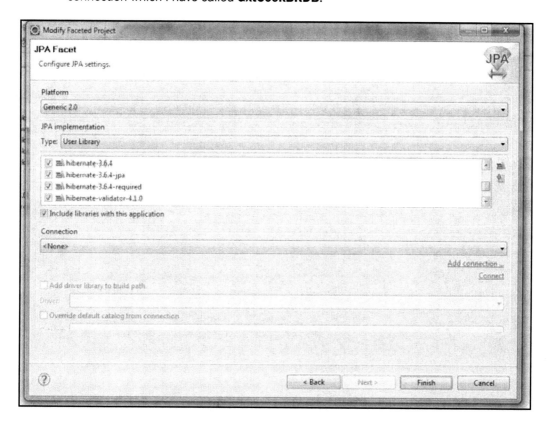

Advanced Tips

5. Choose **MySQL** as the **Connection Profile Types**:

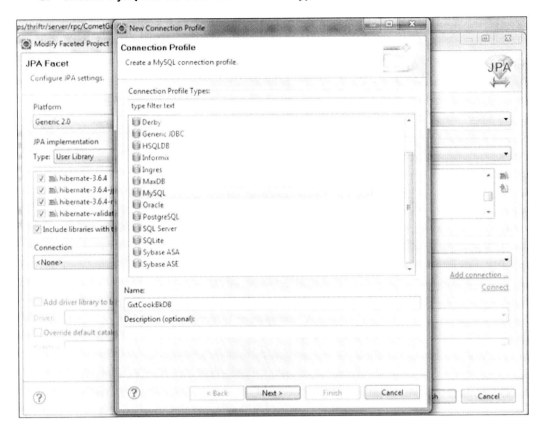

Chapter 11

6. Clicking **Next** on this screen allows us to enter and test the database connection credentials, enter **gxtcookbook** for **Database**, **jdbc:mysql://localhost:3306/gxtcookbook** for **URL**, and then a valid username and password to connect to your installed MySQL RDBMS:

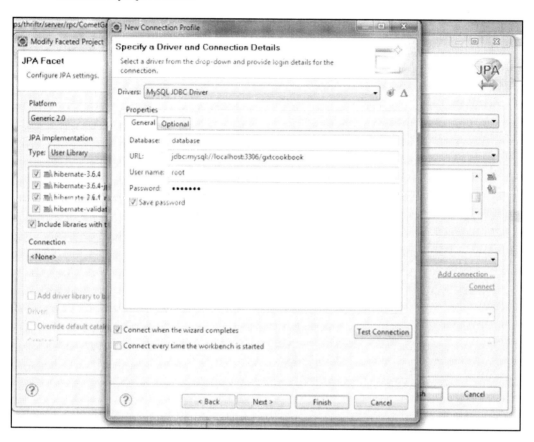

Advanced Tips

7. And when we click finish in the previous screen, we are taken back to the **JPA Facet** screen with the **GxtCookBkDB** connection already selected:

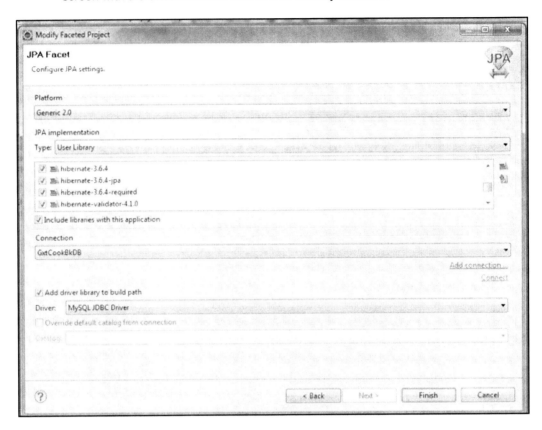

8. As a final step here, check the **Add driver library to build path** field and click **Finish**. These settings will add a new **JPA Content** node under the Eclipse project node, which when expanded reveals a **persistence.xml** file:

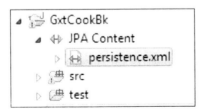

9. Double-click on the **persistence.xml** file to open it. In the **General** tab, enter **org.hibernate.ejb.HibernatePersistence** for the **Persistence Provider** field, click to expand the **Managed classes** field-set and check **Exclude unlisted classes** to prevent extra baggage and requiring you to return here to add your annotated/mapped Java classes with the **Add** button on the right of this field-set.

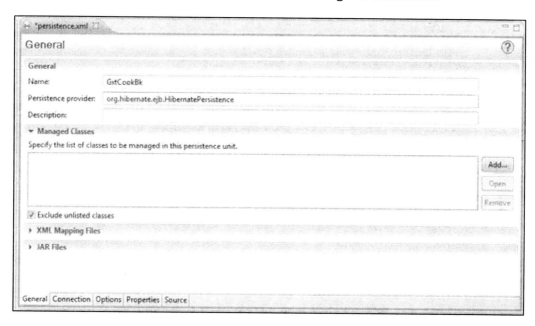

Advanced Tips

10. Under the **Connection** tab, select **Resource Local** for the **Transaction type** field and click **Populate from connection** within the **JDBC connection properties** field-set to fill in the parameters for the GxtCookBkDB connection. Save changes (*Ctrl + S*).

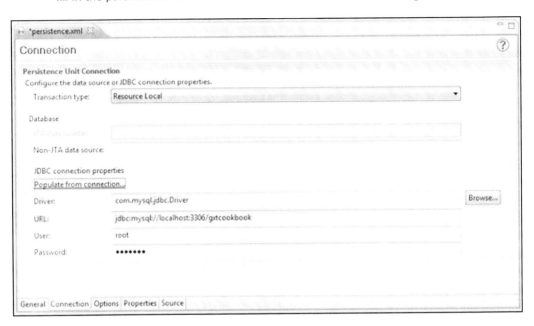

11. Open the eclipse **Data Source Explorer** view (**Window | Show View | Data Source Explorer**) and select the **GxtCookBkDB** connection. Right-click it then click **Connect** to connect to it. Open the DB.sql file in the com.gxtcookbk.code.client.data package in the eclipse editor and then at the top, select the **GxtCookBkDB** connection for the **Name** field and **gxtcookbook** for the **Database** field. Right-click inside the code editor and select **Execute All** to run the SQL statements.

12. Now we need to configure Hibernate for the persistence unit and our database. Right-click the src folder within the project and create a file (**New | Other | General | File**), name it hibernate.cfg.xml and copy the listing given as follows into it. However, you will need to change the username and password values to match your MSQL settings. It is highly recommended that you provide (also within the same folder) a log4j.properties file for better visibility of Hibernate's workings (queries and errors). Also, do not forget to add the .jar files of the added libraries (Hibernate and others) to your war/WEB-INF/lib directory.

```
<?xml version="1.0" encoding="UTF-8"?>
<!DOCTYPE hibernate-configuration PUBLIC "-//Hibernate/Hibernate
Configuration DTD 3.0//EN"
   "http://hibernate.sourceforge.net/hibernate-configuration-
3.0.dtd">
<hibernate-configuration>
```

```
    <session-factory>
       <property name="hibernate.dialect">org.hibernate.dialect.
MySQLDialect</property>
       <property name="hibernate.connection.driver_class">com.mysql.
jdbc.Driver</property>
       <property name="hibernate.connection.url">jdbc:mysql://
localhost:3306/gxtcookbook</property>
       <property name="hibernate.connection.username">root</property>
       <property name="hibernate.connection.password">asAdm1n</
property>
    </session-factory>
</hibernate-configuration>
```

Client/server persistence

With the server environment configured and ready to deal with persistent objects, all that we need to do is give it some POJOs and perhaps arm ourselves with some JPA utility classes to make our work easier. For our recipe, we will create a grid that displays a list of students. The grid will retrieve the student records from the database using JPA and will support deleting and adding students. The add and delete operations on the grid will be persisted to the database using an RPC call that will use JPA.

How to do it...

Create a `Student` class, as usual it implements `BeanModelTag` (or the equivalent `BeanModelMarker` approach) and is `Serializable`, which are requirements for GXT data components and GWT's RPC respectively. Make sure the `Student` class has a default (no argument) constructor, and a `toString()` method. `equals()`, and `hashCode()` are also highly recommended along with the regular getters/setters.

```
    public class Student implements BeanModelTag, Serializable {

      private Long id;

      private String address;

      private String emailId;

      private String lastName;

      private String firstName;

       private Department department;

       private Set<CourseOfStudy> courseOfStudy;

      public Student() {
```

Advanced Tips

```java
      super();
      courseOfStudy = new HashSet<CourseOfStudy>();
   }

   @Override
   public String toString() {
      return "Student [" + lastName + " " + firstName + "]";
   }

   @Override
   public int hashCode() {
      final int prime = 31;
      int result = 1;
      result = prime * result + ((emailId == null) ? 0 : emailId.
hashCode());
      return result;
   }

   @Override
   public boolean equals(Object obj) {
      if (this == obj)
         return true;
      if (obj == null)
         return false;
      if (getClass() != obj.getClass())
         return false;
      Student other = (Student) obj;
      if (emailId == null) {
         if (other.emailId != null)
            return false;
      } else if (!emailId.equals(other.emailId))
         return false;
      return true;
   }
}
```

Next, edit the `Student` class to extend GILEADs `net.sf.gilead.pojo.gwt.LightEntity` and then annotate it (JPA annotations) mapping the class to a database table and its fields to columns within the table.

```java
   @Entity
   @Table(name="students")
   public class Student extends LightEntity implements BeanModelTag,
   Serializable {

      @Id @GeneratedValue
      private Long id;

      @Column(name="address")
      private String address;
```

```java
    @Column(name="email")
    private String emailId;

    @Column(name="lname")
    private String lastName;

    @Column(name="fname")
    private String firstName;

    @ManyToOne
    @JoinColumn(name="department")
    private Department department;

    @OneToMany(mappedBy = "student", targetEntity=CourseOfStudy.class,
fetch=FetchType.EAGER)
    private Set<CourseOfStudy> courseOfStudy;

    public Student() {
      super();
      courseOfStudy = new HashSet<CourseOfStudy>();
    }

........
}
```

Add RPC methods to your `RemoteService` and `RemoteServiceAsync` interface implementations.

```java
    @RemoteServiceRelativePath("remotegateway")
    public interface RemoteGateway extends RemoteService {
    ......

      public Response deleteStudents(ArrayList<Long> losers);
      public Response saveStudents(ArrayList<Student> changes);
      public ListLoadResult<Student> listStudents(ListLoadConfig cfg);
    }

    public interface RemoteGatewayAsync {
    ......

      void deleteStudents(ArrayList<Long> losers, AsyncCallback<Response>
    callback);

      void saveStudents(ArrayList<Student> changes,
          AsyncCallback<Response> callback);

      void listStudents(ListLoadConfig cfg,
          AsyncCallback<ListLoadResult<Student>> callback);

    }
```

Advanced Tips

Now, edit the `RemoteServiceServlet` implementation (`RemoteGatewayImpl`) to extend GILEADs `net.sf.gilead.gwt.PersistentRemoteService` instead, and edit its constructor to configure and set the `PersistentBeanManager`. Also, provide implementations for the methods added to `RemoteGateway` interface.

```java
public class RemoteGatewayImpl extends PersistentRemoteService
implements
    RemoteGateway {

  private HibernateUtil hibernateUtil = null;
  private PersistentBeanManager beanManager = null;
  private final Logger logger = LoggerFactory.getLogger(RemoteGatewayImpl.class);

  public RemoteGatewayImpl() {
    super();

    SessionFactory sessionFactory = new Configuration().configure().buildSessionFactory();
    hibernateUtil = new HibernateUtil(sessionFactory);
    beanManager = GwtConfigurationHelper.initGwtStatelessBeanManager(hibernateUtil);
    setBeanManager(beanManager);

    Validation.byDefaultProvider().configure();
  }

  ......

  @Override
  public Response deleteStudents(ArrayList<Long> losers) {
    Response response = Response.get();
    JpaController<Long, Student> dao = new JpaController<Long, Student>() {};
    try{
      dao.delete(losers);
      response.OK();
    }catch(Exception ex) {
      response.ERR(ex.getMessage());
    }
    return response;
  }

  @Override
  public Response saveStudents(ArrayList<Student> changes) {
    Response response = Response.get();
    ArrayList<Student> fresh = new ArrayList<Student>();
```

```
    ArrayList<Student> modified = new ArrayList<Student>();
    JpaController<Long, Student> dao = new JpaController<Long,
Student>() {};

    for(Student student : changes) {
      if(student.getId() == null){
        fresh.add(student);
      }else{
        modified.add(student);
      }
    }

    try{
      dao.create(fresh);
      dao.edit(modified);
      response.OK();
    }catch(Exception ex) {
      response.ERR(ex.getMessage());
    }
    return response;
  }

  @Override
  public ListLoadResult<Student> listStudents(ListLoadConfig cfg) {
    JpaController<Long, Student> dao = new JpaController<Long,
Student>() {};
    return new BaseListLoadResult<Student>( dao.entities() );
  }
}
```

Finally, set up the client side, a grid to load the student objects, and then some buttons to add, delete, and save records.

How it works...

With the `Student` class extending `LightEntity` and implementing `BeanModelTag` as well as `Serializable`, and the server properly configured, persisting changes for a collection of student records is just a matter of initiating a regular RPC call and sending the modified records to the server to do its bit.

The `Student` class extends the `LightEntity` class from the GILEAD library which provides the low-level plumbing and passage between the output of Hibernate and out GXT frontend, especially in cases where the object being persisted/serialized contains fields that are collections; for example, the `courseOfStudy` object in the `Student` class, which is a Set.

Advanced Tips

The `Student` class is made persistent with JPA's `@Entity` annotation and is mapped to the students table with `@Table(name="students")`. Using `@Id` and `@GeneratedValue`, the Long ID field will uniquely identify student records with an auto generated value. The `address`, `emailed`, `lastName`, and `firstName` String fields are mapped to their corresponding columns with the `@Column` annotation which also contains a `name` attribute explicitly specifying the name of the target column.

In our example, there is a many-to-one relationship between a student and a department (many students to one department) such that there is a foreign key department column (specified with `@JoinColumn`) in the students table pointing to the ID (primary key) of a record in the `departments` table. Hence the `Department` field in the `Student` class is mapped with a `@ManyToOne` and `@JoinColumn` annotation for which there is a corresponding `@OneToMany` mapping in the `Department` class ensuring we have a bi-directional mapping between both entities, thus giving us the ability to fetch a student's department with `student.getDepartment()` and conversely fetch students in a department with `department.getStudents()`.

Since one student can offer many courses and vice-versa, we decompose the obvious and usually problematic many-to-many relationship between `Student` (`students` table) and `Course` (`courses` table) by introducing a look-up `CourseOfStudy` class (`courseofstudy` table). With this in place, the `courseOfStudy` Set in the `Student` class bears a `@OneToMany` mapping that is EAGER (when we load a `Student`, fetch his `CourseOfStudy` list too) and mapped by a `student` field in the `CourseOfStudy` class.

The rest of the `Student` class is regular default constructor, getters/setters, and implementations for `toString()`, `equals()`, and `hashCode()` which any good IDE can auto generate.

`RemoteGateway` and `RemoteGatewayAsync`, our RPC service interfaces, also declare methods for doing CRUD on the student POJO as well as the other newly introduced persistent classes (`Department`, `Course`, and so on). These methods are implemented in the `RemoteGatewayImpl` servlet that is updated to extend GILEAD's `PersistentRemoteService` (which in turn extends GWTs `RemoteServiceServlet`) and given a GWT-configured `PersistentBeanManager` from within its default constructor.

The new RPC methods also follow a general pattern for fetching or saving the POJOs; using a parameterized utility `JpaController` class that configures our persistence unit and connects to the database at runtime, we have handy methods for doing regular database transactions (`find`, `delete`, `edit`, and so on). This class can be extended, to say, `StudentJpaController`, so as to provide an interface (methods) for student-specific database queries.

listStudents() creates an ad-hoc implementation of the abstract JpaController that will load only student objects identified by Long objects. The records are acquired with a simple call to dao.entities() and returned as a BaseListLoadResult when requested from the client after the Grid gets attached.

```
   private void runDelete(){
      final List<BeanModel> selection = grid.getSelectionModel().
getSelection();
      if(selection.size() >= 1){
         grid.mask("Attempting Delete ..");
         ArrayList<Long> losers = new ArrayList<Long>();
         for (BeanModel model : selection) {
            Student student = (Student) model.getBean();
            losers.add(student.getId());
         }

         AsyncCallback<Response> callback = new AsyncCallback<Response>() {
            @Override
            public void onFailure(Throwable caught) {
               grid.unmask();
           Info.display("RPC Error", caught.getMessage());
            }

            @Override
            public void onSuccess(Response result) {
               grid.unmask();
               if(Response.STATUS_OK.equals(result.getStatus())){
                  for (BeanModel model : selection) {
                     grid.getStore().remove(model);
                  }
                     grid.getStore().commitChanges();
                  }else{
                     Info.display("Server Error", result.getMessages().
toString());
                  }
               }
            }
         };

      DataCenter.get().rpcService().deleteStudents(losers, callback);
      }
   }

   private void runSave(){
      if(grid.getStore().getModifiedRecords().size() >= 1){
         grid.mask("Saving ...");

         ArrayList<Student> changes = new ArrayList<Student>();
            for (Record record : grid.getStore().getModifiedRecords()) {
               Student student = (Student) ((BeanModel) record.getModel()).
getBean();
```

Advanced Tips

```
              changes.add(student);
          }

      DataCenter.get().rpcService().saveStudents(changes, new
AsyncCallback<Response>() {
          @Override
          public void onFailure(Throwable caught) {
            grid.unmask();
            Info.display("RPC Error", caught.getMessage());
          }

          @Override
          public void onSuccess(Response result) {
            if(Response.STATUS_OK.equals(result.getStatus())){
          grid.getStore().commitChanges();
          grid.getStore().getLoader().load();
            }else{
               Info.display("Server Error", result.getMessages().
toString());
            }
          }
      });
    }
}

@Override
public void onApply() {
  // A Registry based repo of stores
  DataCenter.init();

  // Create and configure the grid
  List<ColumnConfig> configs = getColumnCfgs();
  CheckBoxSelectionModel<BeanModel> selectionMdl = new CheckBoxSelecti
onModel<BeanModel>();
  configs.add(0, selectionMdl.getColumn());

  ColumnModel cm = new ColumnModel(configs);
  String storeKey = DataCenter.StoreKeys.STUDENT_LIST_STORE.encode();
  final ListStore<BeanModel> store = (ListStore<BeanModel>) Registry.
get(storeKey);
  grid = new EditorGrid<BeanModel>(store, cm);

  grid.addPlugin(selectionMdl);
  grid.setSelectionModel(selectionMdl);

  grid.setBorders(true);
  grid.setSize(650, 135);
  grid.setStripeRows(true);
  grid.setLoadMask(true);
  grid.setAutoExpandColumn("emailId");
  grid.setStyleAttribute("marginBottom", "15px");
```

```java
    grid.addListener(Events.Attach, new Listener<GridEvent<BeanModel>>()
{
      @Override
      public void handleEvent(GridEvent<BeanModel> evt) {
        store.getLoader().load();
      }
    });

    // show it up, equivalent to
    // RootPanel.get().add(grid)
    centerPanel.add(grid);

    ButtonBar btnBar = new ButtonBar();
    btnBar.add(new Button("Add", new SelectionListener<ButtonEvent>() {
      @Override
      public void componentSelected(ButtonEvent evt) {
        BeanModelFactory modelFtry = BeanModelLookup.get().
getFactory(Student.class);
        BeanModel model = modelFtry.createModel(new Student());
        EditorGrid<BeanModel> editorGrid = (EditorGrid<BeanModel>) grid;
        editorGrid.stopEditing();
        editorGrid.getStore().insert(model, 0);
        editorGrid.startEditing(grid.getStore().indexOf(model), 0);
      }
    }));

    btnBar.add(new Button("Delete", new SelectionListener<ButtonEvent>()
{
      @Override
      public void componentSelected(ButtonEvent evt) {
        runDelete();
      }
    }));

    btnBar.add(new Button("Save Changes", new SelectionListener<ButtonE
vent>() {
      @Override
      public void componentSelected(ButtonEvent evt) {
        runSave();
      }
    }));

    // show it up, equivalent to
    // RootPanel.get().add(btnBar)
    centerPanel.add(btnBar);

}
```

Advanced Tips

`ListStore` is maintained centrally by a utility `DataCenter` class that employs the use of GXT's Registry to provision useful application-wide values, objects, and data so that we don't have to duplicate code and effort if we need to display, say, a `Grid`, `ComboBox`, and `ListView` of students.

Deleting students is easy, initiated with the client-side `runDelete()` method which makes an RPC call to the server-side `deleteStudents()` method with an `ArrayList` of the `ids` (primary keys) for the selected `Student` records in the `Grid`. The remote `deleteStudents()` creates a `JpaController` and invokes `delete()` on it, setting an `ok` flag on the wrapper `Response` object that is sent back to the client. The entire operation is very straightforward to client code, having configured and commissioned JPA, Hibernate, and GILEAD to do the heavy lifting.

Similarly, when the *save changes* button is clicked, the `runSave()` method builds a list of modified records (edited or created), obtains the RPC service object from `DataCenter` and invokes the remote `saveStudents()` method with the modified records. `saveStudents()` iterates over the collection of students, separating the edited ones from the newly created (without ID) ones, then calls `create()` and `edit()` on the `JpaController` object to save the changes to the database.

There's more...

Though the details of JPA/Hibernate best practices are outside the scope of this book, I find the following tips to be best suited for GXT application development:

- Strive to use `BeanModelTag` for your persistent classes
- Map/annotate class fields instead of their getter methods
- Try as much as possible not to have more the one EAGER mapping in a given persistent class
- Always implement `toString()`, `equals()`, and `hashCode()` in persistent classes; however, reduce the use of the `id` (primary key) field in these implementations
- Use `Long` instead of `int` for the `id` (primary key) fields in persistent classes

A novel UI with MVP, actions, and a bus

Designing and building a large application has several hurdles which can't be wished away even in the GWT world. In fact, GWT development introduces its own peculiar challenges to the mix, often requiring a slightly different approach to UI development, multiple developers working simultaneously on the same codebase, testing, and so on.

Fortunately, we can always leverage on the software industry's experience and apply patterns for proper development life-cycle management and good design. Some of the patterns to choose from include: Model-view-controller, Model-view-presenter, Presentation-abstraction-control, and so on. Though each pattern has its pros and cons, it has been established that an MVP (Model-View-Presenter) approach works best when developing a GWT-based app.

MVP ensures clearly decoupled components and focuses on making the view as simple as possible allowing us to minimize our use of `GWTTestCase` which needs the presence of a browser, and for the bulk of our code (the presenter), write lightweight JRE tests which cares less about a browser.

With the view reduced to laying()out UI, we can design to have several swappable views for a single model, say a grid()view and a list()view for department models. The presenter contains all of the logic to drive the view (view transition, RPC, and so on) and handle events sourced from the widgets within the view, but must have no knowledge of any UI-based code, thus minimizing the GWT/GXT ties allowing for non `GWTTestCase` to be useful but still keeping the ability to place and control an interface-based view on the screen.

A key component of the MVP mantra is the **event-bus**, another pattern for a robust design. With the presenter sinking events sourced from the widgets within views, the event-bus becomes the traffic cop for firing and registering for application-wide events such as a *department update* event.

Although not a necessity for MVP, actions are recommended for use with views in large scale apps to encapsulate the action for command widgets such that a *create department* action can be tied to a button, and a menu-item at the same time and both widgets when clicked triggers the same routine in the presenter.

These concepts will be demonstrated with a set of Department objects rendered in two swappable views – a Grid and a ListView, both tied to a single `ListStore` and each deciding which actions to present to the user.

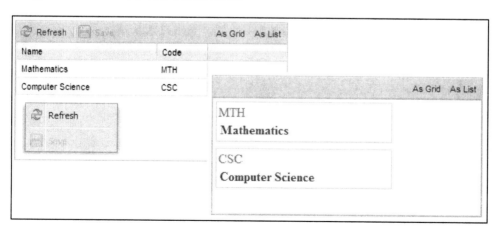

Advanced Tips

Getting ready

Since we are using persistent server-side POJOs, this recipe builds on the foundation of the previous one. If you have not already done so, quickly cover the previous recipe; you'll not only need it to understand this one but the rest of this chapter builds and improves on it.

How to do it...

In order to define our data model (the M in the MVP) we introduce two interfaces on the server. The ModelType interface is a Serializable BeanModelTag and defines getId() and setId() which our POJOs must have. The interface DepartmentModel extends ModelType and further defines the interface for the MvpDepartment POJO. DepartmentModel also becomes what is used to parameterize the arguments and return types for the saveDepartments() and listDepartmentModels() RPC methods in RemoteGateway. These methods are implemented in RemoteGatewayImpl like the other persistence-powered methods discussed in the previous recipe.

We now need to construct our view and presenter. The following class diagram shows the main classes and their relationships:

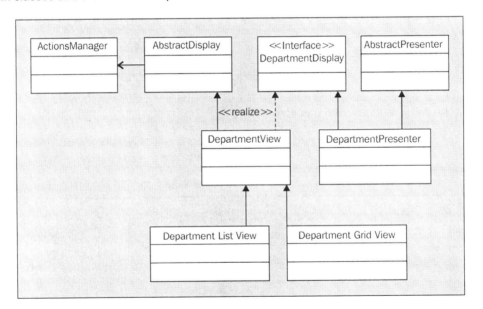

- DepartmentView defines the UI logic that all department views (grid and list) will share. It obtains the central departments store from the DataCenter class and implements the methods inherited from the DepartmentDisplay interface hierarchy.
- The presenter, DepartmentPresenter, implements the AbstractPresenter class and contains a reference to the DepartmentDisplay interface. This is how the presenter interacts with the views (grid or list) without a UI dependency.

- **DepartmentGridView** extends the abstract `DepartmentView` and renders the model (remote `DepartmentModel` objects) in a Grid component.
- **DepartmentListView** extends the abstract `DepartmentView` and renders the model in a `ListView` component.
- **DepartmentPresenter** in the `onBindActions()` method obtains the actions made available in the given view (grid or list implementation) and assigns to them the routine to be performed. Using a slightly modified version of the Actions framework discussed in *Chapter 3, Click-ware: Buttons, Toolbars, and Menus*, here, the view decides (and presents) the actions to be performed on it, but the presenter delegates which logic is executed when the actions are triggered.

```
private ToolBar topBar;
private ContentPanel ctPanel;

private void installView(DepartmentView view){
  ctPanel.removeAll();
   ctPanel.layout();

  topBar.removeAll();
  topBar.layout();
  if(view instanceof DepartmentGridView){
    ActionButton refreshBtn = new ActionButton(DepartmentGridView.
get().refreshAction());
        topBar.add(refreshBtn);
        topBar.add(new SeparatorToolItem());
        ActionButton saveBtn = new ActionButton(DepartmentGridView.
get().saveAction());
        topBar.add(saveBtn);

        Menu ctxMenu = DepartmentGridView.get().ctxMenu();
        ctxMenu.removeAll();
        ((ActionMenu) ctxMenu).add(DepartmentGridView.get().
refreshAction());
        ctxMenu.add(new SeparatorMenuItem());
        ((ActionMenu) ctxMenu).add(DepartmentGridView.get().
saveAction());

        DepartmentPresenter.get().setDisplay(DepartmentGridView.get().
display());
    ctPanel.add(DepartmentGridView.get().viewComponent());
  }else if(view instanceof DepartmentListView){
    DepartmentPresenter.get().setDisplay(DepartmentListView.get().
display());
    ctPanel.add(DepartmentListView.get().viewComponent());
  }

  addControlBtns();
  topBar.layout();
  ctPanel.layout();
}
```

Advanced Tips

```java
  private void asGrid(){
    installView(DepartmentGridView.get());
  }

  private void asList(){
    installView(DepartmentListView.get());
  }

  private void addControlBtns() {
    topBar.add(new FillToolItem());
    topBar.add(new Button("As Grid", new SelectionListener<ButtonEve
nt>() {
        @Override
        public void componentSelected(ButtonEvent evt) {
          if(DepartmentPresenter.get().display().
equals(DepartmentGridView.get().display())){
            return;
          }
          asGrid();
        }
    }));
    topBar.add(new Button("As List", new SelectionListener<ButtonEve
nt>() {
        @Override
        public void componentSelected(ButtonEvent evt) {
          if(DepartmentPresenter.get().display().
equals(DepartmentListView.get().display())){
            return;
          }
          asList();
        }
    }));
  }

  @Override
  public void onApply() {
    ctPanel = new ContentPanel();
    ctPanel.setLayout(new FitLayout());
    ctPanel.setHeaderVisible(false);
    ctPanel.setScrollMode(Scroll.NONE);
    ctPanel.setSize(350, 175);

    topBar = new ToolBar();
    ctPanel.setTopComponent(topBar);

    // show it up, equivalent to
    // RootPanel.get().add(ctPanel)
    centerPanel.add(ctPanel);

    asGrid();
  }
```

How it works...

From the `onApply()` method, we set()up a `ContentPanel` and give it a `ToolBar` at the top; the MVP app ticks off when `asGrid()` is invoked. It displays the server models as a grid by calling `installView()` with the `DepartmentGridView` object. A similar `asList()` method is used to call `installView()` too, but with the `DepartmentListView` object.

Considering that we are swapping between two views (a grid and a list), `installView()` starts out by clearing `ContentPanel` and then populating `ToolBar` and context-menu of the view if it is a `DepartmentGridView` object. At the end of each conditional block, the `DepartmentPresenter` is obtained and given the view to work with using its `setDisplay()` method, before the view gets attached to `ContentPanel`.

To make it easy to swap the views, `installView()` also calls `addControlBtnd()` which appends to the `ToolBar` two buttons used to call `asGrid()` or `asList()` again, but ensuring that a view is displayed if the presenter is not already presenting it.

When a given view is passed to `DepartmentPresenter.get().display()` from `installView()`, the superclass `bindActions()` is called which in turn calls the `onBindActions()` template method that is used to set the `ActionsManager` (which manages a set of actions, can perform them or disable/enable them) and then delegates the routine to be executed when they are triggered from any of the UI widgets they are attached to. `beginActions()` is also another template method used to set the actions to an initial state, like having some disabled until necessary.

`setDisplay()` finishes off by adding a `LoadListener` to the store of the view so that all actions (and by implication, their bound UI widgets) are disabled during load operations and then set to their initial state again with `beginActions()` when the operations complete successfully.

As defined in `onBindActions()`, when the `refreshAction()` is triggered, the view's store is instructed to reload. In the same vein, when the `saveAction()` is triggered, the presenter executes `runSave()` which fires the `SaveDepartment` event (`DepartmentGridView` listens for this event and displays a *saving* mask on the Grid), assembles the modified records, and disables all actions in the view with `view.actionsManager().disableAll()` in preparation for the RPC invocation.

The remote `saveDepartments()` method is called on the central RPC service provided by the `DataCenter` class with a callback that instructs the event-bus to fire `DepartmentSaveERR` in its `onFailure()` handler or `DepartmentSaveOK` in the `onSuccess()` handler after committing changes to the store and re-initializing the actions with `beginActions()`.

Advanced Tips

There's more...

While MVP is a design pattern that can be implemented by the developer, Google created its own implementation of the MVP pattern in GWT 2.1 (see `https://developers.google.com/web-toolkit/doc/latest/DevGuideMvpActivitiesAndPlaces`).

The Google implementation introduces activities, which are the presenters in the MVP pattern and places, which represent a navigation location. Each activity has a corresponding place and an `ActivityMapper` which maps a place to its activity. A `PlaceController` handles navigation to a new place and invokes the `ActivityMapper`, which returns the corresponding activity. The framework then activates the activity, which is responsible for displaying the view and handling its UI actions.

History and view transitions

Traditional websites and simple multi-paged apps are navigated by clicking links (or buttons) which load the destination page. This gives the browser a chance to track the pages the user just left and the one currently being viewed such that clicking the back button on the browser's chrome takes the user to the previously viewed page.

However, modern complex web apps have moved away from the idea of pages to that of screens or views, such that within a single page the user can navigate across several tabs and several overlaid windows, often without the browser knowing that these are valid navigations and therefore not updating its history. This leads to the all too familiar problem of the back/forward buttons on the browser failing to perform against the expectations of most users.

History events are token strings that represent some new state within the application; think of them as markers or bookmarks for a view or screen in the application. We can make the back/forward buttons work as expected by instructing the browser to recognize? our UI transitions as valid navigation if we attach unique markers for each view and push these into the history's stack as we transition.

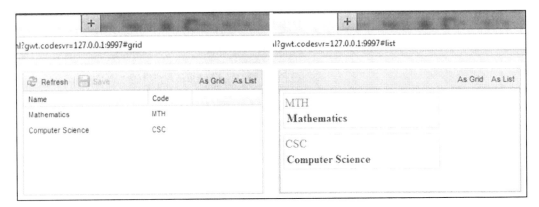

Getting ready

Ensure that your host page contains the usually optional GWT history frame, if not, include it now.

```
<!-- OPTIONAL: include this if you want history support -->
<iframe src="javascript:''" id="__gwt_historyFrame" tabIndex='-1' style="position:absolute;width:0;height:0;border:0"></iframe>
```

How to do it...

Our module has to implement GWT's `ValueChangeHandler` and declare the `onValueChange()` method, this is the method called by the `History` object when we hit the back/forward buttons. We can inspect the marker from the `ValueChangeEvent` parameter and decide which view to show.

Next, the module has to register to receive and handle `History` events having implemented `ValueChangeHandler`.

```java
private class BrowserHistoryRecipe extends ... implements
ValueChangeHandler<String>{

    ....

    @Override
    public void onValueChange(ValueChangeEvent<String> evt) {
      String token = evt.getValue();
      if(token != null && token.equals("list")){
        asList();
      } else if(token != null && token.equals("grid")){
        asGrid();
      }
    }

    @Override
    public void onApply() {
      History.addValueChangeHandler(this);

      ctPanel = new ContentPanel();
      ctPanel.setLayout(new FitLayout());
      ctPanel.setHeaderVisible(false);
      ctPanel.setScrollMode(Scroll.NONE);
      ctPanel.setSize(350, 175);
```

Advanced Tips

```
        topBar = new ToolBar();
        ctPanel.setTopComponent(topBar);

        // show it up, equivalent to
        // RootPanel.get().add(ctPanel)
        centerPanel.add(ctPanel);

        begin();
    }
}
```

A final step is to have an initial state or view, one that is triggered at the start of the application when its history is empty, or to go straight to a view in case it is supplied via a URL or bookmark.

```
private class BrowserHistoryRecipe extends ... implements
ValueChangeHandler<String>{
    ....

    public void begin(){
       if("".equals(History.getToken())){
         History.newItem("grid");
       } else {
         History.fireCurrentHistoryState();
       }
    }
}
```

How it works...

View transitions have to be controlled centrally outside the views themselves; one simple way, as we have done here, is to have a module implement the `ValueChangeHandler` interface and provide implementation for its `onValueChange()` method. The module, therefore, starts out by notifying GWT's history system with `History.addValueChangeHAndler(this)`, that it will listen for and handle `History` events. This translates to the overridden `onValueChange()` method being called wherever we invoke `History.newItem()` with a marker string.

The rest of `onApply` builds the UI (in the same way as the previous recipe) and then calls `begin()` which pushes the grid as a marker into the history's stack if `History.getToken()` is empty (usually when the app is just starting) or instructs the history mechanism to handle the current marker (maybe from URL or bookmark) with `History.fireCurrentHistoryState()`.

Both calls result in a call to `onValueChange()` which obtains the token (marker) from the event object and decides which view or screen to present.

Considering that the entire app is now navigated with the History mechanism, this installation of `addControlBtns()` (from the *A novel UI with MVP, actions, and a bus* recipe) now uses `History.newItem()` to transit between the list or grid instead of calling `asList()` or `asGrid()` directly. This ensures that the back/forward buttons of the browser can take us back and forth through all the views transitions and a direct URL or bookmark will take us to a particular view or screen.

There's more...

In the *There's more...* section of the *A novel UI with MVP, actions, and a bus* recipe, we mentioned that Google has introduced its own MVP implementation with Activities and Places as of GWT version 2.1. Places can be used for history navigation; this can be done by using the `PlaceHistoryHandler`. Note that this history mechanism requires you to implement the GWT MVP pattern implementation (see `https://developers.google.com/web-toolkit/doc/latest/DevGuideMvpActivitiesAndPlaces`).

Real-time server push

Web developers often watch with envy how mobile platforms use *push* technology to send important information and messages from their backends (or from one device) to several mobile devices in real time. It's not clear how to achieve this for the web; consequently many developers settle for polling their backends – asking intermittently *are there updates…*.

While the polling approach is simple and works for the most part, it burdens the client and server unnecessarily, leading to chatty applications, and can quickly impact memory, network, and bandwidth resources.

With push, when an event (for example, `update`) occurs on the server, probably triggered by a client, the server broadcasts a notification (ping) to all registered clients about the update so they can act accordingly. Therefore, as a store manager, I can change the price of an item in my products view then save the change, and have the new price immediately show up on the views of the cashiers at the POS terminals without them having to first refresh their browsers.

Advanced Tips

This recipe augments the code base of the first two recipes of this chapter with push functionality, hence the reuse of MVP nomenclature.

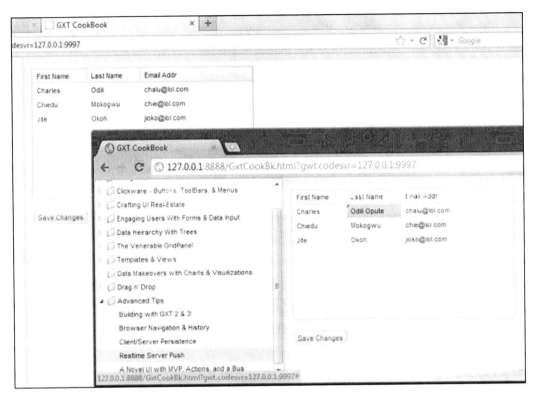

How to do it...

Several APIs promise push functionality for the GWT/GXT apps. However, only a few rise up to the challenge. Download and add `geteventservice` (using 1.0.2) to your build path, and add the following entry to your `.gwt.xml` module file: `<inherits name="de.novanic.eventservice.GWTEventService" />`.

Define `CometGateway` interface to extend GWTs `RemoteService` and declare the `mvpDepartmentsUpdated()` RPC method. Also provide the corresponding `CometGatewayAsync` interface.

```
@RemoteServiceRelativePath("remote/evtgateway")
public interface CometGateway extends RemoteService {
public void mvpDepartmentsUpdated();
}

public interface CometGatewayAsync {
  void mvpDepartmentsUpdated(AsyncCallback<Void> callback);
}
```

The `gwteventservice` API works by triggering events declared on the server which can be listened for, and handled in the client. Define `MvpDepartmentUpdate` in the server to extend the gwteventservice's `Event` class, and define a domain within it to serve as a channel for interested clients to register and listen on. Also define the `MvpDepartmentCometListener` class in the client, that implements gwteventservice's `RemoteEventListener` interface—this is the `listener` class that clients will use to listen for, and handle the remote events (for example, the `MvpDepartmentUpdate` event) when they are broadcast from the server.

```java
public class MvpDepartmentUpdate implements Event {

  public static final String DOMAIN = "mvp_dept_domain";

  public MvpDepartmentUpdate() {
    super();
  }
}

public abstract class MvpDepartmentCometListener implements
RemoteEventListener {

  @Override
  public void apply(Event anEvent) {
    onUpdate((MvpDepartmentUpdate) anEvent);
  }

  public abstract void onUpdate(MvpDepartmentUpdate evt);

}
```

Now add servlet declarations and mappings in the `web.xml` file for the `gwteventservice` servlet and our `CometGatewayImpl` servlet.

```java
public class CometGatewayImpl extends RemoteEventServiceServlet
implements
    CometGateway {

  public CometGatewayImpl() {
    super();
  }

  @Override
  public void mvpDepartmentsUpdated() {
    addEvent(DomainFactory.getDomain(MvpDepartmentUpdate.DOMAIN), new MvpDepartmentUpdate());
  }

}
```

Advanced Tips

```xml
<?xml version="1.0" encoding="UTF-8"?>
.....

<web-app>

  <!-- Servlets -->
  <servlet>
    <servlet-name>EventService</servlet-name>
    <servlet-class>de.novanic.eventservice.service.EventServiceImpl</servlet-class>
  </servlet>
  <servlet>
    <servlet-name>CometGateway</servlet-name>
    <servlet-class>com.gxtcookbook.code.server.comet.CometGatewayImpl</servlet-class>
  </servlet>

  .....

  <!-- Mappings -->
  <servlet-mapping>
    <servlet-name>EventService</servlet-name>
    <url-pattern>/gxtcookbk/gwteventservice</url-pattern>
  </servlet-mapping>
  <servlet-mapping>
    <servlet-name>CometGateway</servlet-name>
    <url-pattern>/gxtcookbk/remote/evtgateway</url-pattern>
  </servlet-mapping>
  .....

</web-app>
```

How it works...

Once again, and true to its calling, the `DataCenter` class provisions the comet service to the rest of the application, much like the `rpc-service` we've been using throughout this chapter. It initializes `cometEventMgr` (used by the client to listen for remote event broadcast by server) and `cometRpcService` (used by the client to instruct the server to broadcast an event) making them available with `cometEventMgr()` and `cometRpcService()` respectively.

```java
public class DataCenter extends BaseObservable {

  ....

  private RemoteGatewayAsync rpcService;
  private RemoteEventService cometEventMgr;
  private CometGatewayAsync cometRpcService;
```

```
    .....
    private DataCenter() {
      super();

      rpcService = (RemoteGatewayAsync) GWT.create(RemoteGateway.class);

      RemoteEventServiceFactory serviceFctry =
    RemoteEventServiceFactory.getInstance();
      cometEventMgr = serviceFctry.getRemoteEventService();
      cometRpcService = (CometGatewayAsync) GWT.create(CometGateway.
    class);

      buildStores();
    }

    public RemoteGatewayAsync rpcService() {
      return rpcService;
    }

    public RemoteEventService cometEventMgr() {
      return cometEventMgr;
    }

    public CometGatewayAsync cometRpcService(){
      return cometRpcService;
    }
    ......
}
```

Considering that our codebase (from the first two recipes in this chapter) builds on the idea of central stores from the `DataCenter` class, a `LiveStore` util class is created and its `listenForCometBroadcast()` method uses the `cometEventMgr` object acquired from the `DataCenter` to listen on the `MvpDepartmentUpdate.DOMAIN` channel with an `MvpDepartmentCometListener` object whose `onUpdate()` method is called with the remote `MvpDepartmentUpdate` event when it occurs.

The `onUpdate()` method here reloads the store (it's a light ping saying *there are updates on the server, go fetch them*) after adding a `LoadListener` to the store's loader which iterates over observers (interested parties in the UI) on the live store, giving them the benefit of doing stuff on the UI with the fresh data.

```
    public class LiveStore {

      public interface UpdateObserver{
        public void broadcastReceived(ListStore<? extends ModelData>
    store, MvpDepartmentUpdate updateEvt);
      }
      ....
```

Advanced Tips

```java
public LiveStore(ListStore<? extends ModelData> listStore) {
   ......

   listenForCometBroadcast();
}

....

private void listenForCometBroadcast(){
   DataCenter.get().cometEventMgr().addListener(DomainFactory.
getDomain(MvpDepartmentUpdate.DOMAIN), new
MvpDepartmentCometListener() {
      @Override
      public void onUpdate(MvpDepartmentUpdate evt) {
         // got fetch the updates;
         // especially for new records
         // that will need id.
         // The observers are called
         // before and after the data arrives
         // to make required UI updates if any.
         store.getLoader().addLoadListener(new
UpdatesLoadListener(evt));
         store.getLoader().load();
      }
   });
}

private class UpdatesLoadListener extends LoadListener{

   private UpdatesLoadListener me;
   private MvpDepartmentUpdate evt;

   public UpdatesLoadListener(MvpDepartmentUpdate event) {
      super();
      evt = event;
      me = this;
   }

   @Override
   public void loaderLoad(LoadEvent le) {
      super.loaderLoad(le);
      for (LiveStore.UpdateObserver observer : observers) {
         observer.broadcastReceived(store, evt);
      }
```

```
            store.getLoader().removeLoadListener(me);
        }
    }

    .....
}
```

The client code (onApply() portion) is exactly the same as the MVP recipe. However, DepartmentPresenter here defines a pushChanges() method which it invokes (from the onSuccess() handler) after an RPC request to persist changes on the server returns. pushChanges() uses cometRpcService to invoke the remote mvpDepartmentsUpdated() method in CometGatewayImpl.

```
    public class DepartmentPresenter extends AbstractPresenter {

    ...

    private void runSave() {
    ....

        DataCenter.get().rpcService().saveDepartments(changes, new AsyncCallback<Response>() {
        ....

                @Override
                public void onSuccess(Response result) {
                  if(Response.STATUS_OK.equals(result.getStatus())){
                    view.display().store().commitChanges();
                    beginActions();
                    MvpEvents.getBus().fireEvent(MvpEvents.DepartmentSaveOK);

                    // used for comet
                    // request the server to notify
                    // others of the changes made
                    pushChanges();
                      }else{
                        Info.display("Server Error", result.getMessages().
toString());
                    MvpEvents.getBus().fireEvent(MvpEvents.
DepartmentSaveERR);
                    }
                  }
        });
```

Advanced Tips

```
    }

    private void pushChanges(){
       DataCenter.get().cometRpcService().mvpDepartmentsUpdated(new
    AsyncCallback<Void>() {
          @Override
          public void onFailure(Throwable caught) {}

          @Override
          public void onSuccess(Void result) {}
       });
    }
}
```

The method broadcasts a `MvpDepartmentUpdate` event on the `MvpDepartmentUpdate.DOMAIN` channel and therefore notifies all clients listening on the channel, as we have done within the `listenForCometBroadcast()` method in `LiveStore`.

12
Theming

In this chapter we will cover the following points:

- ▶ Setting a default theme
- ▶ Registering and using themes
- ▶ Switching themes at runtime
- ▶ Customizing a theme
- ▶ Building a custom theme

Introduction

Themes in GXT, as with other UI platforms, provide a robust way to control the look and feel of the components and widgets available to an application. Besides the collection that ships with the standard GXT distribution, quite a number of GXT themes can be found online, making it possible to change from the bluish look of GXT applications to something different in color and even structure.

A GXT theme defines the set of images and CSS used for its styling of components, and can then be used together with the GXT theme-manager component so that the rest of the API can be dressed in the attire of the said theme.

This chapter will discuss how to use the standard bundled themes and third-party themes as well, before briefly touching on how to begin building custom themes for GXT applications.

Theming

Setting a default theme

There are three built-in themes in the standard GXT distribution: Blue (the all too familiar default), Gray, and Slate. Each of these themes (and any other for that matter) encapsulates a set of images and CSS for the peculiar styling it performs on the UI components.

Although GXT comes with the Blue theme set as default, we can easily change it to any other theme that we deem appropriate; after all it just takes a single line of code.

The following screenshot shows components using the gray theme:

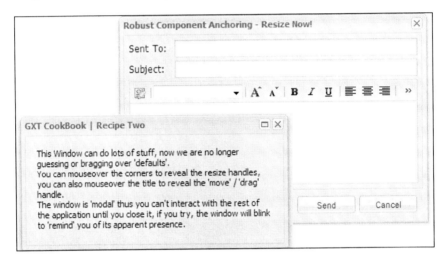

Getting ready

The GXT system expects that theme resources will reside under a `gxt` folder within the web applications root directory and unless otherwise stated by a custom theme. The GXT system will look at this default location whenever it needs to load a theme, therefore one must ensure that things are properly set up upfront.

1. Ensure that there is a `gxt` folder on the floor of your web application's `war` directory, if not, make one.
2. Copy the `images` folder (which contains a `default`, `gray`, and `gxt` folder within it) from the `resources` folder of a GXT distribution into the `gxt` folder so that we now have a path like `gxt/images/gray/s.gif`.
3. Make a `css` folder within the `gxt` folder from step 1 and place in it a copy of the `gxt-gray.css` CSS file from the `resources/css` directory of a GXT distribution. We should now have a valid path to `gxt/css/gxt-gray.css`.
4. Add `<inherits name='com.extjs.gxt.themes.Themes' />` entry to your `.gwt.xml` module file.

How to do it...

It is quite simple to change the default Blue theme to the GXT Gray theme, for example. We just need to do the following:

1. Ensure that the steps in the *Getting ready* section of this recipe have been followed.
2. Invoke `GXT.setDefaultTheme(Theme.GRAY, true)` as the first line in the `onModuleLoad()` method of your entry point. It is very important that this is the very first line within `onModuleLoad()`. Once `GXT.setDefaultTheme(Theme.GRAY, true)` is called, it instructs GXT to use the Gray theme instead of the Blue one.

   ```
   @Override
   public void onModuleLoad() {
     GXT.setDefaultTheme(Theme.GRAY, true);
   }
   ```

How it works...

When calling `GXT.setDefaultTheme(Theme.GRAY, true)` we pass `true` as the second parameter, instructing GXT that we really want to effect the changes right away.

The reason this call must be the very first thing in the `onModuleLoad()` method is that we want to set the theme before GXT starts creating components—a process that will internally initialize the theme system with `GXT.init()` calls in the `Component` class. If `GXT.init()` is called before setting the theme, then our theme change will be ignored.

There's more...

To be very sure that you are ready to be changing themes from within your code, ensure that your entry-point class only implements `com.google.gwt.core.client.EntryPoint` and does not extend any descendant of the GXT `Component` class, as this means the theme would have been set before you get a chance to change it.

Registering and using themes

The Slate and Access themes are also included in a standard GXT distribution as samples of custom themes. However, we cannot just use them like the Gray theme without first being registered with the GXT `ThemeManager`, ensuring that the system will know how to locate the theme and its resources when needed.

Theming

The following screenshot shows components using the slate theme after we register it:

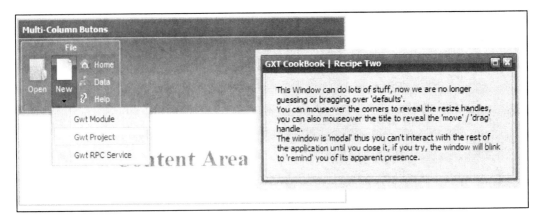

Getting ready

The GXT system expects that theme resources will reside under a `gxt` folder within the web applications root directory and unless otherwise stated by a custom theme, the GXT system will look at this default location whenever it needs to load a theme. Therefore, one must ensure that things are properly set up upfront.

1. Follow the *Getting ready* section of the first recipe (*Setting a default theme*) of this chapter.
2. Copy the `themes` folder (contains a `slate` and `access` folder within it) from the `resources` folder of a GXT distribution into the `gxt` folder so that we now have a path like `gxt/themes/slate/css/xtheme-slate.css`.
3. If you want to use any other third-party theme, place them here just as we have done in step 2.

How to do it...

Register the themes with the static `ThemeManager.register()` method and then use `GXT.setDefaultTheme()` to make any one of them the default. These steps must be taken as the first thing within the `onModuleLoad()` method.

```
@Override
public void onModuleLoad() {
   ThemeManager.register(Slate.SLATE);
   ThemeManager.register(Access.ACCESS);

   GXT.setDefaultTheme(Slate.SLATE, true);
}
```

How it works...

The call to `ThemeManager.register()` is used to make the GXT system aware of the Slate and Access themes and make them available for use with the `GXT.setDefaultTheme()` call. It turns out to be really simple except that you must not do any UI calls or initialization(s) before the `GXT.setDefaultTheme()` call, otherwise the default Blue theme will be used instead of our newly registered ones.

Switching themes at runtime

The GXT system provides a handy way of switching/changing themes dynamically or at runtime, instead of having to always do it in code and recompile to see it in action. Runtime theme switching is done with a `ThemeSelector` widget, which is actually a `ComboBox` extension.

It presents to the user the available themes provided by (and registered with) the `ThemeManager`, such that the user can then select any theme from the list and have it applied immediately.

The following screenshots show the `ThemeSelector` widget and the result of selecting the **Access** theme on a component:

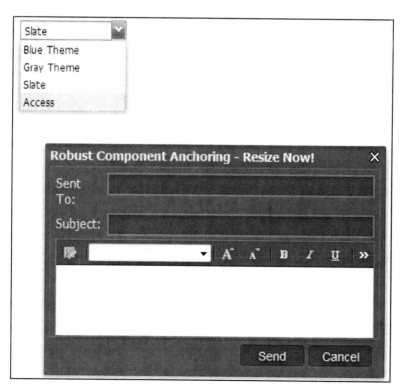

Theming

How to do it...

Create a `ThemeSelector` widget and place it on the screen. From that point, the widget takes control and does all the work needed to change to a theme as long as the themes are placed in the right places expected of them (see the *Getting ready* section of the first recipe, *Setting a default theme*, in this chapter) by the GXT system.

```
@Override
public void onModuleLoad() {
  // Although not needed but
  // if you ever call GXT.setDefaultTheme()
  // when you intend to switch themes
  // later with the ThemeSelector, then
  // make sure the GXT.setDefaultTheme() call
  // is given false as second parameter
  // because true as second parameter will
  // force the theme specified as first
  // parameter to be enabled even when the app
  // is reloading after a selection has been
  // made with the ThemeSelector.
  ThemeManager.register(Access.ACCESS);
  ThemeManager.register(Slate.SLATE);
  GXT.setDefaultTheme(Slate.SLATE, false);

    ThemeSelector selector = new ThemeSelector();
    selector.setWidth(125);

    // Equivalent to
    // RootPanel.get().add(selector);
    centerPanel.add(selector);
}
```

How it works...

`ThemeSelector` is a `ComboBox` derivative that simplifies the selection and change process of available themes. When the user makes a selection from the presented themes, it loads the theme by re-loading the application with the selected theme set as default, thereby eliminating the need to use `GXT.setDefaultTheme()` from code.

Chapter 12

Customizing a theme

GXT themes are mechanisms for controlling how UI components are presented to the user and they can be used *as-is* or customized with CSS and images. Therefore, one can decide to use the standard Blue theme but alter the way certain components look by styling them with CSS and changing some of their images.

Building a custom theme from scratch offers a good level of control; however it may suffice to just modify certain aspects of an already satisfying theme with images and CSS.

We will demonstrate such styling by altering the default presentation of panels and portlets in GXT using CSS and then switch the images used in by the `Grid` component with a set of custom images specified with a `XImage` implementation.

The following screenshot shows a re-styled Portlet component with CSS overrides:

Here we show a re-styled `Grid` component with custom images:

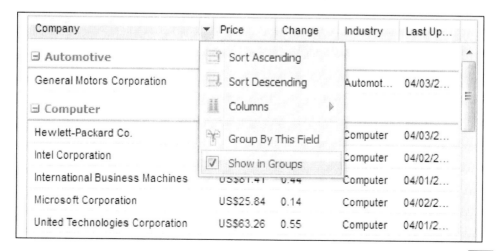

Theming

How to do it...

Perform the following steps for this recipe:

1. Edit the project's CSS file and add the following CSS rules to re-style our panels and portlets:

    ```css
    .x-panel-tc {
      background-image:none;
      background-image: url("resources/images/default/window/top-bottom.png");
    }

    .x-panel-tr {
      background-image: url("resources/images/default/window/right-corners.png");
    }

    .x-panel-tl {
      background-image: url("resources/images/default/window/left-corners.png");
    }

    .x-panel-bl {
      background-image: url("resources/images/default/window/left-corners.png");
    }

    .x-panel-br{
      background-image: url("resources/images/default/window/right-corners.png");
    }
    ```

2. To use a different set of images for the `Grid` component, create an interface that extends GXT's `XImage` interface and overrides the required methods.

    ```java
    public interface CustomImages extends XImages {

      @Resource("sort-asc.gif")
      AbstractImagePrototype grid_sortAsc();

      @Resource("sort-desc.gif")
      AbstractImagePrototype grid_sortDesc();

      @Resource("columns.gif")
      AbstractImagePrototype grid_columns();

      @Resource("group-by.gif")
      AbstractImagePrototype grid_groupBy();
    }
    ```

3. Then reset `GXT.IMAGES` as follows:

    ```java
    GXT.IMAGES = (XImages) GWT.create(CustomImages.class);
    ```

How it works...

The host page for a GWT project usually includes a link to the project's CSS file and this is where local/custom styling to the UI is done. Here we simply set the styling for all panel-based components to use the images for the window instead. I particularly like the view of the GXT window because of its flatness and round corners. The CSS rules ensure that our `Panel` components wear a similar look as the `Window` components.

The second code listing shows a `CustomImages` interface that extends the GXT `XImage` interface and overrides some of the images used for a `Grid` component. After executing `GXT.IMAGES = (XImages) GWT.create(CustomImages.class)`, all `Grid` components in the system will use the images we have specified (instead of the default ones), which according to our code is expected to reside within the same package as the `CustomImages` interface.

Building a custom theme

When alterations to an existing theme via CSS and images get overwhelming, then it's time to build your own custom theme, which is not really far from the concept of styling an existing theme with CSS and images.

We will demonstrate this by making a minimal custom theme which I want to call Chrome.

How to do it...

Let's list the steps required to complete the task.

1. Ensure that there is a `gxt` folder on the floor of your web application's `war` directory, otherwise make one.
2. Ensure that there is a `themes` folder within it, if not, make one and then also make a `chrome` folder for the Chrome theme.
3. Place a `css` folder within the `chrome` folder created in step 2, and then place a `css` file named `xtheme-chrome.css` inside it.
4. Within the `chrome` folder created in step 2, create an `images/chrome` folder and place any custom images you want to use for the theme.
5. Create a `Chrome` class that extends the GXT `Theme` class. Implement the constructor to indicate the name for the theme and a path to the `xtheme-chrome.css`. Register the theme with GXT `ThemeManager` and then use it as any other theme.

    ```java
    public class Chrome extends Theme {

        public static Theme CHROME = new Chrome();

        public Chrome() {
    ```

Theming

```
    super("chrome", "Chrome", "gxt/themes/chrome/css/
xtheme-chrome.css");
  }

  public Chrome(String name){
    super("chrome", name, "gxt/themes/chrome/css/xtheme-chrome.
css");
  }

}
```

How it works...

The `xtheme-chrome.css` file defines the CSS rules for the Chrome theme. Inside the file, we specify colors and images (from the `images/chrome` folder within the `theme` folder) to use with the theme. We can also alter the structure of components in this CSS file such that our tabs will wear a totally different look from that of a GXT `TabPanel`.

A `Chrome` class is then created to extend the GXT `Theme` class. It specifies the name of the theme and the path to the `xtheme-chrome.css` file it uses for styling.

Once registered with `ThemeManager`, it becomes available like the Blue, Gray, or Slate theme and can be used in code or with a `ThemeSelector` to change the theme of any given GXT application.

A
Event Handling— Making Those GUIs Do Something

We want to see how to get GUIs to respond to user actions such as clicking on a button, typing text, or dragging the mouse. These user actions are called **events**, and responding to them is called **event handling**.

The event loop

In a GUI-based program, all processing revolves around something called the **event loop**. The process is as follows:

1. The program sits there, waiting for the user to do something.
2. The user does something (generates an event).
3. The program responds in some way.
4. Go back to step 1.

Event handling 101

In Java (and most other programming environments), event handling is based on the observer design pattern. In this pattern, an object maintains one or more dependent objects and notifies them of any changes. In event handling, listeners or handlers are registered to a UI component and listen for events coming from the component. A listener contains a method which contains the code we want to run when an event happens.

Event Handling—Making Those GUIs Do Something

When an event happens to a component, that event is passed on to all the listeners for that component; some of which might then respond to the event. When they have done this, they go back to listening.

Control flow of delegation event model

The source component registers an event listener, which is responsible for handling the event. The event is fired by the component and an event object is passed to the listener.

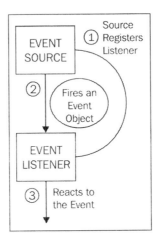

The following are the steps we need to take to handle events:

1. Set up the GUI component.
2. Create a `Listener` object, for example, a `SelectionListener` for handling button clicks.
3. Associate the `Listener` object with the component we want to respond to, using the `addListener()` method, or `addSelectionListener()` which is recommended for a `SelectionListener`.

That's basically all there is to event handling.

A simple example – button presses

A simple form of event is the pressing of a button; this generates a `ButtonEvent`, which we will listen for with a `SelectionListener`. It is relatively easy to write the code to handle a button-press, so let's write one!

```
Button btn = new Button("Button Text");

SelectionListener<ButtonEvent> listener;
listener = new SelectionListener<ButtonEvent>() {
  @Override
  public void componentSelected(ButtonEvent evt) {
      String msg = evt.getButton().getText();
    Info.display("Message", "Clicked - " + msg);
  }
};

btn.addSelectionListener(listener);
```

Anonymous inner classes

Anonymous inner classes are unnamed inner classes (a class within a class), which help to simplify your code especially in event handling. The previous example can now be re-written as follows:

```
Button btn = new Button("Button Text",
new SelectionListener<ButtonEvent>() {
    @Override
    public void componentSelected(ButtonEvent evt) {
        String msg = evt.getButton().getText();
      Info.display("Message", "Clicked - " + msg);
   }
});
```

The use of anonymous inner classes in event handlers is quite common. However, for code clarity, these handlers should be very short code snippets.

Summary

To respond to events, we create listener objects.

- A listener is an object whose class implements an appropriate interface; in GXT it's the `Listener` interface
- `SelectionListener` is a listener implementation used to listen for selections such as button presses
- The method `handleEvent()`, or `componentSelected()` in the case of a button, contains the code to run when the event is fired
- The listener is attached to a GUI component using the `addListener()` method or `addSelectionListener()` for a button

As of version 2.0, GWT uses handlers for its event handling. GXT version 3.0 will move from using listeners to using handlers, so that it will be compatible with the GWT event handling mechanism. This compatibility will also allow GXT 3.0 to add support for GWT `UIBinder`. `UIBinder` is used for building a UI in a declarative way, using an XML file, in order to cut down on boilerplate code and provide more flexible layouts.

Custom Icons in GXT

The GXT toolkit contains many cool widgets, but there's no pre-built collection of icons for garnishing the UIs we often want to build. Even if there was such a collection, it's just a matter of time before we start wanting to use custom icons here and there. The solution is quite simple and extensible too.

GXT icons

We will create a custom interface that extends `ClientBundle` and call it `Icons`, to encapsulate methods that return the icon images as instances of `ImageResource`.

```
public interface Icons extends ClientBundle {
   ImageResource people();
   ImageResource home();
   ImageResource orgchart();
}
```

Our sample `Icons` interface extends `ClientBundle` and declares three methods, each named with the exact name of an image placed in the same package as the `Icons` interface. Having created the interface, we can use it with tabs, buttons, and other GXT components, usually components that implement the `IconSupport` interface. However, we will need to convert the `ImageResource` object from our `Icons` interface to an `AbstractImagePrototype` object, which GXT components accept.

```
Icons ICONS = GWT.create(Icons.class);
TabItem homeTab = new TabItem("Home");
homeTab.setIcon(AbstractImagePrototype.create(ICONS.home()));
Button btn = new Button("Btn Text");
btn.setIcon(AbstractImagePrototype.create(ICONS.people()));
```

Note that the image itself can reside in the same package as the interface, or have its path specified with the `@Source` annotation.

Custom Icons in GXT

Leveraging icons in the wild

There is a huge collection of icon sets floating on the web that we can take advantage of, especially in making our UI look radically different. Some popular ones include *Silk*, *Tango*, *Fugue*, and *SweetiePlus*.

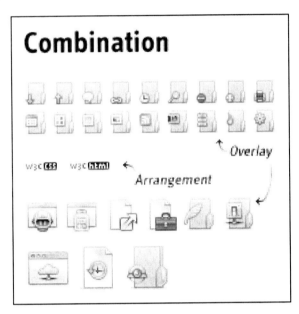

The `Icons` interface that we currently have is not so flexible. If we want to combine icons from the *Silk* and *Tango* sets, then we must dump all the image files in that same package folder, risking over-writing some. Also, if we want to use only the *Tango* icons, we will have problems since there's no namespace structure.

To make it easy to use all these icons and others yet to be discovered, in an intuitive way, we'll re-factor the `Icons` interface to serve as a factory while the `ClientBundleinterface` will be extended to provide, say a `SilkIcons` interface for the *Silk* collection, and a `FugueIcons` interface for the *Fugue* icons set.

```
// The Icons "factory"
package com.example.client.icons;

public interface Icons {

   SilkIcons Silk = GWT.create(SilkIcons.class);
   FugueIcons Fugue = GWT.create(FugueIcons.class);

}
```

```
// Silk icons set
package com.example.client.icons.silk;

public interface SilkIcons extends ClientBundle{

   ImageResource accept();
}

// Fugue icons set
package com.example.client.icons.fugue;

public interface FugueIcons extends ClientBundle {
   FugueX32 x32 = GWT.create(FugueX32.class);
   ImageResource acorn();
}

// Fugue 32x32icons set

public interface FugueX32 extends ClientBundle {
   ImageResource folder();
   ImageResource document();
}
```

This makes for a fluid interface from the client code perspective, such as `Icons.Fugue.x32.document()`. Our earlier example will now be as follows:

```
TabItem homeTab = new TabItem("Terms");
homeTab.setIcon(AbstractImagePrototype.create(Icons.Silk.accept()));

Button btn = new Button("Document");
btn.setScale(ButtonScale.LARGE);
btn.setIconAlign(IconAlign.TOP);
btn.setIcon(AbstractImagePrototype.create((Icons.Fugue.x32.document())));
```

GWT-RPC

The GWT RPC framework makes it easy for the client and server components of your web application to exchange Java objects over HTTP. The server-side code that gets invoked from the client is often referred to as a service. The implementation of a GWT RPC service is based on the well-known Java servlet architecture. Within the client code, you'll use an automatically generated proxy class to make calls to the service. GWT will handle serialization of the Java objects passing the arguments back and forth in the method calls and the return value.

GWT RPC is not the same as web services based on SOAP or REST. It is a lightweight HTTP-based client server protocol specific for GWT.

Components of the GWT RPC mechanism

When you set up a GWT project, using either the Google command line tools or the eclipse GWT plugin, a specific package structure is created for you. The package structure is designed to help you differentiate between client code, server code, and code that will be shared between the client and server.

Packages of the form `<package-base>.client` and `<package-base>.shared` will be compiled into JavaScript by default (as specified in the GWT XML configuration file with the `source` tag), while packages of the form `<package-base>.server` are by default the place for server-side code.

When setting up GWT RPC, you will focus on these three elements involved in calling procedures running on remote servers:

1. The service that runs on the server (the method you are calling).
2. The client code that invokes the service.
3. The Java data objects that pass between the client and server.

GWT-RPC

Both the server and the client have the ability to serialize and deserialize data so the data objects can be passed between them as ordinary text.

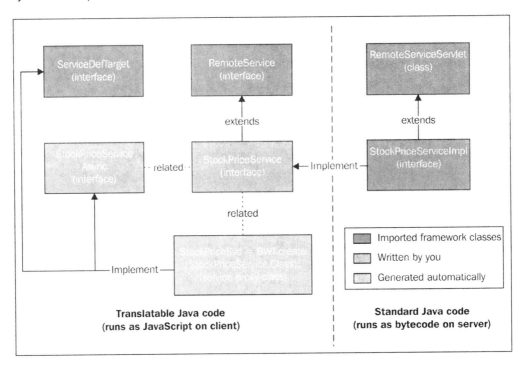

GWT-RPC development steps

The following steps describe how to implement a service using GWT RPC:

- Define the main service interface
    - Implement the `RemoteService` interface
    - Define the regular methods without explicit HTTP
    - Use the `@RemoteServiceRelativePath` to point at servlet
- Define the callback (Async) version of the service interface
    - If the main interface is `FooService`, define `FooServiceAsync`
- Make the service servlet
    - Extend the `RemoteServiceServlet`, implement the `service` interface
    - Supply the URL-pattern in `web.xml` that matches the relative path

- Create and use the service proxy
    - Call `GWT.create(FooService.class)`
    - Define the client-side callback objects with the `onSuccess` and `onFailure` methods implemented

A service implementation must extend `RemoteServiceServlet` and must implement the associated service interface. Notice that the service implementation does not implement the asynchronous version of the service interface. Every service implementation is ultimately a servlet, but rather than extending `HttpServlet`, it extends `RemoteServiceServlet` instead. `RemoteServiceServlet` automatically handles serialization of the data being passed between the client and the server and invokes the intended method in your service implementation.

RPC data types

Server methods can accept and return complex types with packing and unpacking handled automatically even though client-side code is JavaScript (not Java) at runtime.

Legal types

The following is a list of legal data types that can be passed over the network using GWT RPC:

- Primitives
    - `int`, `double`, `boolean`, and so on
- Wrappers
    - `Integer`, `Double`, `Boolean`, and so on
- A subset of standard Java types
    - `ArrayList`, `Date`, `HashMap`, `HashSet`, `String`, and so on
    - For a full list see http://code.google.com/webtoolkit/doc/latest/RefJreEmulation.html
- Custom classes that implement `Serializable`
- Arrays containing any of the given types

Note that we can also cut down on the GWT JavaScript size, by instructing GWT not to generate serialization and deserialization code for some classes.

GWT-RPC

We can do this by specifying a list of blacklisted classes in the GWT module XML file. For example:

```xml
<extend-configuration-property name="rpc.blacklist"
value="com.google.gwt.user.client.ui.ChangeListenerCollection"/>
```

A simple example

The following example shows a simple GWT RPC greeting service, which is generated automatically when you create a GWT project.

Define the main service interface

We create an interface that implements `RemoteService` and define our remote methods in it. We annotate the service with the `@RemoteServiceRelativePath` annotation, which specifies the path to the service implementation servlet on the server.

```java
import com.google.gwt.user.client.rpc.RemoteService;
import com.google.gwt.user.client.rpc.RemoteServiceRelativePath;

@RemoteServiceRelativePath("greet")
public interface GreetingService extends RemoteService {
   String greetServer(String name) throws IllegalArgumentException;
}
```

Define the callback version of the service interface

We define the asynchronous version of our interface, by adding our remote methods with the same parameters as they were defined in the service interface, but without a return value. Instead, we add another parameter which is the `AsyncCallback` class parameterized by our object return type.

In this example, we return `String` from the `greetServer()` method so we pass `AsyncCallback<String>` as the callback class.

```java
import com.google.gwt.user.client.rpc.AsyncCallback;

public interface GreetingServiceAsync {
   void greetServer(String input, AsyncCallback<String> callback)
   throws IllegalArgumentException;

}
```

Create the service servlet

Now, we create implementation of our service interface. This is the actual service that will be invoked on the server side. Our service implementation needs to extend the `RemoteServiceServlet` and implement our service method.

```
import com.bitrunk.gwtrpc.client.GreetingService;
import com.google.gwt.user.server.rpc.RemoteServiceServlet;

public class GreetingServiceImpl extends RemoteServiceServlet implements
    GreetingService {

  public String greetServer(String input) throws
IllegalArgumentException {
    return "Hello, " + input;
  }
}
```

Our service implementation is actually a servlet. It needs to be defined in the web application deployment descriptor `web.xml`. Note that the URL mapping of the servlet is composed of `<web application root>/<service-path>`. The `<service-path>` is the same URL path defined in our service interface using the `@RemoteServiceRelativePath` annotation.

```
// web.xml
<web-app>

  <!-- Servlets -->
  <servlet>
    <servlet-name>greetServlet</servlet-name>
    <servlet-class>com.bitrunk.gwtrpc.server.GreetingServiceImpl</servlet-class>
  </servlet>

  <servlet-mapping>
    <servlet-name>greetServlet</servlet-name>
    <url-pattern>/gwtrpc/greet</url-pattern>
  </servlet-mapping>

  <!-- Default page to serve -->
  <welcome-file-list>
    <welcome-file>GwtRPC.html</welcome-file>
  </welcome-file-list>

</web-app>
```

GWT-RPC

Create and use the service proxy

To invoke our RPC service on the client side, we create an instance of our `GreetingServiceAsync` interface using a call to `GWT.create()`, passing the service interface. We can now call the `asynchronous` method and pass it to our `callback` class.

The `callback` class contains the `onFailure` method, which is called in case of an exception and the `onSuccess` method which is called if the remote call succeeds.

```
private GreetingServiceAsync greetingService = GWT.
create(GreetingService.class);

...

greetingService.greetServer(textToServer,
    new AsyncCallback<String>() {
  public void onFailure(Throwable caught) {
    // Show the RPC error message to the user
      // if the called service method throws an exception
      // defined in a throws clause then handle it here.
  }

  public void onSuccess(String result) {
    // Show success message to the user   or update some UI
  }
});
```

The GWT RPC service knows the URL of the service by the value of the `RemoteServiceRelativePath` annotation defined in the service interface. That value is appended to a URL which includes the GWT module name. In case we want to invoke a service that belongs to a different GWT module, we will need to explicitly specify the service URL. This can be done using the `ServiceDefTarget` interface:

```
ServiceDefTarget endPoint = (ServiceDefTarget) greetService;
endPoint.setServiceEntryPoint(GWT.getHostPageBaseURL() + "/gxtcookbk/
greet");
```

Handling exceptions

When a remote procedure call fails, the cause falls into one of two categories: an unexpected exception or a checked exception. In either case, you want to handle the exception and, if necessary, provide feedback to the user.

Unexpected exceptions

Any number of unexpected occurrences could cause the call to a remote procedure to fail: the network could be down, the HTTP server on the other end might not be listening, the DNS server could be on fire, and so forth.

Another type of unexpected exception can occur if GWT is able to invoke the service method, but the service implementation throws an undeclared exception. For example, a bug may cause a `NullPointerException`.

When unexpected exceptions occur in the service implementation, you can find the full stack trace in the development mode log. On the client side, the `onFailure(Throwable)` callback method will receive an `InvocationException` with the generic message: *The call failed on the server; see server log for details.*

Checked exceptions

If you know that a service method might throw a particular type of exception and you want the client-side code to be able to handle it, you can use checked exceptions. GWT supports the `throws` keyword so you can add it to your service interface methods as needed. When checked exceptions occur in an RPC service method, GWT will serialize the exception and send it back to the caller on the client for handling.

Summary

RPC is a powerful technique for constructing distributed, client-server based applications. It is based on extending the notion of conventional or local procedure, so that the called procedure need not exist in the same address space as the calling procedure. GWT automatically generates most of the classes required for RPC.

Jakarta Commons–FileUpload

`FileUpload` is an aptly named library that makes it easy to add file upload capability to a Java web application. By using its clear API, a user can send files to a web server for easy processing by simply making a selection from a web form. A file upload request comprises of an ordered list of items that are encoded according to RFC 1867 - "Form-based File Upload in HTML".

`FileUpload` can parse such a request and provide your application with a list of the individual uploaded items. Each such item implements the `FileItem` interface, regardless of its underlying implementation.

Using `FileUpload` creates new file items using a `FileItemFactory`. This is what gives `FileUpload` most of its flexibility. The factory has ultimate control over how each item is created. The factory implementation that currently ships with `FileUpload` stores the item's data in memory or on disk, depending on the size of the item (for example, bytes of data). However, this behavior can be customized to suit your application.

Each file item has a number of properties that might be of interest for your application. For example, every item has a name and a content type, and can provide an `InputStream` to access its data. The `FileItem` interface provides the methods to make such a determination, and to access the data in the most appropriate manner.

Handling uploads

Before you can work with the uploaded items, you'll need to parse the request itself. Ensuring that the request is actually a file upload request is not so difficult, but `FileUpload` makes it really simple by providing a static method to do just that. The result of a parse is a list of file items, each of which implements the `FileItem` interface but in most cases, you'll want to handle file uploads differently from regular form fields, so you might process the list as the following:

```java
import java.io.File;
import java.io.IOException;
import java.text.SimpleDateFormat;
import java.util.Date;
import java.util.List;

import javax.servlet.ServletException;
import javax.servlet.http.HttpServlet;
import javax.servlet.http.HttpServletRequest;
import javax.servlet.http.HttpServletResponse;
import javax.servlet.http.HttpSession;

import org.apache.commons.fileupload.FileItem;
import org.apache.commons.fileupload.FileItemFactory;
import org.apache.commons.fileupload.FileUploadException;
import org.apache.commons.fileupload.disk.DiskFileItemFactory;
import org.apache.commons.fileupload.servlet.ServletFileUpload;
import org.slf4j.Logger;
import org.slf4j.LoggerFactory;

public class FileUploadServlet extends HttpServlet {

  private final Logger logger = LoggerFactory.getLogger(FileUploadServlet.class);

  public FileUploadServlet(){
    super();
  }

  @SuppressWarnings("unchecked")
  @Override
    protected void doPost(HttpServletRequest req, HttpServletResponse resp) throws ServletException, IOException {
      String status = "No Uploads !";

      if(ServletFileUpload.isMultipartContent(req)){
        try{
          FileItemFactory fileItemFactory = new DiskFileItemFactory();
          ServletFileUpload uploadHandlr = new ServletFileUpload(fileItemFactory);
```

```java
                    List<FileItem> uploadItems = uploadHandlr.parseRequest(req);
                    handleFile(uploadItems, req.getSession());
                    status = "Done Uploading " + uploadItems.get(0).getName();
                    logger.info(status);
            } catch (FileUploadException ex) {
                status = ex.getMessage();
                logger.error(ex.getMessage());
            } catch (Exception ex){
                status = ex.getMessage();
                logger.error(ex.getMessage());
            }
        }
        resp.getWriter().print(status);
            super.doPost(req, resp);
    }

        private boolean ensureFilesDir(String path){
            File dir = new File(path);
            boolean status = dir.exists();
            if(!status){
                status = dir.mkdirs();
            }
            return status;
        }
    public void handleFile(List<FileItem> fileItems, HttpSession session) throws Exception {
        String filePath = "";
            String fileSeparator = System.getProperty("file.separator");
            String basepath = "files" + fileSeparator + "gtxuploads";
            String filesDir = session.getServletContext().getRealPath(basepath);

        SimpleDateFormat fmt = new SimpleDateFormat("MMM-yyyy");
            String datePrefix = fmt.format(new Date());

        File file = null;
        ensureFilesDir(filesDir);
        for (FileItem fileItem : fileItems) {
          if(!fileItem.isFormField()){
            filePath = filesDir + fileSeparator + datePrefix + "_" + fileItem.getName();
                file = new File(filePath);
                fileItem.write(file);
        }
      }
    }
```

Jakarta Commons - FileUpload

The `FileUpload` servlet must be defined in the `web.xml` deployment descriptor. For our example, we need to add the following servlet mapping to the `web.xml` file:

```xml
<servlet>
  <servlet-name>FileUploadServlet</servlet-name>
  <servlet-class>com.gxtcookbook.code.server.FileUploadServlet</servlet-class>
</servlet>
<servlet-mapping>
  <servlet-name>FileUploadServlet</servlet-name>
  <url-pattern>gxtcookbk/uploadgateway</url-pattern>
</servlet-mapping>
```

Our `FileUploadServlet` can now be invoked from the client. We can call our `FileUploadServlet` using a GXT `FormPanel` with a `FileUploadField`:

```java
FormPanel panel = new FormPanel();
panel.setHeading("File Upload");
panel.setFrame(true);
panel.setAction(GWT.getModuleBaseURL() + "/uploadgateway");
panel.setEncoding(Encoding.MULTIPART);
panel.setMethod(Method.POST);
panel.setWidth(350);

TextField<String> fileName = new TextField<String>();
fileName.setFieldLabel("Name");
panel.add(fileName);

FileUploadField file = new FileUploadField();
file.setAllowBlank(false);
file.setName("uploadedfile");
file.setFieldLabel("File");
panel.add(file);
```

Tracking upload progress

If you expect really large file uploads, then it would be nice to report to your users, how much is already received. Even HTML pages allow implementing a progress bar by returning a multipart/replace response, or something like that. Tracking the upload progress may be done by supplying a `ProgressListener`.

`ProgressListener` is called quite frequently, depending on the servlet engine and other environment factors it may be called for any network packet. In other words, your `ProgressListener` may become a performance problem! A typical solution might be to reduce the activity of `ProgressListener` to only emit a message if the number of megabytes has changed beyond a range. The following example shows a `ProgressListener` which implements this solution. We will probably want to communicate the progress to the progress bar on the client. The *Real-time server push* recipe in *Chapter 11, Advanced Tips*, can be used as a starting point for implementing pushing updates to the client.

```
/Create a progress listener
ProgressListener progressListener = new ProgressListener(){
  private long megaBytes = -1;
  // only update the percent if more than a MB has been uploaded.
  public void update(long pBytesRead, long pContentLength, int pItems)
{
    long mBytes = pBytesRead / 1000000;
    if (megaBytes == mBytes) {
      return;
    }
    megaBytes = mBytes;
    // compute percent uploaded.
    if(pContentLength > 0) {
      float percent = pBytesRead / pContentLength;
      // percent needs to be communicated to the client
      // progress bar
    }

  }
};
```

Index

Symbols

@Column annotation 290
@Entity annotation 290
@GeneratedValue annotation 290
@Id annotation 290
@JoinColumn annotation 290
@ManyToOne annotation 290
@RemoteServiceRelativePath 330
@Source annotation 325
<tpl> tag 213

A

AbstractImagePrototype object 146, 325
AccordionLayout
  about 77
  navigation, organizing with 77-79
actionPerformed() method 73
actions
  organizing, with menu 55-58
  organizing, with split buttons 55-58
ActivityMapper 300
addAggregationRow() method 175
addChartConfig() method 235
addControlBtnd() method 299
addHeaderGroup() method 169, 171
addListener() method 322
add() method 274
addPlugin() method 201, 221, 223
addSelectionListener() method 49, 322
addStyleName() method 63
addTab() method 274
addText() method 13
addWindow button 23

advanced tips, GXT
  about 275
  bus 294-299
  client/server persistence 285–294
  client/server persistence setup 276-284
  history events 300 303
  novel UI, with MVP 294-299
  real-time server push 303-310
  view transitions 300-303
advanced windows
  building 10-12
afterCommit() method 243
AggregationRowConfig 172
Ajax 7
AnchorLayout 80
anonymous inner classes 323
area chart
  about 235
  using 235, 236
  working 238
asGrid() method 299
asList() method 299
asynchronous trees
  building 155-157
attached 76
automatic pagination 183-185

B

bar chart
  about 226
  using 227, 228
  working 229
BaseModel class 112
basic grid
  numbered rows 162-165
  re-orderable columns 162-165

basic tree
  building 141-144
basic validation
  simple form, building with 102-109
basic window
  creating 8, 9
basic wizard
  building, with CardLayout 85-91
BeanLib
  downloading 277
BeanModel
  about 198
  overview 199
  working 200
BeanModelTag interface 112, 198
beginActions() method 299
BorderLayout
  about 82
  UI cardinality 82-84
bottom navigation tabs
  creating 29, 30
bound model
  customizing, for ComboBox 113-116
BoxComponent 149
bus 294-299
ButtonBar instance 32
ButtonBar object 46, 143
ButtonEvent 323
button presses
  about 323
  example 323
buttons
  about 48
  aligning 50-52
  creating, with icons 48, 49
  creating, with text 48, 49

C

callback version
  defining, for service interface 332
CardLayout
  about 85
  basic wizard, building with 85-91
cell data
  formatting 166-168

chart
  about 225
  area chart 235
  bar chart 226
  line chart 232
  pie chart 230
checkboxes
  used, for selecting record 176-179
checkbox selection
  trees, building with 152-155
CheckBoxSelectionModel plugin 177
checked exceptions 335
Chrome version 17, 252
client/server persistence
  about 285-287
  setting up 276-284
  working 289-294
column aggregation 171
column data
  aggregating 172-176
column grouping 168
column headers
  grouping 168-171
ColumnLayout
  about 94
  grids, building with 94-96
ColumnModel 172
ColumnModel class 172
ColumnModel object 163
ComboBox
  about 110, 113
  bound model, customizing 113-116
  displays, customizing 217-220
combos
  linking 117-120
  options, displaying with 110-113
Comet 96
commitChanges() method 182
compare() method 159, 160
component
  data, visualizing from 238-243
ComponentPlugin interface 162
components
  drag-and-drop (DnD), implementing 255-258
  dragging 252-254
  snapping 79-82

componentSelected() method 15, 32, 55
components, GWT RPC mechanism 329
configureCombo() method 220
configurePanel() method 214
configurePortlet() method 99
ContentPanel 54, 79, 107
ContentPanel class 183
ContextMenu
  trees, augmenting with 149-152
context menus 149
contextual switching 52, 53
control flow, delegation event model 322
createIfSupported() method 248
CSS3 47
ctPanel ContentPanel 52
ctxMenu instance 152
custom DnD
  implementing, on tabs 269-274
custom rendering
  for grid groups 189-192
custom sorting, trees 158-160
custom tab icons
  tabbed content, building with 26-28
custom theme
  building 319
  working 320
CylinderBarChart 229

D

dashboards
  about 96
  building 97-99
data
  binding, into forms 127-134
  formatting, with basic template 207-209
  grouping, in grids 187-189
  visualizing, from component 238-243
DataCenter class 294
data formatting 165
default theme
  setting 312, 313
delegation event model
  control flow 322
department update event 295

details
  providing, with RowExpander plugin 221-223
development steps, GWT RPC 330, 331
DHTML 7
dialog 13
Dialog class 15
Dialog object 14
dialog windows
  creating 13-15
displays
  customizing, for ComboBox 217-220
Document Object Model (DOM) 75
drag-and-drop (DnD)
  about 251
  across components 259, 264
  from desktop, with HTML5 265-269
  implementations 252
  within components 255-258
draggable buttons 252
Draggable class 253
drawChart() method 247
DropTarget instance 274

E

enable checkbox selection comment 155
equals() method 285, 290
event-bus 295
event handling
  about 321
  steps 322
event loop 321
events 321
exceptions
  handling 334

F

Facebook 96
fetchData() method 247
FileItemFactory 337
FileItem interface 337
FileModel class 143
FileService class 157
file upload
  handling 124-127

FileUpload
  about 337
  using 337
FileUploadField widget 125
FileUploadServlet class 127
FilledBarchart 229
fillRect() method 250
Firefox version 8.0 252
FitLayout 54, 77
for keyword 213
formatChangeCol() method 176
FormBinding class 128
FormLayout 81
FormPanel 80, 81, 103, 107
forms
  about 101
  building, with basic validation 102-109
  data, binding into 127-134
  options, displaying with combos 110-113
FugueIcons interface 326

G

getActive() method 91
getAdvTemplate() method 220
getAll() method 143, 149, 152, 155
getCheckedSelection() method 155
getColumnCfgs() method 182
getContext2d() method 248
getCustomer() method 209, 217
getCustomers() method 200
getFirstName() method 113
getFolderChildren() method 157
getFullName() method 113
getLastName() method 113
getNext() method 91
getPrevious() method 91
getStringValue() method 146
getTemplate() method 209, 213, 217, 220, 223, 264
getValue() method 109
getValues() method 109
GILEAD
  downloading 277
Gmail 96
greetServer() method 332

Grid Component
  cell data, formatting 166-168
  column data, aggregating 172-176
  column headers, grouping 168-171
  custom rendering, for grid groups 189-192
  intuitive record filtering 201-203
  live data group summaries 192-198
  records, selecting with checkboxes 176, 177
GridDragSource class 256
GridDropTarget class 256
GridFilter plugin 200
GridGroupRenderer interface 190
Grid object 35
grids
  about 161
  automatic pagination 183, 185
  building, with ColumnLayout 94-96
  data, grouping in 187-189
  overview 162
  validated data, entering into 179-182
groupBy() method 189-192
GWT Panels 75
GWT RPC 96, 329
GWT RPC mechanism
  components 329
  development steps 330, 331
  example 332
GXT
  about 29
  advanced tips 275
  asynchronous trees, building 155-157
  basic tree, building 141-144
  combos, linking 117-120
  components, dragging 252-254
  custom sorting, within trees 158-160
  data, binding into forms 127-134
  file upload, handling 124-127
  icons 325
  icons, leveraging 326, 327
  multiple input selection, capturing 121-124
  node labels, customizing 144-146
  options, displaying with combos 110-113
  simple form, building with basic validation 102-109
  slider field, building 134-137

trees, augmenting with
    ContextMenu 149-152
trees, building with checkbox
    selection 152-155
trees, decorating with icons 146-149
GXT application development
    tips 294
GXT button 48
GXT Chart API 248
GXT components
    dragging 252-254
GXT layouts 75, 76
GXT library 75
GXT theme 311
GXT toolkit 33, 325
GXT windows 18

H

handleAppend() method 264
hasChildren() method 157
hashCode() method 285, 290
hasNext() method 91
hasPrevious() method 91
Hibernate
    downloading 277
Hibernate Validator
    downloading 277
hideAll() method 24
hierarchical data model 139
history events 300-303
horizontal aligning, RowLayout 92, 94
HTML 5
    about 47, 102, 248
    drag-and-drop (DnD), from desktop 265-269
HTML 5 canvas element
    visualizations, drawing 248-250
HTML backend 102
HtmlContainer class 32
HTML frontend 102

I

icons
    about 325
    buttons, creating with 48, 49
    leveraging 326, 327
    trees, decorating with 146-149

Icons interface 325, 326
IconSupport interface 325
IE 9 252
if conditional logic 214
ImageBundle 26
ImageResource object 325
initBlink() method 39
installView() method 299
int parameter 39
intuitive record filtering 201, 203
InvocationException 335
isBlinking() method 39

J

Java 321
Java Persistence Architecture (JPA) 275, 276
JSON 96
JSONP 96
JSR 258 96

L

LayoutContainer 9, 75
LayoutContainer panel 28
layouts 75, 76
Lazy-Rendering 76
leaves 139
legal data types, RPC 331
lexicographic schemes 158
LightEntity class 289
line chart
    about 232
    using 233, 234
    working 234
listCustomers() method 116, 214
listener 321
Listener object 322
ListLoadconfig object 121
ListStore 110, 294
listStudents() method 291
ListView 110, 255, 259
live data group summaries 192-198
loaderBeforeLoad() method 120
load() method 157, 200
Log4J
    downloading 277

log4j.properties file 284
logic
  performing, in templates 210-214

M

main service interface
  defining 332
makeLinks() method 79
math
  performing, in templates 214, 217
menu
  menuactions, organizing with 55-58
MenuItem object 152
MessageBox.alert() call 17
MessageBox class 15, 18
MessageBox.confirm() call 17
MessageBox object 17
MessageBox.prompt() call 18
messages
  users, pre-empting with 15-18
mixedBtn button 49
Mockingbird 252
ModelStringProvider interface 146 144
Model-View-Presenter (MVP) pattern 275
multi-column buttons
  crafting, in ToolBar 61-64
multiple input selection
  capturing 121-124

N

navigate() method 91
navigation
  organizing, with AccordionLayout 77, 79
node labels
  customizing 144-146
novel UI, with MVP 294-299
NullPointerException 335
numbered rows 162-165

O

onApply() method 209, 220, 223,
    250, 254, 258, 299
onBindActions() method 297, 299
onDragDrop() handler 274
onDragDrop() method 274

onDragEnter() method 274
onDragStart() method 260
onFailure() method 331
onFailure(Throwable) callback method 335
onModuleLoad() method 182, 247, 313, 314
on/off toggle buttons
  creating 52-54
onRender method 46
onRender() method 46
onResponseReceived() method 247
onSuccess() method 149, 331
onValueChange() method 301
options
  displaying, with combos 110-113
overwrite() method 209

P

pagination 183
PagingModelMemoryProxy 185
PagingToolBar 183
Params object 207
parent/child relationship 139
particular tab
  selecting 40-42
persistence 276
pie chart
  about 230
  using 230
  working 232
PlaceController 300
PlaceHistoryHandler 303
POJO (Plain Old Java Object) 112, 276
portlet specification 96
ProgressListener 341

R

RadioGroup 108
real-time server push 303-310
record
  selecting, with checkboxes 176-179
refreshAction() method 299
rejectChanges() method 182
remote data
  visualizing 244-246
RemoteGateway 290
RemoteGatewayAsync 290

RemoteService interface 330
RemoteServiceRelativePath annotation 334
render() method 190
re-orderable columns 162-165
root 139
RowData object 92
RowEditor plugin
  about 179, 182
  details, providing with 221, 223
RowExpander plugin 220
RowLayout
  about 92
  horizontal aligning 92-94
  vertical aligning 92-94
RPC
  legal data types 331
RpcProxy 185, 186
RpcProxy instance 156
RpcProxy() method 113
RSA cryptography 214
runAction() method 73
runDelete() method 294
runSave() method 294

S

saveAction() method 299
saveDepartments() method 299
saveStudents() method 294
scrollable tab strip
  tab panel, creating with 30, 32
SelectionListener 15, 322
ServiceDefTarget interface 334
service interface
  callback version, defining 332
service proxy
  creating 334
  using 334
service servlet
  creating 333
setAction() method 127
setActiveItem() method 85
setAllowBlank() method 127
setAllowSelfAsSource() method 256, 258
setArrowAlign() method 64
setAutoExpandColumn() method 165
setBlinkModal() method 10

setBottomComponent() method 183, 185
setBoxLabel() method 109
setButtonAlignment() method 52
setChartModel() method 233
setCheckable() method 153
setCheckNodes() method 153
setCheckStyle() method 153
setClosable() method 10
setCloseContextMenu() method 28, 42
setColour() method 235
setColumnReordering() method 258
setColumnWidth() method 99
setConstrain() method 253
setContainer() method 253, 254
setContextMenu() method 150
setDisplayField() method 116
setDisplay() method 299
setDisplayProperty() method 141, 144, 259
setDraggable() method 12
setEditor() method 182
setEnabled() method 73
setFeedBack() method 256, 264
setFillStyle() method 250
setFrame() method 54
setGroupable() method 192
setGroupRenderer() method 192
setGroupRenderer() method 190
setHeaderVisible() method 107, 112
setHeading() method 8, 10, 14
setHeight() method 42
setIconProvider() method 147
setItemSelector() method 264
setLabelProvider() method 141, 144, 145
setLabelSeparator() method 112
setLocal() method 201
setMaximizable() method 10, 12
setMaxValue() method 109
setMenu() method 57
setMessage() method 134
setMinValue() method 109
setModal() method 10
setModelProcessor() method 114
setName() method 109
setOperation() method 264
setPropertyEditor() method 109
setRegex() method 108
setRenderer() method 176

setResizable() method 12
setSelectedStyle() method 264
setSize() method 8, 10, 54, 107, 112
setStripeRows() method 165
setStyleAttribute() method 107, 112
setTemplate() method 218, 220, 221, 223
setText() method 235
setTopComponent() method 183
setTrackMouseOver() method 141
setUseQueryCache() method 120
setValidator() method 127
setView() method 189, 190
setWidth() method 42
setXAxis() method 233
setYAxis() method 233
several click-wares
   single action, binding to 64-74
showAll() method 24
show() method 8, 13, 14
showTabStrip() method 46
simple form
   building, with basic validation 102-109
single action
   binding, to several click-wares 64-74
slices 230
slider field
   building 134-137
SplitButton button 24
split buttons
   actions, organizing with 55-58
startBlinking() method 39
strategy pattern 137
Student class 285, 289
supportDrag() method 274
supportDrop() method 274

T

tabbed content
   building, with custom tab icons 26-28
TabItem class 28
tab notification 35-39
tab panel
   creating, with scrollable tab strip 30-32
TabPanel class 28, 32, 45

tabs
   about 25
   adding, programmatically 33-35
   custom DnD, implementing on 269-274
   locating 40-42
   removing, programmatically 33-35
   searching for 40-42
   selecting 40-42
   usage 26
tab strip
   about 30
   displaying, for multiple tabs 42-46
   tab panel, creating with 30, 32
template class 206
Template object 207
template parser. *See* template processor
template processor 205
templates
   about 205, 206
   data, formatting with 207-209
   logic, performing in 210-214
   math, performing in 214-217
text
   buttons, creating with 48, 49
textBtn button 49
the hideTabStrip() method 46
themes
   customizing 317-319
   registering 313, 314
   switching, at runtime 315, 316
   using 315
ThemeSelector widget 315
   working 316
theming 311
throws keyword 335
ToggleButton class 55
ToggleButton object 32
ToolBar
   about 58
   building 59, 60
   multi-column buttons, crafting in 61-64
toString() method 285, 290
TreeDragSource class 256
TreeDropTarget class 256
TreeGrid 255
TreePanel 255
TreePanel class 140

TreePanel instance 155
TreePanel object 143
trees
  augmenting, with ContextMenu 149-152
  building 141-144
  building, with checkbox selection 152-155
  custom sorting 158-160
  decorating, with icons 146-149
TreeStore class 160
TreeStore instance 140, 143, 155
tree structure 139, 140
Twitter 96, 226

U

UI cardinality
  with BorderLayout 82-84
unexpected exceptions 335
upload handling 338, 340
upload progress
  tracking 341
uploads
  handling 338, 340
users
  pre-empting, with messages 15-18

V

validated data
  entering, into grid 179-182
vertical aligning, RowLayout 92, 94
VerticalPanel class 9
viewport 10, 254

view transitions 300-303
visualizations
  about 225
  drawing, on HTML 5 canvas
    element 248, 250

W

Web2.x communication systems 96
web form
  HTML backend 102
  HTML frontend 102
WebSockets 96
Window class 14
WindowListener class 23
window management system
  building 18-24
windowMinimize() method 23
Window object 12
Windows 7
WiseStripTabPanel class 43, 45
WizardPanel 91

X

XHR 96
XMLHttpRequest object 47
XTemplate 205
XTemplate class 210
xWindow variable 12

Thank you for buying
ExtGWT Rich Internet Application Cookbook

About Packt Publishing

Packt, pronounced 'packed', published its first book "*Mastering phpMyAdmin for Effective MySQL Management*" in April 2004 and subsequently continued to specialize in publishing highly focused books on specific technologies and solutions.

Our books and publications share the experiences of your fellow IT professionals in adapting and customizing today's systems, applications, and frameworks. Our solution based books give you the knowledge and power to customize the software and technologies you're using to get the job done. Packt books are more specific and less general than the IT books you have seen in the past. Our unique business model allows us to bring you more focused information, giving you more of what you need to know, and less of what you don't.

Packt is a modern, yet unique publishing company, which focuses on producing quality, cutting-edge books for communities of developers, administrators, and newbies alike. For more information, please visit our website: `www.packtpub.com`.

About Packt Open Source

In 2010, Packt launched two new brands, Packt Open Source and Packt Enterprise, in order to continue its focus on specialization. This book is part of the Packt Open Source brand, home to books published on software built around Open Source licences, and offering information to anybody from advanced developers to budding web designers. The Open Source brand also runs Packt's Open Source Royalty Scheme, by which Packt gives a royalty to each Open Source project about whose software a book is sold.

Writing for Packt

We welcome all inquiries from people who are interested in authoring. Book proposals should be sent to author@packtpub.com. If your book idea is still at an early stage and you would like to discuss it first before writing a formal book proposal, contact us; one of our commissioning editors will get in touch with you.

We're not just looking for published authors; if you have strong technical skills but no writing experience, our experienced editors can help you develop a writing career, or simply get some additional reward for your expertise.

Ext GWT 2.0: Beginner's Guide

ISBN: 978-1-849511-84-1   Paperback: 320 pages

Take the user experience of your website to a new level with Ext GWT

1. Explore the full range of features of the Ext GWT library through practical, step-by-step examples
2. Discover how to combine simple building blocks into powerful components
3. Create powerful Rich Internet Applications with features normally only found in desktop applications
4. Learn how to structure applications using MVC for maximum reliability and maintainability

Learning Ext JS 3.2

ISBN: 978-1-849511-20-9   Paperback: 432 pages

Build dynamic, desktop-style user interfaces for your data-driven web applications using Ext JS

1. Learn to build consistent, attractive web interfaces with the framework components
2. Integrate your existing data and web services with Ext JS data support
3. Enhance your JavaScript skills by using Ext's DOM and AJAX helpers
4. Extend Ext JS through custom components

Please check www.PacktPub.com for information on our titles

Ext JS 3.0 Cookbook

ISBN: 978-1-847198-70-9   Paperback: 376 pages

109 great recipes for building impressive rich internet applications using the Ext JS JavaScript library

1. Master the Ext JS widgets and learn to create custom components to suit your needs
2. Build striking native and custom layouts, forms, grids, listviews, treeviews, charts, tab panels, menus, toolbars and much more for your real-world user interfaces
3. Packed with easy-to-follow examples to exercise all of the features of the Ext JS library
4. Part of Packt's Cookbook series: Each recipe is a carefully organized sequence of instructions to complete the task as efficiently as possible

Google Web Toolkit 2 Application Development Cookbook

ISBN: 978-1-849512-00-8   Paperback: 244 pages

Over 70 simple but incredibly effective practical recipes to develop web applications using GWT with JPA, MySQL, and iReport

1. Create impressive, complex browser-based web applications with GWT 2
2. Learn the most effective ways to create reports with parameters, variables, and subreports using iReport
3. Create Swing-like web-based GUIs using the Ext GWT class library

Please check **www.PacktPub.com** for information on our titles

CPSIA information can be obtained at www.ICGtesting.com
Printed in the USA
LVOW050024121012

302502LV00018B/15/P